The Afghanistan Challenge

Hard Realities and Strategic Choices

Edited by
Hans-Georg Ehrhart and
Charles C. Pentland

McGill-Queen's University Press
Montreal & Kingston • London • Ithaca

SCHOOL OF
Policy Studies

Publications Unit
Policy Studies Building
138 Union Street
Kingston, ON, Canada
K7L 3N6
www.queensu.ca/sps/

Library and Archives Canada Cataloguing in Publication

The Afghanistan challenge : hard realities and strategic choices / edited by Hans-Georg Ehrhart and Charles C. Pentland.

Co-published by: Institute for Peace Research & Security Policy, School of Policy Studies and McGill-Queen's University Press.

Includes bibliographical references.
ISBN 978-1-55339-241-5

1. Afghan War, 2001-. 2. Afghanistan—History—2001-. 3. Afghan War, 2001- —Participation, Canadian. 4. Afghan War, 2001- —Participation, German. 5. North Atlantic Treaty Organization—Armed Forces—Afghanistan. I. Ehrhart, Hans-Georg, 1955- II. Pentland, Charles III. Queen's University (Kingston, Ont.). Centre for International Relations IV. Queen's University (Kingston, Ont.). School of Policy Studies V. Universität Hamburg. Institut für Friedensforschung und Sicherheitspolitik

DS371.412.A44 2009   958.104'7   C2009-901779-2

Contents

PART II

Acknowledgements

This book is the product of an international conference on NATO and the International Engagement in Afghanistan, held in Hamburg on 13–14 December 2007. Hosted by the German Armed Forces General and Staff Academy, the conference was sponsored by the Institute for Peace Research and Security Policy at the University of Hamburg (IFSH) and the Centre for International Relations (QCIR) at Queen's University in Kingston, Ontario, Canada. The sponsors wish to acknowledge the generous support of NATO's Public Diplomacy Division and the Security and Defence Forum of Canada's Department of National Defence.

In developing the manuscript for publication, the editors have received advice, support, and technical assistance from a number of quarters. Dr Knut Kirste and Megan Minnion at NATO headquarters provided useful guidance early in the project. Britta Fisch of IFSH managed the conference and publication accounts, and Heather Gilmartin translated some of the chapters. On the Canadian side, Maureen Bartram at the QCIR provided administrative support, and Mark Howes, Valerie Jarus, Meghan Stouffer, and Ellie Barton in the Publications Unit of the School of Policy Studies at Queen's University undertook the technical preparation of the manuscript for McGill-Queen's University Press.

Chapter 1

Introduction

HANS-GEORG EHRHART AND CHARLES C. PENTLAND

Since the fall of 2001, Afghanistan has been a rich source of lessons in the conduct of international missions in failed or fragile states. Handed the primordial task of providing a secure environment for a comprehensive United Nations mission to nurture stability, good governance, and economic development in that troubled country, the members of the North Atlantic Treaty Organization (NATO) have confronted an especially steep learning curve. Debates among and within NATO members about objectives, strategies, and tactics, along with a lack of coordination and burden-sharing, continue to raise questions about the prospects of the mission, and about the future of the alliance.

For NATO and its twenty-six members, just about everything regarding the Afghanistan mission is new. It is the first operation outside the alliance's original European theatre. It is the first ground combat operation conducted by the allies, although largely in parallel rather than truly combined. For the ten new members inducted in 1999 and 2004, it is their first real experience of multilateral, diplomatic, and military coordination through the alliance, however haphazard and ineffective those processes may sometimes seem.

Canada and Germany are among the largest contributors to NATO's mission, after the United States and the United Kingdom. Canadian and German troops are in different parts of the country, doing quite different things. Canada's higher ratio of combat to development work is reflected in a higher rate of casualties. Canadians have sometimes joined in criticisms directed at Germany and some other European allies for their unwillingness to take on riskier military tasks in Afghanistan's southern and eastern provinces. Some Germans, in turn, have chided

The Afghanistan Challenge: Hard Realities and Strategic Choices, ed. H.-G. Ehrhart and C.C. Pentland. Montreal and Kingston: McGill-Queen's University Press, Queen's Policy Studies Series. © 2009 The School of Policy Studies, Queen's University at Kingston. All rights reserved.

Canada (along with the US and the UK) for stressing war-fighting at the expense of more pacific approaches centred on development.

The Canadian and the German positions in this intra-alliance debate reflect, in part, the differences between the relatively quiescent security environment of Regional Command North, which makes possible real progress on development and governance, and the chronic volatility of Regional Command South, which has given primacy to defeating, and defending against, the insurgency. That the Germans are in the north and the Canadians in the south is also, however, a reflection of how politicians and the public in each country have come to think about the role of the military and the conduct of multilateral missions in dangerous and impoverished places. More than a decade after German military missions abroad became politically permissible, they remain hedged about with caveats and require justification at home as exercises in peacekeeping and development. By contrast, Canada's leaders—especially since 2006—have presented the Afghan mission to the public as a necessary break with outmoded images of peacekeeping, and as an opportunity to transform the military (especially the army) into a force better fitted for the "new wars" of the twenty-first century, of which Afghanistan is the first.

As befits traditionally close allies, there is mutual respect between Canadians and Germans on many levels. That said, the divergent evolution of their political and strategic cultures and their different experiences in the Afghan theatre have led to a degree of mutual incomprehension and impatience and, in turn, to some intermittently sharp exchanges across the Atlantic among politicians, the military, journalists, and academics. In its more thoughtful forms, this Canadian-German dialogue is a bilateral distillation of the larger debate, both operational and existential, within the alliance.

This collection of scholarly essays by leading German and Canadian experts assesses the present state and future prospects of the Afghanistan mission, both to advance the dialogue and to suggest better approaches to the policy questions that continue to confront the alliance. The product of a workshop held in Hamburg in December 2007 sponsored by the Institute for Peace Research and Security Policy at the University of Hamburg, Queen's University's Centre for International Relations, and the German Armed Forces General and Staff Academy, these papers as revised and collected here reflect the state of the intra-alliance debate over the Afghanistan mission in mid-2008. Although some chapters are explicitly prescriptive in their conclusions, this book does not claim, or even aspire, to embody a shared view of the mission—its origins, current state, or prospects—or to arrive at a consensus on the way forward.

The authors—from the overlapping worlds of international public service, foreign and defence policy research centres, universities, the media, and the military—represent a variety of professions and perspectives. Correspondingly, their analyses of the Afghan situation range from close-to-the-ground explorations of Afghan society and culture on the one hand, to the assessment of strategic debates at the highest level within and among NATO allies on the other. No chapter is devoid of criticism, whether of the conduct of the mission, the process of analysis and policy-making in the international community, the performance of the Afghan government, the policies of neighbouring states, or the quality of debate in and among NATO members. Some contributors see evidence of continuing progress toward at least some of the goals set out in the Afghanistan Compact of 2006. Others express something closer to despair or fatalism. Most lie somewhere in between: focusing on one facet of Afghan society or on one sector of the international mission, they find in the details of their chosen subject some modest advances to celebrate amid a growing conviction that a change of direction is in order, and perhaps a recalibration of the goals sought.

The first part of the book consists of eight chapters examining various facets of the international mission in Afghanistan: the political and institutional framework at the international level; the situation on the ground with respect to security, governance, and development; and the policies of important neighbouring states. The second part explores the variances in Canadian and German approaches as these play out in domestic politics, alliance diplomacy, and the critical issues of security sector reform.

The central strategic framework of the international mission is the Afghanistan Compact between the Afghan government and the international community, presented in January 2006 and later endorsed by the United Nations Security Council. Citha Maass in her chapter first clarifies the relationship between the Compact and its predecessor, the Bonn Agreement, and identifies their common features. To what extent, she asks, does the Compact's approach deviate from Bonn, aiming to correct its deficiencies? The mission, she notes, is expected to fall far short of many of the Compact's benchmarks. Should all the blame for this be placed on the deteriorating security situation, or have other factors prevented the international and national actors from achieving their targets on time? Has the Compact even set the right priorities for sustainable stabilization and development, or is it based on unsound assumptions? She then assesses the current state of the reform process. Are the setbacks caused only by tactical mistakes, susceptible of correction if the timelines are extended? Or is a strategic revision needed? Maass concludes with some basic recommendations that ought to be considered by a mid-term review.

The chapter by Conrad Schetter and Rainer Glassner explores the limits of the widely used term *warlordism* as a depiction of the structures of violence in Afghanistan. While not denying the existence of warlords, they argue that the manifold forms of individual leadership in Afghanistan and the variability of local security arrangements call into question the positing of a simple linear axis between warlords at one pole and the modern state at the other. The argument proceeds from a discussion of the term *warlord* in order to arrive at a concise and practicable definition. The authors then turn to an analysis of the balance of power and influence between the centre and the periphery in Afghanistan. Through case studies of Kunduz, Kandahar, and Paktia, they examine in detail the security situation on the provincial level, demonstrating the enormous variety of arrangements by which security is managed. Schetter and Glassner suggest, moreover, that the prevailing discourse of warlordism has been challenged by the re-emergence of the Taliban in the last few years. The labelling of actors in Afghanistan, they argue, is influenced more by the concerns and interests of the intervening powers than by the realities on the ground. The chapter concludes by suggesting better ways to understand or define the local security architecture in Afghanistan.

Florian Kühn's chapter also explores deeply rooted traditions and indigenous power structures that help explain the difficulty of imposing an externally designed order on Afghanistan. While the previous chapter focused on security structures, Kühn's emphasizes political economy—Afghanistan's long history as, in his words, a "rentier state." He shows how the type of economic structure peculiar to such states has shaped the process of state formation in Afghanistan for more than a century, if not longer. Having first defined "rent-seeking" and the characteristics of rentier states, he interprets Afghan history from the time of the British presence, through the period of Soviet-American competition for influence and the Soviet occupation, to the rise and fall of the Taliban. Kühn shows how rentier structures adapted to these changing circumstances and how their survival accounts for many of the difficulties in building a modern Afghan state under international tutelage. The concluding section describes the interplay between drug rentiers and the political rentiers embedded in the state, and the unintended consequence of the international presence in strengthening the very dependencies it claims to oppose.

The next two chapters explore different elements of that international presence. Lara Olson and Andrea Charron examine myths and realities in the role of non-governmental organizations (NGOs) in international development generally, and in Afghanistan in particular, and review NGOs' efforts to influence broader international strategies for security, development, and peace in Afghanistan. They first describe the context and note the dominance of integrated civil-military approaches in Afghanistan, turning then to examine the NGO sector's relationship with state actors and state-building. Following a review of the roles NGOs have historically played in Afghanistan, in the final section they look at the current, persistent advocacy by NGOs concerning strategic issues for the international mission. NGOs seek to prioritize humanitarian space, civilian protection, human rights, women's rights, agriculture, civil society development, subnational government, and community- and national-level peace-building. Olsen and Charron argue that inclusive and responsive consultative processes on these larger strategic issues are needed; NGOs and civil society groups must work directly with Afghan communities if better coordination and better outcomes are to emerge.

Mihai Carp's chapter reflects NATO's assessment of the state of play six years after its initial engagement in Afghanistan. The challenges, he notes, remain daunting. At the same time, the 2008 Summit in Bucharest showed that NATO and its partners, including the Afghans themselves and those from other international organizations, remained committed for the long haul and determined to consolidate the progress achieved to date. Despite concerns that had been mounting for months over insurgent activity, the absence of effective governance in large parts of the country, weak and corrupt Afghan institutions and officials, and last but not least, intra-alliance squabbles, Bucharest contributed to a new sense of momentum that must now be exploited to the fullest. Long-term success will depend not only on the effective implementation of a comprehensive approach whereby all actors in Afghanistan assume their respective roles in a coordinated fashion but also on tangible Afghan ownership, notably in the security sector. Carp argues that the international community can build on common ground as there is a clear realization that the costs of failure in Afghanistan are too great to contemplate and would have direct consequences not only for the well-being of the Afghans themselves but for wider regional and international security.

Afghanistan is in a tough neighbourhood, and two of its toughest neighbours are Pakistan and Iran. Christian Wagner's chapter shows how the Pakistani army's costly battles in the tribal areas, the deterioration of Islamabad's bilateral relationship with Kabul, and international criticism of the Pakistani military's advances against Islamist extremists (which are often seen as half-hearted) have all helped to shift Pakistan's foreign policy focus, traditionally centred on India, more strongly toward Afghanistan. However, relations with Afghanistan will remain dependent on those with India. Pakistan's interest in Afghanistan since the 1990s can only be understood within the context of its conflict with India over Kashmir and the military's domestic dominance. That said, until the end of the 1980s there was hardly any connection between Pakistan's conflicts with India over Kashmir and with Afghanistan. Only then did the Pakistani military leadership begin to link the two conflicts more strongly. Yet this strategy has come under increasing pressure since the attacks of 11 September 2001. Sorting through the complexities of this situation, Wagner's chapter first discusses the army's role in Pakistan and then the relationships among Pakistan, India, and Afghanistan. It ends with a brief discussion of future prospects.

Janet Kursawe's chapter discusses Afghanistan's other difficult neighbour, Iran. Teheran's policy toward Afghanistan, she argues, has been shaped by five main factors beyond its opposition to the United States and the sanctions it has imposed on the Islamic Republic. The first is transborder issues, principally the flow of drugs, refugees, migrant labour, the arms trade, and water. The second is Iran's claim to Shia leadership and hence the duty to protect the Shia minority in Afghanistan from persecution. Third, and related, is the imperative to oppose extreme Sunni Islamism in Pakistan and the Gulf. The fourth factor is Iran's pragmatic recognition of the need for selective cooperation on shared regional interests with the United States and other powers. The fifth is the ambition of Iran's leaders to carve out a sphere of Persian cultural influence in the region. Kursawe shows how these factors played out through Iran's strategies in Afghanistan, which centred on reconstruction, culture and education, propaganda, and support for anti-government forces—nuanced, two-track strategies that seem to be paying off in increased influence.

To close out the first section of the book, Hans-Georg Ehrhart and Roland Kaestner provide a strategic assessment of the international engagement in Afghanistan. Their analysis starts with an evaluation of the situation in each of the three main issue areas: security, governance, and development. They then turn their attention to mid- and long-term trends and processes with respect to population growth, resources, culture, society, economy, and politics, and their likely impact on the evolving situation on the ground. In the light of this analysis, the authors present and comment on a number of policy options for the international community. They recommend a strategic change emphasizing five points: more modest strategic objectives, "Afghanisation" of security, decentralization of governance structures, more local administration of development assistance, and more involvement of regional actors in the management of the Afghan conflict.

The essays in the second part of this book explore the perceptions, debates, and strategies that comprise the Canadian and German approaches to the Afghanistan mission. Kim Nossal leads off by challenging the widespread public view that the Canadian House of Commons decided, in its resolution of March 2008, simply to terminate Canada's military mission to Afghanistan in December 2011. Reviewing the history of the Afghanistan debate in Canada, he points out that from 2001 to 2008, every decision to change or extend the mission specified a time period or a withdrawal date. Debates surrounding each decision, particularly those taken in 2006 and 2008, revealed deep divisions in public opinion among the four political parties in the House and within the Liberal party (in opposition after January 2006). The parliamentary debate in March 2008 evoked a list of reasons why withdrawing in 2009—as two opposition parties had proposed—was a bad idea; the alternative end date of December 2011 emerged "by default." Nossal points out that this outcome reflected a degree of dubious logic and legerdemain on many sides, not least in setting such a deadline given the realities on the ground and in the alliance. These contradictions, he argues, can be resolved if attention is paid to the literal wording of the motion, which calls for a military redeployment out of Kandahar, not necessarily a full exit from Afghanistan.

David Haglund's chapter focuses on two "striking ironies" that have emerged in the transatlantic dimensions of this debate. The first concerns the remarkable role reversal experienced by Ottawa, all of a sudden a NATO capital that has found itself lecturing other allied capitals on the need to make a more credible commitment to the common effort. For so much of NATO's history, this used to be a criticism launched at Canada itself. The second irony inheres in the manner in which the current dispute calls into question one of the cherished myths of certain Canadian atlanticists, namely, those who have managed to convince themselves that there existed a "special relationship" forged within alliance circles between the Canadians and the Germans, conceived in their minds to be the alliance's gold-dust twins. Haglund's chapter addresses both issues, and asks whether caveats attached by Berlin to the *Bundeswehr* deployment in Afghanistan constitute a derogation from alliance solidarity.

Both the Canadian and the German missions in Afghanistan are officially multidimensional and integrated, focused on security, governance, and development, although they continue to differ in the emphasis they need or can afford to place on each of these three themes. Drawing on his experience as the military commander of the governance-oriented Strategic Advisory Team in Kabul, Mike Capstick points out that there has been very little analysis of Canada's "whole of government" approach (formerly "3D"—defence, diplomacy, and development). "Whole of government" is based on the idea that no single element of national power is, on its own, sufficient to deal with all the complexities of failed and failing states; therefore, a coordinated and concentrated effort is necessary to secure the strategic effects desired by the international community, by Canada and, most importantly, by the people most vulnerable to state failure. To illustrate how this concept should work, Capstick discusses how the military is supporting the Afghanistan Compact and Afghanistan's National Development Strategy. Although the analysis concentrates on the Canadian Forces' contribution, it recognizes the subordinate, supporting role that the military plays in those areas that are within the competence of Foreign Affairs, the Canadian International

Development Agency, and the other federal departments and agencies involved in the Afghan mission. Invoking Thucydides, Capstick insists that Canada's fundamental aim is to help the weak of Afghanistan develop the strength they need to deny the strong the ability to "exact what they can." This objective is clearly informed by the long-standing values of "peace, order, and good government" articulated in Canada's constitution.

Christoph Reuter also draws on vast experience in Afghanistan, in his case as a journalist. His central thesis is that the international community is living in a kind of bubble, ignoring the realities in Afghanistan. Because the internationals do not really know what kind of war they are fighting, they are on the way to losing it. They are creating their own enemies by ignoring basic cultural values and by allying with the wrong forces. Reinforcing the observations of Schetter, Glassner, and Kühn, Reuter criticizes the international community for constructing a simplified picture of "good guys and bad guys," ignoring the complexity of Afghan society. German soldiers, he argues, are walking a tightrope dealing with an unknown enemy in a fractured country and facing much criticism at home. Changing Afghanistan is a long-term endeavour that has to start with the Afghan people and their interests.

The last two chapters explore the critical issue of security sector reform in Afghanistan. Involvement in the international mission, writes David Law, has been important for Canada in several respects. It has provoked a major change in Canada's approach to security and in its understanding of its role on the international stage. It has had a significant impact on the country's understanding of governance, particularly as concerns the way its central governmental departments coordinate their actions abroad. It has initiated a long-overdue debate about the nature and needs of effective development assistance in conflict zones and fragile states, and the overall relationship between development and security. As this has happened, security sector reform (SSR) has begun to assume an increasingly important place in Canada's policies in Afghanistan and elsewhere. Law's chapter traces the internal and external factors that set the stage for this development prior to the Canadian deployment. He then provides an overview of the main features of Canada's SSR role in the country: what Canada has been doing, how it has been pursuing its activities, and how its approach compares with that of other countries. In conclusion, Law assesses the impact of Canada's SSR efforts at home and in Afghanistan, putting forward some recommendations for Canadian policy-makers that may also be relevant to their counterparts in other countries.

One of those other countries is, of course, Germany, also deeply immersed in security sector reform in Afghanistan. Michael Brzoska in his chapter notes that the creation of an effective police force is seen as crucial for the country's future, but that police reform is generally judged to have been a quantitative and qualitative failure. With an emphasis on Germany's contribution, Brzoska describes and assesses police reform in Afghanistan. After an introductory section outlining the German approach, he evaluates the successes and failures of the police program along various standard dimensions of social security reform. He then briefly discusses the parallel US-led program and the European Union program that succeeded the German one, arguing that the German program was well meant but too small and inadequately rooted in knowledge of the situation in Afghanistan. The German program was slow to react when the security situation deteriorated, and it lost much of its impact when the United States decided to invest in police reform in grand style. The US program is churning out much larger numbers of police, but largely in the role of auxiliary to the military. Thus, the police reform effort remains woefully inadequate. Brzoska observes that there is no shared understanding of the police's priorities in security provision, that police forces remain closely tied to both traditional and new leaders, and that corruption is a major problem. Depending on the course of the war in Afghanistan, he concludes that the police will either become largely a military-style force or will need to be rebuilt, yet again, from the ground up.

Since the late spring of 2008, when these chapters were submitted, the security situation in Afghanistan has deteriorated, with a more variegated insurgency controlling larger swathes of rural territory and showing a continuing capacity to adapt to the technology and tactics of the international forces. Political change in Pakistan has not produced better results in dealing with the insurgency's bases in the Federally Administered Tribal Areas (FATA) and elsewhere. The incidence of attacks has increased, and the number of Afghan civilians killed (by all sides) in 2008 has risen over that of 2007. Tangible progress in training and expanding the Afghan National Army is offset by continuing frustration with other elements of security sector reform, notably with the police.

In the fall 2008 electoral campaign, Canada's prime minister modified the earlier decision to withdraw from Kandahar by the end of 2011 into a broader commitment to terminate Canada's combat role in Afghanistan by the same date. Neither this nor the earlier diplomatic offensive that had surrounded the NATO Summit in Bucharest did much to alter the reluctance of many NATO allies to upgrade their military contributions to the Afghan mission. The major commitments to increase force levels have come from Germany (in the north), France (in a combat role in the east), and the United States (in the south). The new American administration is committed to a further increase of 17,000. Whether this will suffice and whether, as some suggest, more boots on the ground will mean less call for the air strikes that have created such ill will between Afghans and the international community, remains to be seen.

The picture with respect to governance and development also remains mixed, at best. The termination, in August 2008, of Canada's Strategic Advisory Team (whose work is described in Mike Capstick's chapter) has simply removed one point of international influence on a national government widely perceived as weak and corrupt. Modest improvement in governance at the provincial level does not go far to balance the anxieties surrounding the impending presidential elections, which were recently postponed on questionable constitutional grounds. Meanwhile, progress in development and human rights—notoriously difficult to measure at the best of times—remains hostage to insecurity and administrative incapacity.

Several contributors to this volume call, to differing degrees, for a reassessment of the international community's objectives, strategies, and tactics in Afghanistan. Such a reassessment is in fact under way and will be accelerated by the new American administration. With respect to objectives, ambition is giving way to realistic minimalism: perhaps not a Jeffersonian democracy but at least a relatively stable polity whose remote regions cannot again harbour threats to the rest of the world. With respect to strategy and tactics, there is a growing recognition that superior technology and even the expected Iraq-like surge are unlikely to suffice. As several of our German authors insist, there is no substitute for getting to know the territory and the political culture and trying to work with, not against, the grain of traditional regional and local power structures. While this volume has no policy agenda beyond that of critical assessment, our hope is that it will make some contribution to these current reassessments, so vital for the future of Afghanistan, NATO, and the global order.

Part I

Chapter 2

Assessing the Afghanistan Compact:
Is the International Community Defaulting
on the Compact or Is the Compact the
Wrong Approach?

Citha D. Maass

Introduction

The growing concern that Afghanistan might slip back into instability or even civil war has raised questions about whether the international approach in Afghanistan has been appropriate to the specific Afghan conditions. Had the Bonn Process laid a solid foundation for a gradually progressing recovery of the war-torn country, delays in the implementation of the ambitious Afghanistan Compact[1] would not have caused serious doubts about the basic method of implementation. Since the Compact has not been even halfway implemented, only a preliminary assessment can be made as to why it has been missing its benchmarks.

In this chapter, the relationship between the Compact and the Bonn Agreement[2] will be clarified. The first section asks: What are the common features of both frameworks? How and to what extent does the Compact's approach deviate from the Bonn Process and attempt to correct some of the latter's deficiencies?

The second section explores why the Compact is expected to fall far short of the many benchmarks. Is it only the deteriorating security situation that should be blamed? Or are there other reasons that have prevented the international and national actors from achieving the time-bound rehabilitation targets? This leads to the question of whether the Compact has set the right priorities for sustainable stabilization and development. Has the Compact been based on unsound assumptions?

Third, this chapter assesses the current state of the reform process. Are the setbacks caused by tactical mistakes correctable if the timelines are extended? Or is a strategic revision needed? Finally, some basic recommendations are made that might be considered by a mid-term review.

The Compact: Same Basic Philosophy but Adjusted Strategy

The relationship between the Compact and the Bonn Agreement can be summarized as follows: both have been shaped by the same long-term vision of establishing a "liberal market democracy" in Afghanistan. Apart from the same ultimate goal, however, the Compact has sought to correct certain deficiencies that became obvious during efforts to implement the Bonn Agreement. Both have been understood by the United Nations and the international community as political documents: they function as strategic frameworks for the multisectored peace-building effort and demonstrate the political commitment of international donors to the long recovery process of Afghanistan.

Although both documents emphasize "Afghan ownership," their political nature differs due to the distinctive political processes by which they were conceptualized. The Bonn Agreement was the outcome of intensive political negotiations between, on the one hand, the victorious Afghan war factions and military allies of the United States in their fight against the Taliban regime, and on the other the UN, the dominant US negotiator Zalmay Khalilzad, and various international diplomats. The Bonn Agreement fell short of a peace treaty, but served a similar purpose. It was a political compromise between those external and internal forces that had defeated the Taliban, or had benefited from their collapse, on how to initiate the political process of installing an Afghan government elected by the Afghan people. The final document was officially approved by those Afghan and international representatives who participated in the Bonn I conference in November–December 2001.

Although the Compact was also designed as a political document, it should basically be considered a strategic planning framework. It was conceptualized primarily by Afghan and international technocrats close to the World Bank institutions, and the consultation process was rather restricted. The Compact itself was presented at the international conference on Afghanistan in London on 31 January 2006. In contrast to the Bonn Agreement, it was not officially signed, and thus not legally binding. To compensate for this, it was later endorsed by the UN Security Council as the "central strategic framework" for rebuilding Afghanistan.[3]

In addition, just as the Bonn Agreement served as the basic document for the overall Bonn Process, the Compact is the central document of a much broader process. It is directly linked to two other planning documents: the *Afghanistan National Development Strategy Summary Report: An Interim Strategy* (hereafter referred to as the *I-ANDS Summary Report*)[4] and *Afghanistan's Millennium Development Goals: Report 2005, Vision 2020* (referred to as *Millennium Goals*).[5] Thus, the Compact in fact refers to the broader strategic framework constituted by all three documents, of which the *I-ANDS Summary Report* is still a work in progress. Contrary to the Bonn Process, however, the Compact—understood as a process—envisages a much more complex strategic planning effort. The linkage between the three documents indicates the new approach pursued in the Compact, incorporating lessons learned from the Bonn Process. In particular, the Compact departs from its predecessor, the Bonn Agreement, in the following respects:

- *Time frame:* What seems to be a mere technicality can actually be viewed as a lesson learned—to prolong the planning term. Initially the Bonn Process had been scheduled for only three years, but it soon needed to be extended by another year. In recognition that more time is required to rebuild the war-ravaged country, the Compact is designed for five years: 2006–2010. It aims at a long-term commitment by international donors and a corresponding planning process by the Afghan government, which has aligned it with the *Millennium Goals* report whose targets are to be met in 2020.
- *Political responsibility and ownership:* While the Bonn Agreement was a "pact among Afghans to be monitored and assisted by the United Nations," the Compact intends to provide a "framework for *partnership* between the [Afghan] Government and the international community."[6] It claims to emphasize Afghan ownership and to upgrade the responsibility of the Government of Afghanistan.
- *Concept:* The most important lesson learned is the broadening of sectoral planning. The Bonn Agreement focused only on the governance pillar by building Afghan government institutions. It was complemented by the Military Technical Agreement, which provided the security pillar by establishing the International Security Assistance Force.[7] However, economic development as the third pillar was neglected. Now this shortcoming has been eliminated as the Compact combines all three pillars in the same conceptual framework.

The Compact has directly succeeded the Bonn Agreement. It specifies the obligations of the international community as well as those of the Government of Afghanistan. The Compact has empowered the Afghan government to take the lead in setting development priorities and enforcing principles for improved aid effectiveness, such as transparency and accountability on the part of the Afghan government and international donors (Annex II). With regard to the obligations of the Government of

Afghanistan, the Compact summarizes the *immediate* goals, adopts the benchmarks and datelines of the *I-ANDS Summary Report*, and confirms Kabul's commitment.

The *I-ANDS Summary Report* outlines the *medium-term* goals, introduces a framework for development planning, and establishes a mechanism for fiscal adjustments ranging from one to fifteen years. It specifies the three pillars also mentioned in the Compact: (i) security, (ii) governance, rule of law and human rights, and (iii) economic and social development. In addition, five cross-cutting themes are mentioned.[8] Of particular importance is the vision that determines the Government of Afghanistan's strategy of development.

The *Millennium Goals* report articulates the *long-term* overarching goals for the future well-being of the Afghan people and for re-establishing Afghanistan's role in the international community. The report's planning framework declares the intention of the Government of Afghanistan to contribute to the global task of achieving the eight goals specified in the Millennium Declaration adopted by the UN General Assembly in September 2000. In view of the war legacy, the Afghan *Millennium Goals* report has extended the UN dateline of 2015 to the year 2020. Since Afghanistan is the fifth poorest country in the world, the Afghan government is focusing particularly on the first goal, namely, to eradicate extreme poverty and hunger. This goal is to be achieved by an anti-poverty strategy combined with promotion of sustained economic growth.

The development strategy is not only highly ambitious but also ideologically loaded with a vision that, surprisingly, combines ancient Islamic statecraft with present-day theories about the market economy. The technocrats who prepared the strategy sought to legitimize it by linking it to the ancient concept of the Circle of Justice, which dates back to a famous Islamic scholar of the ninth century.[9] Islamic teachings on the Circle of Justice asserted that a government needed basic components that were interdependent: armed forces to ensure security, state income to maintain the army, prosperity and development to fill the coffers of the state, and justice and good governance to guarantee the wealth and well-being of the people. The authors have clothed the millennium development strategy in ancient Islamic thought in order to claim that "this government's vision for Afghanistan is fully consistent with our Islamic and cultural values as stated in our Constitution," thus pre-empting potential criticism from anti-reform forces.[10]

This reference to an ancient concept also serves to legitimize the ambitious task of the *I-ANDS Summary Report*: "Like the Circle of Justice, this vision has mutually reinforcing security, political and economic dimensions." If the government does not simultaneously progress on all three pillars, it risks a "circle of injustice." [11] Having read these lofty intentions, one wonders what strategy the Government of Afghanistan will pursue to turn its promises into reality.

For each pillar, a specific vision has been formulated. The security vision aims at creating a "peaceful and just society" based on the state's monopoly of the use of force. The governance vision intends to develop Afghanistan into a "stable and mature Islamic constitutional democracy." Interestingly, the government's role in regulating the economy is specifically mentioned: the government should act as an "enabler of the private sector, not its competitor." Finally, the economic vision identifies the ideological centrepiece of the development strategy: "to build a liberal market economy." The private sector is considered the driving force for development, poverty alleviation, and progressive elimination of the drug economy, thus allowing "all Afghans to live in dignity."[12]

The priority sectors of economic and social development are detailed at great length. This prioritization reveals who the actual owners of the development strategy are: the technocrats of the World Bank institutions. De facto, the Government of Afghanistan has to follow their orders regardless of its officially claimed "leadership." This explains why the link to Islamic tradition has been so necessary: it provides the Afghan government with a political argument to counter resistance both from criminalized drug profiteers and from power-driven Islamist forces, be they Taliban or Islamists in governmental or parliamentarian ranks.

Thus, the Compact spells out the conceptual approach that also underpinned the Bonn Agreement: the liberal peace thesis. Also known as liberal market democracy, this approach is based on the premise that "democratization and marketization would foster domestic peace."[13] When the then UN Secretary General Boutros-Ghali introduced his *Agenda for Peace* in 1992,[14] the UN adopted a broad peace-building concept. Since then, the concept of liberal market democracy has ruled UN peace-building missions. Boutros-Ghali's successor, Kofi Annan, considered it a "highly effective means of preventing conflict, both within and between states."[15] Consequently, the international peace-building efforts in Afghanistan have been based on this approach regardless of whether it was appropriate for conditions in this particular "failed state."

Missing the Benchmarks: Encountering the Afghan Reality

When the Compact was presented at the London Conference in January 2006, cynics (or realists?) instantly considered it a worthless document. They argued that at the very moment of its release, its benchmarks needed to be revised. Thus, no one who was familiar with the situation in Afghanistan was surprised to learn that the newly formed Joint Coordination and Monitoring Board decided as one of its first actions to postpone all timelines for three months.[16] Although this revision was merely bureaucratic, it already pointed to flaws in the general political approach.

The eulogies of the world leaders at the London Conference were soon belied by the dramatic rise of the insurgency from May 2006 onward. This development raised questions as to whether politicians and technocrats alike had been willing at all to assess the state of recovery realistically and to tailor the Compact to Afghanistan's most pressing needs. The euphoria at the London Conference had sprung from the belief that with the inauguration of the newly elected Afghan parliament in December 2005, the Bonn Process had finally concluded with successful institution-building. Relief over the two rounds of relatively peaceful elections for the presidency and the parliament in 2004 and 2005 misled the United Nations, the international community, and the Afghan government to assume that the new institutions would soon function effectively and deliver basic public services to the poverty-stricken Afghan people.

When the world leaders and President Karzai adopted the Compact at the conference, however, warning signs had already appeared. Voter turnout in the parliamentary elections had significantly declined compared with that of the presidential elections. Disillusionment about the performance of the Karzai government and the pervasive corruption had been openly voiced. The Karzai government had not succeeded in establishing its monopoly of power in the southern and eastern parts of the country. Donor funds piled up in the ministerial coffers in Kabul because they could not be invested for lack of administration and absorptive capacity in the provincial hinterland. The eroding legitimacy of the Karzai government in general, and the growing anger among Pashtun tribes who felt discriminated against in the distribution of international development projects in particular, paved the way for the insurgency. The more the Pashtun tribes felt alienated from Kabul, the easier it became for the Taliban-led insurgents from across the Pakistani border to make inroads with the local tribes. The question arose whether the world leaders, the Karzai government, and the technocrats who authored the Compact had deceived themselves with wishful thinking, simply ignoring the warning signs.

By the second anniversary of the London Conference in January 2008, it was obvious not only that the timelines needed to be further extended but also that the benchmarks needed to be revised. International as well as Afghan officials who had been involved in implementing the Compact tended to blame the deteriorating security situation and the threats emanating from Pakistan for the shortfalls. However, these contingencies did not sufficiently explain the disappointing progress.

This analysis leads to the following conclusion: the adoption of the Compact in London was based on a faulty assessment of the overall political situation. With regard to security, the political authors of the Compact and their technocratic experts entertained false hopes that the Taliban had been wiped out. They might not have anticipated the degree to which the Taliban-led insurgency would subsequently gain momentum, but they should certainly have taken into account that the high command under Mullah Omar had started to regroup the neo-Taliban insurgents on both sides of the Durand Line, mustering covert support through intimidation as well as willing cooperation among the local Pashtuns. This misjudgment played a major role in preventing the Compact from being implemented according to schedule. Other reasons contributing to the disappointing progress included an overestimation of the functional capability of the newly established state institutions, the poor performance of the Karzai government, and the unwillingness of the international donors to better coordinate their priorities and policies.

Thus, the Compact got on the wrong track from the very beginning. This does not, however, imply that the conceptual approach was also inappropriate. Compared with the Bonn Agreement, the most significant improvement was that the Compact provided an overarching framework for reforming all three basic sectors: security, governance, and economic development. The approach reflected the lessons learned from the international debate on post-1992 peace-building efforts: no development without security, and no sustainable peace without development. And to achieve these goals, an effective government and functioning state institutions were needed. According to the international debate about externally supported peace-building in postwar countries, the Compact set the right priorities by emphasizing the interdependence among the three pillars. From a theoretical point of view it was the correct concept. In view of the political situation, however, the crucial question was this: Had the essential prerequisites on the ground already been established? Or was the approach too ambitious at that early phase of rebuilding Afghanistan after decades of war? The latter claim can be considered correct, as a few examples will illustrate.

Security

The security vision focused on the Government of Afghanistan's ability to provide security for its citizens and uphold the law. The Compact specifically referred to security sector reform (SSR) as enabling the Afghan government to fulfil this task. The Compact emphasized the "strong support" that the NATO-led International Security Assistance Force, the US-led Operation Enduring Freedom, and the partner nations would provide for implementing the five pillars of SSR:[17] building the Afghan National Army (key partner nation: US); building the Afghan National Police (key partner nation: Germany, succeeded in June 2007 by the European Union); countering narcotics (key partner nation: UK); and disbanding illegal armed groups (key partner nation: Japan). Reform of the justice sector, previously the fifth pillar of SSR, was now subsumed into the governance pillar (key partner nation: Italy, from July 2007 onward strongly assisted by the European Union).

Occasional reports about small achievements could not obscure the fact that hardly any progress was made—with countering narcotics, disbanding illegal armed groups, and reforming the justice sector having the worst record. In view of the precarious security situation, it was of utmost importance to establish functioning Afghan security forces. The buildup of a professionalized army was progressing reasonably, but development of the Afghan National Police was falling alarmingly short of the benchmark set in the Compact: "By end-2010, a fully constituted, professional, functional and ethnically balanced Afghan National Police and Afghan Border Police with a combined force of up to 62,000 will be able to meet the security needs of the country effectively and will be increasingly fiscally sustainable."[18] The gap between this ambitious goal and political reality soon became obvious. The blame had to be shared by all involved actors: the technocrats who defined the benchmarks and timelines; the Government of Afghanistan, which should have politically enforced the multiphase reform process; and the international community, whose joint efforts were essential for implementing police reform and training.

The technocrats set goals in the Compact that were far too ambitious and totally unrealistic under Afghan circumstances, even if the growing Taliban-led insurgency had not severely impeded the police reform. Furthermore, the Afghan government in general, and President Hamid Karzai and the Ministry of Interior in particular, obstructed the speedy implementation of reform in various ways. In June 2006, Karzai tried to sabotage the second phase of the rank-and-pay reform by nominating appointees with criminal records.[19] The Ministry of Interior was considered one of "Kabul's most corrupt ministries"[20] because it appointed chiefs of police who were deeply involved in protection, patronage, and networks of drug trafficking and other criminal activities.

The international community, too, caused a slowdown in the reform process because it did not sufficiently coordinate its contributions. Leading states quarrelled over which of the rival philosophies was more appropriate for Afghan conditions: the German vision of a civilian law-and-order force, or the US vision of a security force with a counter-insurgency role. To respond to the growing insurgency, the US pushed through quick fixes such as the impromptu creation of the Afghan National Auxiliary Police. This was to be a tribal militia of 11,271 men, who were to receive the same pay as ordinary police after only ten days of training.[21] The scheme watered down the initial concept of a rank-and-pay reform, an agreement that had been reached by the leading states involved in police reform and signed by President Karzai in December 2005. Furthermore, when Germany could no longer live up to the obligations of the "lead nation" in police reform, it handed over the task to the European Union. Under the European Security and Defence Policy, the EU Police Mission (EUPOL) was launched in mid-June 2007.[22] It soon became obvious, however, that the mission's complement of about 190 police mentors from various European member states could neither be filled nor would meet the much higher demands on the ground. Not only has the mission remained heavily understaffed, but it is also doubtful whether mentoring is the appropriate approach to raising the low standard of the Afghan National Police.

In view of these manifold obstacles, the police force is currently assessed as underpaid, understaffed, and ill-equipped, with an illiteracy rate of about 70 percent, an annual attrition rate of 15–30 percent (estimates for 2006), and a high degree of corruption. In spite of all these shortcomings, the Afghan National Police force has been increasingly deployed in the forefront of counter-insurgency or targeted by suicide attacks, and so has suffered a dramatic increase in casualties: 138 police officers died and 183 were wounded in 2004–2005, 627 died and 1,090 were wounded from 2006 through July 2007,[23] and the figures are still rising. Only recently has the international community woken up to this dramatic deficit in the Compact's implementation. While the United States reacted by significantly increasing its support, the European Union and Germany have basically confined themselves to paying lip service to making the EUPOL mission more effective. Thus, the prospects of overcoming the structural deficits in the foreseeable future are bleak.

Governance, Rule of Law, and Human Rights

The Bonn Process had focused on institution-building with the result that the legal basis for governance and protection of human rights has been provided by the Afghanistan Constitution, and the principal institutions of the three constitutional branches of government (Supreme Court, Lower House, and Upper House of the National Assembly) have been established. Thanks to these accomplishments, the authors of the Compact obviously assumed that the new political system had been sufficiently stabilized. Therefore, they saw good prospects for the new system to further advance toward the goal outlined in the governance vision: to establish a stable and mature Islamic constitutional democracy. This explains why the Compact has such lofty aims, declaring, for example, that the Government of Afghanistan will

- "rapidly expand its capacity to provide basic services to the population throughout the country";
- establish "a more effective, accountable and transparent administration at all levels of government";

- "implement measurable improvements in fighting corruption"; and
- together with the international community, give "a priority" to reforming the justice sector.[24]

At first glance, the development strategy with which the Afghan government sought to reach these goals seemed to tackle the key problem. The *I-ANDS Summary Report* stated that the "government's overall aim is to enhance governance, by establishing and strengthening government institutions at the central and sub-national level in order to achieve measurable improvements in the delivery of services and the protection of rights of all Afghans."[25] A long list of benchmarks followed: a number of commissions, committees, and other institutions would be set up and national legislation or international conventions ratified by specified deadlines.

Establishing public commissions is a necessary precondition for governing a state. Yet the mere fact that a commission has been set up does not guarantee that the quality of governance has improved. Similarly, signing a law or ratifying an international convention as such does not prove that the standard of rule of law has been raised or better protection of human rights ensured. What actually matters is *how* these commissions perform and whether the new legislation is effectively enforced on a regular basis. This leads to the crucial question of whether, so far, the governance strategy has succeeded in translating progress on paper into visible improvements in everyday life for the ordinary Afghan citizen. If not—and all indications have been pointing in this direction—President Karzai will suffer a further decline in his legitimacy. As a consequence, the image of the international community is likely to be tarnished as well, since it is held responsible by the Afghan public for the performance of the Karzai government.

The Western donors' exaggerated promises of replacing the tyranny of the Taliban with a liberal market democracy have tarnished the reputation of the international community and the Karzai government. The political rhetoric of the Bush administration in particular, but also of other Western donors in general, unduly raised expectations of quick and visible progress. Instead of dampening inappropriate expectations, the Compact's overambitious goals even further nurtured false hopes. This unfounded optimism predisposed the Afghan population as well as the public in the donor countries to assume that Afghanistan could easily jump from the Middle Ages of the Taliban regime into the enlightened world of twenty-first-century Western democracies. Consequently, the long-standing experience that newly established institutions need time to mature and gradually build in-house capacity before they can effectively function slipped the minds of the Afghan and international public.

No one should be surprised that the ensuing frustration among the public in Afghanistan and in the donor countries has intensified as a result of the Compact's approach of combining unrealistic political estimations with lengthy technocratic planning procedures in which

- expectations of rapid democratic progress were exaggerated;
- progress in state-building was overestimated due to the fact that formal institution-building was not accompanied by performance requirements for the new institutions;
- progress was often measured merely by bureaucratic benchmarks and unrealistic quantitative indicators; and
- operational guidelines were missing entirely or are still being drafted and redrafted, although the Compact has already entered into its third year of implementation.

Another inappropriate planning approach has been particularly obvious in the governance pillar but can also be observed in the other two pillars: the tendency to restrict the strategy to bureaucratic or formal institutional reforms without realizing or wanting to acknowledge the highly sensitive, broader political implications of these reforms. The faulty logic of the World Bank draft paper issued in July 2007 on how to establish governance at the subnational level in Afghanistan may illustrate this.[26] Building up a provincial administration and linking it with the national ministerial bureaucracy was rightly considered an urgent task. The draft paper comprehensively identified existing deficiencies and recommended a detailed strategy to establish a subnational institutional structure. However, insufficient attention was paid to the political implications: implementing such a reform would immediately rekindle the political debate on the structure of the Afghan political system, in particular the controversy over centralism versus federalism (or, to use a less controversial term, devolution). This had been one of the most fiercely debated issues during the Constitutional Loya Jirga in December 2003–January 2004. At that time, after much backroom pressure and bribery, a presidential system with a highly centralized state structure was adopted by the delegates and laid down in the new Afghan constitution.[27] The *technocratic* attempt to establish the missing institutional link between national and provincial administrations has opened up a *political* Pandora's box, with the consequence that the urgently needed reform of subnational governance has been further delayed.

The mix of negative repercussions for the daily lives of the Afghan public and the extended technocratic planning and lack of political commitment on the side of the Karzai government can best be illustrated by the fate of the anti-corruption strategy. Admittedly, fighting corruption is an extremely difficult task in any country. However, the degree to which corruption has infected public institutions, political life, and the fledgling private economy has turned Afghanistan into one of the most corrupt countries by any measure. The authors of the Compact realized that this could undermine efforts to stabilize the fragile political system, but they reacted in a typical bureaucratic manner. For example, the Government of Afghanistan in the first volume of the *I-ANDS Report* correctly diagnosed the problem in early 2006, but over a year passed before the Compact's authors reacted. The *I-ANDS Report* stated:

> Many civil servants are still recruited through a system of patronage and rarely by merit. This is because the pay scale of civil servants is insufficient to attract, retain, and motivate skilled and qualified staff. This causes corruption by civil servants, ensuring that the public sector remains short of educated, skilled and professional human resources, while many more skilled people are hired by the aid community.[28]

Although the Compact's authors were aware how urgently actions were needed, the first draft of the so-called *Anti-Corruption Roadmap* was not published until April 2007.[29] A few months later the first draft was replaced by a second one.[30] Even more elaborate, it painstakingly listed a whole range of causes for corruption, but disappointingly concluded by recommending a "national anti-corruption foundation strategy."

Yet it would be unfair to blame only the technocrats, for the real cause of the problem lay elsewhere. The prevailing opinion of ordinary Afghans in all parts of the country could be summarized thus: "Corruption was 'worse than ever,' people said, as aid flows and the illegal economy helped enriched [*sic*] the powerful."[31] A pilot survey published by Integrity Watch Afghanistan in January 2007 concluded: "Some 60 percent of respondents perceived President Karzai's administration to be more corrupt than that of the Taliban, mujahidin or the Communist periods."[32] Three conclusions can be drawn from this widespread perception:

- It reveals the limitations under which the Compact's authors had to work, be it with regard to corruption or other issues of governance. To do justice to the technocrats, it should be mentioned that they had actually identified this problem in the first draft of the *Anti-corruption Roadmap*: "The political dimension of anti-corruption cannot be ignored. Corruption is not only a criminal activity, but also a means for enrichment and empowerment of political elites."[33]
- If the Karzai government lacks the political will to dismiss corrupt governors, police chiefs, or high-ranking officials[34] and, generally speaking, to reform the dysfunctional state institutions, then the chances of overcoming bad governance will be slim.
- Finally, the reference to the inflow of international aid money demonstrates that the international community must also be blamed for directly fuelling corruption.[35] The international donors were accused by the Afghan public of having indirectly contributed to

corruption because they had been tolerating corrupt practices and the disappointing functioning of the Karzai government for too long.

Economic and Development Pillar

The economic vision aimed at building a liberal market economy. Conforming with this vision, the Afghan finance minister Anwar-ul-Haq Ahadi noted in October 2007 that the "freedom of the individual to initiate economic activity was most important" and that this had been deliberately decided by the Afghan government.[36] He added that Afghanistan has now laid the foundation for a market-based economy. The German Office for Foreign Trade (BFAI) confirmed that the course for a "relatively liberal trade regime" had been set, but cautioned against excessive expectations by pointing out structural problems and the weakness of private consumption.[37]

A strategy of promoting economic development that will be more specific than the interim Afghanistan National Development Strategy still has to be finalized. In spite of all the obstacles impeding overall progress since the London Conference, the final strategy can be expected to follow the same basic philosophy that shaped planning from the beginning and that was reiterated in the first volume of the *I-ANDS Report*: "Our strategy will provide the enabling environment for the private sector to create legal employment."[38] Interestingly, the report identified not one but two core aims: "private sector-led growth" and "eliminating the narcotics economy." The emphasis on the second aim indicated a new element. Compared with the initial Compact paper presented at the London Conference, now it was felt that more attention had to be paid to countering narcotics, even though, in principle, such efforts have so far remained confined to drafting and revising a national counter-narcotics strategy.[39]

Assessing socioeconomic progress is hampered by a methodological problem that has been common to war-torn countries in general but, in the case of Afghanistan, has been further aggravated by the sheer length and devastation of the war. Even after seven years of internationally funded reconstruction, statistical data are still missing, unreliable, or incomparable (due to different criteria and methodologies applied), and the long awaited population census has not yet been completed. Consequently, both planning and evaluation have been suffering from weak, incoherent, or simply unavailable information, in particular statistical data.

The lack of trustworthy data has directly affected political discussions in Afghanistan and donor countries alike. It has fuelled a highly polarized controversy: On the one hand Afghan and international politicians justify their commitment by citing extraordinary growth rates. On the other, domestic and international critics quote other statistics to demonstrate how little progress has actually been achieved and under what miserable conditions the vast majority of the Afghan people still have to live—when they survive at all. More and more publications are released, alternating between success stories about jump-starting some economic sectors and negative stories about program failure due to poor management, corruption stemming from overfunding, or ignorance of real needs. The chance to educate the international and Afghan publics about the enormous challenge of developing the shattered economy has unfortunately been missed. Instead, widespread mistrust has been nurtured: officials of the Afghan and donor governments are suspected of having obscured the actual state of affairs. This contradictory picture has discouraged independent assessments as to whether or not the economic strategy as originally conceived has proved to be appropriate.

As is often the case in the early phase of reconstructing the economies of war-torn countries, one finds unexpected quick successes side by side with well-conceived but ultimately fruitless efforts. Even if corruption and the drug economy are put aside, the crux of the problem in Afghanistan is that any progress achieved so far has to be judged against the background of an extremely low level of socioeconomic development in absolute terms. If the baseline is more or less zero, even a small improvement will make growth rates skyrocket. Politicians have exploited the difference between relative and absolute progress by focusing only on one side of the coin. Different interpretations of the growth rate of the gross domestic product (GDP) may illustrate the issue.

In order to demonstrate remarkable progress, politicians and technocrats have preferred to cite the estimated growth rates of real GDP: 2002–03 = 28.6 percent; 2003–04 = 15.7 percent; 2004–05 = 8.0 percent; 2005–06 = 14.0 percent; and 2006–07 = 8.0 percent.[40] With an estimated population of 25.7 million (fiscal year 2005–06[41]), the increase in the nominal figures in millions of US dollars was less impressive: 2002–03 = $4,084; 2003–04 = $4,585; 2004–05 = $5,971; 2005–06 = $7,309; and 2006–07 = $8,399.[42] However, GDP growth rates alone cannot serve as a sufficient indicator of economic progress and structural reforms because they do not reveal what has caused the growth, what role has been played by the high international subsidies for the various trust funds, and what the relationship has been between the "licit" economy and the "illicit" one (narcotics and smuggling).

The reverse side of the coin has been the dismal outlook projected by social indicators. Official documents of the World Bank institutions dryly state, "poverty rate: no account." However, the Afghan government in the *I-ANDS Report* was frank enough to admit that poverty in Afghanistan is pervasive. Social indices such as the UN Human Development Index place Afghanistan among the six poorest countries worldwide, the other five being African states.[43] In this context the estimated absolute figures of the GDP per capita in US dollars were revealing: 2002–03 = $182;

2003–04 = $199; 2004–05 = $253; 2005–06 = $294; and 2006–07 = $344. How could an Afghan family, which normally has five to seven children, survive on US$344 for a whole year? And how did those families survive who had no jobs at all? The three different ways to measure GDP growth belie the words of the politicians and technocrats: what began as a success story turned into proof of absolute poverty on a worldwide scale. Beyond the continuing controversy over interpreting GDP growth is the point that socioeconomic progress cannot be evaluated on the basis of a single, though significant, macroeconomic indicator.

The second review under the three-year poverty reduction and growth facility arrangement, prepared by the International Monetary Fund (IMF) for the Afghan government, pinpointed the causes of the contradictory development: "Progress in implementing the structural reform agenda has been mixed owing mainly to capacity constraints and an increasingly difficult political environment."[44] How urgently a structural reform was needed was demonstrated by the deficits of the "aid architecture," for which both the international donors and the Government of Afghanistan had to be held responsible. Among the various factors that caused the deficits, two should be examined in more detail. The first points to conceptual flaws of externally induced stabilization and reconstruction efforts: the supply-driven nature of the aid architecture. The second indicates another basic dilemma in aid delivery: budgetary constraints and the lack of institutional linkages inside the government structure of the recipient country.

Although the first issue is not unique to Afghanistan, there the repercussions have been particularly detrimental. Because of the worldwide shock under which the international donors responded to the Bush administration's call for a "global war on terrorism," the aid architecture in Afghanistan has been not only heavily supply-driven but also strongly biased in favour of military assistance and emergency relief. This bias ignores a lesson learned from external interventions in other postwar countries: from the very beginning, short-term relief projects should be combined with a long-term reconstruction strategy. Only if both approaches are conceptually combined can the grand strategy meet the imperative of building sustainable structures and lasting domestic capacity.

In Afghanistan, however, assistance has mostly been given according to the priorities of the donors. Often, spending procedures are determined not by local needs in Afghanistan but by the fiscal constraints of the donors, who have to spend surplus aid money before the end of the fiscal year. The supply-driven character of aid limits attempts to impose certain conditions on the Government of Afghanistan or on particular Afghan partners. "Such a situation produces a 'Samaritan's Dilemma' in which the donor is driven to give, but the incentive for the recipient to expend effort is weaker since there is assured assistance."[45]

The second factor may be called the delivery dilemma: donors bypass the national government in Kabul and fund projects directly because the national ministries lack internal structures and capacity to invest the foreign aid effectively. However, since the Afghan government has been insufficiently funded, it has been unable to improve its governance and deliver public services, thus losing its legitimacy among the Afghan people. Without going into too many details, the following figures for the Afghan budget year 1384 (2005–06) illustrate the delivery dilemma.

In 2004 the Government of Afghanistan revised its system of budget reporting. Henceforth, aid that is directly spent by donors is reported under the "External Budget." In addition, further funds are channelled by donors through the Afghan government's budget. These contributions (also called "budget funding"), together with (so far limited) domestic revenue raised by the government itself through customs duties and taxes, are reported under the "Core Budget." In 2005–06, 55 percent of the total expenditure was funded by the Afghan government through its governmental Core Budget, while the remaining 45 percent bypassed the government budget and was directly spent by the donors (External Budget). In the following year, 2006–07, donors channelled more funds through the government budget, but at the same time reduced their overall assistance. Thus, although the Government of Afghanistan spent a higher share (61 percent) through its Core Budget compared with 39 percent through its External Budget, the cake itself became smaller. [46]

Yet, this was not the end of the delivery dilemma. As stated in the IMF report on poverty reduction and growth facility (*Second Review*), not only a lack of capacity but also the absence of fiscal linkages between the national line ministries in Kabul and their respective departments in the provinces prevented the Afghan government from promoting economic growth in the countryside. This part of the problem becomes obvious when the Core Budget is analyzed. It comprises two categories. The first is "ordinary," for recurring expenses such as salaries, operations, and maintenance. More relevant is the second category, "development," for new investments—which are the driving force of economic progress and the reduction of poverty.

In 2005–06, the Ministry of Rural Rehabilitation and Development excelled over all other line ministries with an execution rate of 71 percent of its development budget. It was followed by the Ministry of Public Health with an execution rate of 63 percent and the Ministry of Higher Education with a rate of 60 percent. At the opposite end was the Ministry for Counter Narcotics with an execution rate of 0 percent (!), and the Ministry of Commerce with a rate of 3 percent. The average disbursement rate was 39 percent.[47] In other words, a high percentage of international aid funds and (limited) domestic revenue simply gathered dust in the coffers of the national line ministries—or may have disappeared into unknown pockets. At the same time, provincial departments of the line ministries were thirsting for funds from Kabul but received too few. Thus, the provincial authorities turned to the international donors, who responded by giving money directly, which was reported under the External Budget—a vicious circle indeed!

To conclude, the strategic core component of the Afghanistan National Development Strategy—promoting private sector-led growth—needs to be looked at. As the IMF *Second Review* stated, "We were unable to implement a number of other program commitments. In particular, we were unable to adopt a comprehensive restructuring/divestment plan for public enterprises engaged in commercial activities."[48] The report also revealed the actual state of planning: one month earlier, in May 2007, the World Bank had submitted a document called "Afghanistan: Privatization Strategy Note" with the aim of facilitating the development of a privatization strategy.[49] If no privatization strategy has yet been conceptualized, how and when will the private sector start functioning as a driving force in building a liberal market economy? The odds are formidable: a deteriorating security situation, disillusioned private investors, and insufficient GDP growth. Do the strategic priorities of the Afghanistan National Development Strategy really constitute an appropriate response to coping with such a challenge?

Tactical Mistakes or Strategic Failure?

What assessment can be made of the reform process after six years of international peace-building efforts and two years of implementing the Compact? Two different schools of thought can be distinguished. Proponents of the first school see the glass of water as half full. They argue that more time is needed so that the reform schemes envisaged in the Compact can become effective. They blame the seemingly unexpected emergence of the reorganized Taliban (neo-Taliban) for the delays in the time-bound development mechanism. They concede tactical mistakes which, however, they believe can be rectified when the Afghan government and the newly established Joint Coordination and Monitoring Board have overcome their bureaucratic teething troubles and learned to better coordinate their activities. And they expect the reform process to speed up as soon as the backbone of the neo-Taliban insurgency has been broken.

Proponents of the second school consider the glass of water half empty. They argue that the implementation of the Compact's reform agenda has been severely impeded by the legacy of the Bonn Agreement. They see the Compact's approach as endangered by the structural weakness of the governance pillar. If the newly established state institutions are not functioning at all or are distorted by patronage and corruption, basic prerequisites for promoting a democratic system and market economy are missing. In their view, the delays in implementing the Compact indicate a strategic failure of the international peace-building efforts.

If progress in building the three pillars is weighed against setbacks, and if one takes into consideration the structural constraints in all reform sectors as well as the complex security risks posed by a heterogeneous alliance of ideological insurgents, power brokers, and drug barons, one has to reject the argument of the first school of thought. The turning point in favour of sustainable stabilization and lasting economic recovery has not been reached. It is beyond doubt that the international community has been seriously defaulting on the Compact. If deadlines are merely extended, but the current strategy is not revised, the international intervention in Afghanistan is at risk of failing in principle.

If the glass of water is already half empty, as argued by the second school of thought, the question arises: What to do? Can the process be reversed before the glass is completely empty? Is the strategy of the international community already doomed to fail? Or is there a realistic chance of a mid-course correction of the Compact's flawed approach?

The current debate among NATO allies and in the public of some donor countries seems to be taking a counterproductive turn. There is no doubt that an insurgency has to be fought by military means. For this purpose, certain military capabilities are clearly wanted on a larger scale. In this context the urgent call of the NATO Secretary General to increase the number of deployed troops seems justified. However, the recent change of paradigm—now emphasizing counter-insurgency instead of counter-terrorism—should be complemented by a strategic reassessment. More troops for specific counter-insurgency tasks are needed, but the increase in size should be carefully adjusted to the security situation on the ground and the perceptions of the local population. A rise in military forces should be cautiously balanced against the risk that the foreign troops could be perceived as occupying forces if their strength is too great. Here, the recent quantitative argument that compares the ratio of foreign troops to population in Afghanistan to the ratio in Iraq or the Balkan states is not helpful.

The new emphasis on counter-insurgency implies a further strategic rethinking: insurgencies have to be fought not only by military means but also by efforts in the governance and development pillars. Since the NATO summit in Riga in late October 2006, this strategy has become part of the political rhetoric but has yet to generate any concrete outcomes. In this context, a basic strategic flaw of the security reform concept should be considered. The intentions of the Military Technical Agreement, which emphasized the assistance role of the International Security Assistance Force (ISAF), have been further pursued in the Compact. It has reinforced the international commitment to build the national security forces so that the Government of Afghanistan will ultimately hold a monopoly on the use of force. Alarmed by the growing insurgency, even a large part of the US Operation Enduring Freedom forces have become involved in training the Afghan National Army, although they have not been mandated with this task. With regard to training the Afghan National Police, the efforts of the initial lead country, Germany, proved to be inadequate. Therefore, the United States stepped in but outsourced the training to the private US security company Dyncorp. At the same time, the ISAF's area of operation was broadened and its numbers increased.

All these efforts have, however, culminated in a paradox. The more the international forces have become involved in building the Afghan security forces, trying to maintain basic security in some parts of the country and to contain the insurgency in others, the less the Afghan government seems to be progressing toward establishing its monopoly of the use of force. While the buildup of the Afghan army has advanced reasonably well, though behind schedule, the performance of the national police has been alarmingly poor.

If the vast majority of the Afghan people still want the international forces to remain in the country because the Government of Afghanistan is seen as too weak and incapable of protecting its own people, then it can be concluded that the Karzai government has lost its credibility and is not expected to establish its monopoly of the use of force. So far, the international strategy of "Afghan ownership" in the security sector has failed: the people do not trust their own government, fearing that it may fall and the country relapse into violence the moment the international forces withdraw.

An important lesson can be learned from this paradox. Contrary to the current international debate, which focuses on the security sector and military strength, and also contrary to the emphasis the Compact has placed on private sector-led growth, the main bottleneck is obviously constituted by the deficiencies of the governance pillar. Two conclusions can be drawn:

- Unless governance is improved, efforts in the security sector will not lead to adequate results.
- Instead of promoting one particular sector, a revised strategy should start from the assumption that interdependence and mutual re-enforcement of all three pillars is the key to stabilization and sustainable development.

What Next?

A mid-term review of the Compact could offer the occasion for a general strategic revision. The following recommendations should be considered:

- The Compact should replace the lofty aims of the security vision, the governance vision, and the economic vision with more realistic and credible goals.
- The international community may need to redefine the envisioned end state, since the establishment of a liberal market democracy does not seem feasible in the foreseeable future. This should be accompanied by downgrading criteria and realistically identifying the aims of donors' engagement.
- A public debate in the donor countries is urgently needed in order to clarify the national interests and values that determine their engagement in Afghanistan.
- Inadequate governance has been identified as a major bottleneck. In order to avoid the above mentioned "Samaritan's Dilemma," the donors should set certain conditions on their assistance.
- Donors should put their own house in order by better coordinating their assistance.
- Finally, instead of prioritizing the security sector, the interdependence of all three pillars should serve as a guiding principle.

Notes

1. "The Afghanistan Compact: Building on Success; The London Conference on Afghanistan," 31 January–1 February 2006, http://www.ands.gov.af/admin/ands/ands_docs/upload/UploadFolder/Afghanistan%20Compact.pdf.
2. "Agreement on Provisional Arrangements in Afghanistan Pending the Reestablishment of Permanent Government Institutions" (Bonn Agreement; Bonn, 5 December 2001), http://www0.un.org/News/dh/latest/afghan/afghan-agree.htm.
3. International Crisis Group, "Afghanistan's Endangered Compact: Policy Briefing," Asia Briefing No. 59 (Kabul/Brussels, 29 January 2007), 5, http://www.crisisgroup.org/library/documents/asia/south_asia/b59_afghanistans_endangered_compact.pdf.
4. Government of the Islamic Republic of Afghanistan, *Afghanistan National Development Strategy Summary Report: An Interim Strategy for Security, Governance, Economic Growth and Poverty Reduction* (hereafter referred to as the *I-ANDS Summary Report*), http://www.reliefweb.int/rw/RWFiles2006.nsf/FilesByRWDocUNIDFileName/KHII-6LK3R2-unama-afg-30jan1.pdf/$File/unama-afg-30jan1.pdf. In addition to the I-ANDS Summary Report, only the first of three volumes has been published. A final version of the interim strategy has yet to be worked out.
5. *Afghanistan's Millennium Development Goals: Report 2005, Vision 2020*, http://www.ands.gov.af/src/src/MDGs_Reps/FINALMDG%20%20REPORT%20_Saturday%201327.pdf.

6. Government of Afghanistan, *I-ANDS Summary Report*, 5 (emphasis added).

7. "Military Technical Agreement between the International Security Assistance Force and the Interim Administration of Afghanistan," 4 January 2002, http://www.operations.mod.uk/isafmta.doc.

8. The five cross-cutting themes are gender equity, counter narcotics, regional cooperation, anti-corruption, and environment. See *I-ANDS Summary Report*, 20.

9. The Islamic scholar Ibn Qutayba is quoted in the *I-ANDS Summary Report*, 1: "There can be no government without an army, no army without money, no money without prosperity, and no prosperity without justice and good administration."

10. Government of Afghanistan, *I-ANDS Summary Report*, 3.

11. Ibid., 3.

12. Ibid., 3-4

13.   Roland Paris, *At War's End: Building Peace after Civil Conflict* (Cambridge: Cambridge University Press, 2004), 6.

14. Boutros Boutros-Ghali, *An Agenda for Peace: Preventive Diplomacy, Peacemaking and Peace-Keeping* (New York: United Nations, 1992).

15. Paris, *At War's End*, 42.

16. International Crisis Group, "Endangered Compact," 10. In order to emphasize the "partnership" between the Government of Afghanistan and the international community, the Joint Coordination and Monitoring Board was co-chaired by a representative of President Hamid Karzai and the special representative of the UN Secretary General, Tom Koenigs, and jointly manned by Afghan officials and international experts.

17. "Afghanistan Compact," 3.

18. "Afghanistan Compact," Annex 1, Benchmarks and Timelines: Security, 6.

19. Contrary to the recommendations of the joint Afghan-International Selection Committee, Karzai nominated appointees who had links to illegal armed groups or who were known human rights abusers, warlords, drug-traffickers, or influential criminals. Only when the major international donors involved in the police reform strongly intervened could Karzai's appointees be forced out of their new positions. See Andrew Wilder, "Cops or Robbers? The Struggle to Reform the Afghan National Police" (Issues Paper Series, Afghan Research and Evaluation Unit, Kabul, July 2007), 40-42, www.areu.org.af.

20. Wilder, "Cops or Robbers," 52-53.

21. International Crisis Group, "Reforming Afghanistan's Police," Asia Report No. 138 (30 August 2007), 13-14, http://www.crisisgroup.org/library/documents/asia/south_asia/138_reforming_afghanistan_s_police.pdf.

22. Council of the European Union, "EU Police Mission in Afghanistan Starts," News release, Brussels, 15 June 2007, http://www.consilium.europa.eu/ueDocs/cms_Data/docs/pressData/en/esdp/94719.pdf.

23. Wilder, "Cops or Robbers," Figure 5, 45.

24. "Afghanistan Compact," Governance, Rule of Law and Human Rights, 3.

25. Government of Afghanistan, *I-ANDS Summary Report*, 13.

26. World Bank, "Service Delivery and Governance at the Sub-national Level in Afghanistan" (July 2007), http://siteresources.worldbank.org/SOUTHASIAEXT/Resources/Publications/448813-1185293547967/4024814-1185293572457/report.pdf.

27. International Crisis Group, "Afghanistan: The Constitutional Loya Jirga" (Afghanistan Briefing, Kabul/Brussels, 12 December 2003), http://www.crisisgroup.org/library/documents/asia/2_afgh_the_constitutional_loya_jirga.pdf.

28. Government of Afghanistan, *Afghanistan National Development Strategy (I-ANDS): An Interim Strategy for Security, Governance, Economic Growth and Poverty Reduction*, 1:58, http://www.ands.gov.af/admin/ands/ands_docs/upload/UploadFolder/I-ANDS%20Volume%20One%20-%20Final%20English.pdf.

29. Government of Afghanistan, *Anti-Corruption Roadmap for the Islamic Republic of Afghanistan* (Draft, April 2007), http://www.ands.gov.af/ands/jcmb/src/jcmb5/5D.%20Anti-Corruption%20Roadmap%20GoA%20-%20English.pdf.

30. Government of Afghanistan, *Afghanistan National Development Strategy: Draft National Anti-Corruption Strategy* (2007), Item V, http://www.ands.gov.af/ands/jcmb/site/src/Meeting%20and%20Documents/Sixth%20%20JCMB/pdfs/Eng/12-Draft%20Anti%20Corruption%20Strategy%2020%2009%2007.pdf.

31. Astri Suhrke, "Reconstruction as Modernisation: The 'Post-Conflict' Project of Afghanistan," *Third World Quarterly* 28, no. 7 (2007): 1305.

32. Yama Torabi and Lorenzo Delesgues, "Afghan Perceptions of Corruption: A Survey across Thirteen Provinces" (Integrity Watch Afghanistan, January 2007), 7, http://iwaweb.org/uploadedFiles/Tor_Afgha_345_Afghan%20Perception%20of%20Corruption%20Draft.pdf.

33. Government of Afghanistan, *Anti-Corruption Roadmap*, 3.

34. International Crisis Group, "Endangered Compact," 11.

35. Lorenzo Delesgues and Yama Torabi, "Reconstruction National Integrity System Survey: Afghanistan 2007, Final Draft" (Integrity Watch Afghanistan, London, 2007), http://www.reliefweb.int/rw/RWFiles2007.nsf/FilesByRWDocUnidFilename/KHII-7FN7BB-full_report.pdf/$File/full_report.pdf.

36. Beth Ellen Cole, "Afghanistan's Economy: On the Right Road, But Still a Long Way to Go" (USIP Briefing, United States Institute of Peace, November 2007), 1. The paper summarized a public event at USIP on 23 October 2007, at which Afghan Finance Minister Ahadi spoke about the state of Afghanistan's economy. Available at http://www.usip.org/pubs/usipeace_briefings/2007/1108_afghanistan_economy.html.

37. Martin Böll, "Wirtschaftstrends kompakt: Afghanistan 2006–07" (Köln, BFAI 2007), 5, http://www.bfai.de/ext/anlagen/PubAnlage_3043.pdf.

38. Government of Afghanistan, *I-ANDS: Interim Strategy*, 1: 73.

39. Government of the Islamic Republic of Afghanistan, Ministry of Counter-Narcotics, "National Drug Control Strategy: An Updated Five-Year Strategy for Tackling the Illicit Drug Problem" (Kabul, January 2006), http://www.fco.gov.uk/Files/kfile/NDCSfinal%20_Jan%202006,0.pdf.
40. International Monetary Fund (IMF), *Islamic Republic of Afghanistan: Second Review under the Three-Year Arrangement under the Poverty Reduction and Growth Facility – Staff Report*, IMF Report No. 07/252 (Washington, July 2007), Table 1, 16, http://www.imf.org/external/pubs/ft/scr/2007/cr07252.pdf.
41. The Afghan fiscal year is from 21 March to 20 March.
42. IMF, *Second Review*, Table 1, 16.
43. Government of Afghanistan, *I-ANDS: Interim Strategy*, 45. According to the UN Human Resource Index, the other five countries were Burkina Faso, Burundi, Mali, Niger, and Sierra Leone.
44. IMF, *Second Review* (21 June 2007), Attachment II, 26.
45. Elinor Ostrum et al., "Aid, Incentives, and Sustainability: An Institutional Analysis (SIDA, Stockholm, 2001), quoted in Hamish Nixon, Publication Series on Promoting Democracy under Conditions of State Fragility, vol. 2, International Assistance and Governance in Afghanistan (Berlin: Heinrich Böll Foundation, 2007), 18, http://www.boell.de/alt/downloads/nahost/Demokratie-vol2-i.pdf.
46. These figures are taken from Nixon, *International Assistance and Governance*, 18-20. All figures are from the Afghan Ministry of Finance.
47. Ibid., 20.
48. IMF, *Second Review*, 26.
49. Ibid.

Chapter 3

The Changing Face of Warlordism in Afghanistan

Conrad Schetter and Rainer Glassner

Introduction

Triggered by the terrorist attacks of 9/11, the international intervention in Afghanistan has catapulted the country into the centre of international political attention. The military intervention by the US forces and allies, which started in October 2001 and led to the collapse of the Taliban regime that autumn, left a power vacuum that was immediately filled by hundreds of commanders as well as by tribal and religious leaders. These "big men" either possessed certain legitimacy or controlled the means of violence to a sufficient degree. This development was further strengthened by the US strategy to use Afghan militias to back up its fight against the remnants of al Qaeda and the Taliban.[1]

Thus the world suddenly became aware of structures of violence that had developed during twenty-two years of continuous war in the absence of a functioning state and that could hardly be changed by a military intervention from one day to the next. Consequently, the internationally stimulated peace process in Afghanistan has been repeatedly shaken by recurring acts of violence and weakened by an inadequate designation of clear responsibilities for security tasks. This volatile situation was seen by international observers as a complete lack of security and as the core obstacle at all political stages of the peace process—the Emergency Loya Jirga in June 2002, the Constitutional Loya Jirga in December 2003, the presidential elections in September 2004, and the parliamentary elections in September 2005. None less than Lakhdar Brahimi, the United Nations

Special Envoy to Afghanistan from 2001 to 2003, coined the saying that Afghanistan is in need of three things: "security, security, and security."

Notions of "security" are varied and can have contradictory meanings. In the case of Afghanistan, international policy-makers, journalists, and researchers heavily stressed the lack of physical security, circumscribing it with the term *warlordism*.[2] This labelling was the expression of a modern, state-centric understanding of physical security, which generally assumes that state institutions hold the monopoly of violence. Contrary to this blueprint, individual actors—so-called warlords—were identified as those who de facto controlled the means of violence. Between 2002 and 2006, virtually no influential political figure in Afghanistan could elude this label, which subsequently became the category for all actors spoiling or even casting doubts on the international agenda for the Afghan peace process. Hereby the term *jang salar* (Dari for "warlord"), which had never been used in Afghan parlance in the past, found its way into Afghan rhetoric and is used—in contrast to the usual term *commander*—in a very biased and negative sense.

The aim of this paper is to show that the term *warlordism* and its associated perceptions are not sufficient to characterize the structures of violence in Afghanistan. While we do not deny the existence of warlords in Afghanistan, the manifold forms of individual leadership as well as the local differences regarding security arrangements are so significant that they could be positioned on a continuum between warlords at one end and the modern state at the other. To support our argument, we will first discuss the term *warlord* to reach a concise and practicable definition. Second, we will discuss the balance of power and influence between the centre and the periphery in Afghanistan. Based on this analysis, we will examine the security situation on the provincial level in three case studies (Kunduz, Kandahar, and Paktia). We intend to demonstrate that the variety of security arrangements on the local level is enormous. Moreover, we intend to show that the paradigm of warlords has been challenged by the re-emergence of the Taliban during the last three years, which indicates that the labelling of actors in Afghanistan is much more influenced by the concerns and interests of the interventionists than by the realities on the ground. Drawing from these examples, we will elaborate various patterns that are of primary importance for defining the local security architecture.

Warlordism – A Contradictory Term

Especially since the beginning of the intervention in Afghanistan, the dominance of so-called warlords has been stressed as the major security threat.[3] The most prominent individual examples of these warlords are Rashid Dostum, Mohammad Fahim, and Ismail Khan, who have become the archetypes or icons of today's warlordism. The persistent argument is that their arbitrary habits and their control of the means of violence are the main impediments to establishing countrywide peace and security.

In view of the omnipresence of the term *warlord* in the recent literature on Afghanistan to describe the lack of security,[4] it makes sense to shed light on the etymology of this word. Within the general debate on state collapse in recent years, the competing elites who gained control of the security sector and looted the country for their own profit were called warlords.[5] However, the etymological understanding of the term *warlord* has been criticized from various points of view. For some, the term bears the negative connotation of one-sided warfare. Others object that the positive suffix "-lord" elevates the respective actors to the status of noblemen. However, when looking closely at a whole series of different Afghan actors commonly labelled as warlords, it is striking that they neither draw their income from warfare per se, nor show honourable or baronial behaviour. Accordingly, it can be argued that the label is misleading because it is used for a great variety of actors who seldom have much in common.[6] In light of this fact, the use of the term has to be questioned. However, since this expression was picked up very quickly by journalists, analysts, and policy-makers, it is currently well established in public awareness. Hence, it has to be stressed that the term, even though it lacks a necessary differentiation and sharpness, tackles the problem in a catchy way as no other term does; thus military grades such as "commander" or "general" assume a legality and formality that these actors usually do not have, while descriptors such as "leader," "big man," or "power-holder" lack the aspect of violence. Moreover, the discussion of the term *warlord* has also spread among the Afghans. Thus former members of the Northern Alliance suspect the label *warlord* as an attempt to sideline them on the national level.[7]

While the term *warlord* has met with criticism as well as with public reception and popularity, the deeper problem lies with the perceptions that usually go along with the use of this label. Two main perceptions can be identified which often turn out to be chimaeras: first, that warlords are a counterweight to the state;[8] and second, that warlords are motivated solely by personal economic profit and enrichment. Concerning the first, the term *warlord* is commonly linked to actors who are diametrically opposed to, or hostile toward, the state. They are identified as the "bad guys" boycotting or spoiling the peace process and jeopardizing the establishment of a well-organized and regulated state power. Thus this point of view carries the risk of sustaining a bipolar semantic order, which rarely exists in reality. Instead, most of the so-called warlords operate in a limbo of power. On the one hand they take over state functions and posts as governors, ministers, police chiefs, or military officers; on the other hand they pursue their own interests and do not hesitate to deploy state resources to accomplish their private goals.[9] Although the emergence of so-called warlords is tied to the weakness or fragility of the state,[10] warlordism should not be understood as an antipode to the state. On the contrary, the relationship between warlords and the state can be described as a process in which the former take over state positions and simultaneously disregard the obligation to fulfill state functions and obey state rules.

The other perception prevailing among academics, journalists, and policy-makers is that warlords are modern robber barons: they are viewed as relentlessly exploiting the ordinary population out of greed for individual, material profit.[11] According to this narrative, wars are fragmented along the profit interests of single actors and are perceived as economic struggles over lootable resources.[12] This line of argument lacks the socioeconomic contextualization of single actors. Most of these warlords are embedded in certain social and economic contexts and are part of reciprocal interpersonal networks. The loyalty of their militiamen depends not only on economic benefits but also on family, clan, tribal, ethnic, or religious ties. Many of the Afghan warlords spend their revenues to strengthen their networks. Likewise, the exchange of women through marriage is a common strategy to tighten relationships with important allies. Thus it is misleading to confine warlords to the military sphere. Functional differentiations between politics, economics, and the military are virtually non-existent in non-modern societies such as Afghanistan. Moreover, social status is not necessarily defined by wealth. In most cases, it is achieved by conforming to a certain positive archetype of Afghan society such as the "brave warrior" (Rashid Dostum) or the "wise emir" (Ismail Khan). Thus individual behaviour is associated with ideal figures of Afghan society in a positive way.

Based on the closer examination of the academic discussion on warlordism, we decided not to reject the term *warlord* completely but to define it more narrowly and precisely. Hereby we attempt to elude a judgmental or negative connotation as well as a blurry or excessively flexible definition. Our aim is to provide a definition that focuses on the functional characteristics of these actors. That way, we first underpin the association of the actors with the control of the means of physical violence. Second, we focus on the relationship between actors and structures. Hereby we understand warlords as actors who are able to make decisions without necessarily being controlled by institutional bodies of the state or society. Thus warlords control the means of physical violence—private as well as state owned—and have the potential and capacity to decide by themselves about its use.

Peripherization of the Centre

Warlordism is often regarded as a local phenomenon that can be interpreted as a power struggle between the centre and the periphery.[13]

However, the interactions are much more complicated because the centre and the periphery cannot be separated from each other, as each side endeavours to influence the other. In recent years, the centre has not been in a position to strengthen its power in the periphery, while the periphery has gained the ability to impose its interests on the centre. So we can talk about a "peripherization of the centre" in Afghanistan. To illustrate this argument we will provide some examples.

In the past, the Afghan state never developed beyond an embryonic status. The protracted war since 1979 has destroyed the remaining state structures completely. Thus the government established by the interventionists in December 2001 possessed neither a well-founded authority nor a degree of legitimacy in the eyes of the people. Hence the primary objective of the Afghan government was to re-establish a state-owned monopoly of violence and to dismantle local militias. In both processes the international community supported the Afghan government. However, the disarmament, demobilization, and reintegration (DDR) process (2003–2005) as well as the subsequent disbandment of illegal armed groups (DIAG) process (since 2005 and planned to be completed by 2011), although able to collect a certain number of weapons, were not able to disband the clientelistic structures linking the commanders and their militiamen.[14] In most cases, influential warlords were able to preserve their power by taking over a formal position or by transferring their militias to regular units of the army and the police. Consequently, the security sector of the state is made up to a large extent of warlords and their militias.[15]

In addition, President Hamid Karzai's strategy of restricting the power of those warlords who received a position in the state apparatus was only partially successful. Karzai decided to rotate governors, ministers, and police chiefs from one position to another to prevent them from establishing their own power bases. In the beginning, Karzai gained some respectable results; for example, in 2004 he removed Ismail Khan from the governorship of Herat and appointed him as the Minister of Energy and Water in Kabul, and shifted Gul Agha Shrizai from the governorship in Kandahar to that in Nangarhar. In recent years, though, this policy has faltered: the targeted warlords along with the local elites have resisted this policy more and more successfully. Usually it is enough to prevent a decision of the government when local elites are able to mobilize their clients and demonstrate that the enforcement of the state decision will lead to destabilization and increased violence. This reversal of a government decision is illustrated by the recent example of Karzai's appointment of Juma Khan Hamdard as the new governor first of Jawzjan and then of Kunduz province. Hamdard, who is an ethnic Pashtun and a former member of Hikmatyar's Hezb-i-Islami, had been allied or fighting with many of today's warlords in northern Afghanistan during the

1990s. In May 2007 Rashid Dostum, the dominant warlord in northern Afghanistan, organized a demonstration against the then governor Hamdard in Sheberghan, the provincial capital of Jawzjan. Hamdard was accused of incompetence and ethnic prejudice. The demonstration turned violent and left at least ten people dead and forty injured. To prevent a destabilization of the situation in Jawzjan, Karzai withdrew Hamdard from there and appointed him as governor of Kunduz. When rumours of this decision became public at the end of 2007, protests immediately started. Local elites related to the local warlord Mir Alam, who had fought against Hamdard in the 1990s, organized protests and signed an official letter threatening dire consequences if the central government stuck to this appointment. Again Karzai found himself in an uncomfortable position and withdrew his decision.

The political centre in Kabul is strongly influenced by local politics. Local elites endeavour to develop close relationships with office-holders in the central government and with members of the parliament in Kabul. Local elites are often interwoven with political decision-makers in Kabul by family ties. Thus local elites exert special influence on decision-making processes in the capital, which in turn has an immediate impact on local politics. For example, in Farkhar district in the province of Takhar, the Afghan Interior Ministry intended to displace Abdul Ali, the chief of police. Abdul Ali managed to defend his position by using his family networks with high-ranking officials in the Kabul government, who directly influenced the decision in his favour.

These examples not only show that the government is facing tremendous local resistance in its efforts to implement its decisions beyond the capital but also underline that local elites heavily constrain the government's sphere of activities. This dynamic highlights why the localization of power is of such tremendous significance for understanding Afghan politics.[16]

The Localization of Power

As demonstrated above, the term *warlord* is not sufficient to describe the current (in)security in Afghanistan. There is not a uniform type of actor, nor can these actors be accurately described by a single term. However, alongside the variety of actors, regional and local differences play a crucial role. We intend to show that on the local level different social, economic, and political factors have resulted in different security architectures. Moreover, it would be a mistake to position these security architectures on a continuum between the state at one end and the warlords at the other: many more variables define the security situation. In all three case studies—Kandahar, Kunduz, and Paktia—we chose the provincial level as the level of research for the sake of clarity, while we are aware that local dynamics make the situation much more complex at the subprovincial level.

Kandahar: Feudal Warlordism

The city of Kandahar is not only the capital of the province of the same name but also the main centre of southern Afghanistan. Kandahar has played an important role in Afghan history: Afghans perceive it as the birthplace of modern Afghanistan, and the city served as the stronghold and secret capital for the Taliban. Since the movement was ousted from Kandahar in December 2001, the province has been dominated by a handful of strong warlords collaborating with the government, as well as by the Taliban and international anti-terror forces.

To understand the emergence of warlordism in Kandahar, it is important to take the socioeconomic structures of the province into consideration. The Pashtun confederations of the Durrani and Ghilzai, which comprise several tribes, have been competing for the control of Kandahar city since the eighteenth century.[17] In contrast to the Pashtuns of eastern Afghanistan, the tribes of Kandahar are structured in a simple hierarchical manner. Already during the eighteenth century a small landowning aristocracy had emerged within each tribe. The aristocracy managed to seize the economic resources and to control local decision-making processes, while ordinary tribesmen often ended up as their clients (*hamsayagan*). Thus tribal coherence has been built not only on common tribal identities and values but also on access to economic resources, patronage, and protection.

These socioeconomic structures are reflected in the security architecture of today's Kandahar province. Within each large tribe we find a single warlord or a few powerful ones stemming from landlord or business families and maintaining their own private militias.[18] The powerful elite of Kandahar province encompasses no more than a half-dozen men.[19] These warlords compete for the control of core government positions in order to extend their regional influence. They have already succeeded in taking over core positions in the Kandahar provincial administration and have placed their clients within the civil administration as well as in key local security posts. Especially within the security sector, the warlords managed to transform their militias into regular army units during the DDR process.[20] To illustrate these structures of violence, it is useful to focus on two prominent warlords: Ahmad Wali Karzai and Gul Agha Shirzai.

Ahmad Wali Karzai is the younger brother of President Hamid Karzai and the head of the provincial council of Kandahar province.[21] The Karzai family has been influential in the Kandahar region for decades and belongs to the leading families of the Popalzai tribe, to which the king's family also belongs. Ahmad Wali Karzai makes use of his proximity to Hamid Karzai while at the same time being the main representative of the Popalzai tribe in southern Afghanistan. Furthermore, he is said to control a big share of the drug trade in the region.[22]

After the Popalzai, the Barakzai are the second-biggest tribe in Kandahar province.[23] The most prominent member of the Barakzai is Gul Agha Shirzai. In contrast to Ahmad Wali Karzai, Gul Agha Shirzai is not descended from the tribal aristocracy. Yet his father, Haji Latif, was an important mujahidin commander in the 1980s, and his family gained influence due to its large property holdings. Gul Agha Shirzai served twice as provincial governor of Kandahar and for a short period as a minister in Hamid Karzai's cabinet. He has to be considered one of the most powerful men in Kandahar, not least since he integrated his militias into the Afghan National Police during the DDR process. His militias also assisted the coalition forces in fighting insurgency groups.

The situation in Kandahar is strongly influenced by the US-driven "war against terrorism" and by the operations of the anti-government resistance. While valid information about the latter is rare, it is worth noting that the opponents of the coalition forces are highly embedded in the local communities. Thus rural districts such as Panjwaye, Naish, Arghistan, Khakrez, and Ghorak have been time and again under the control of the Taliban and thus backbones of the anti-government resistance. It was in these districts that the Taliban movement started its rapid military expansion in the mid-1990s. Here the population shares the norms and values of the former Taliban regime. Moreover, the local population still perceives the physical security provided by the Taliban as more reliable than that established by the government and the coalition forces.[24] A common claim is that the harsh and uncompromising exercise of power by the Taliban eliminated banditry and created a certain accountability in everyday life. In addition, the military operations of the coalition forces have tightened the relationship between the Taliban and the local population. Military actions such as routine house searches violate local customs such as concealing womenfolk from men's eyes. Due to the high intensity of violent interactions between the Taliban and the coalition forces, the local elites have been forced either to align themselves with the latter forces or to adopt a "spoiler" position. The dramatic increase of violence and instability,[25] along with increasing anti-government sentiments, has made local institutions such as *shuras* ineffective in bridging the gap between the government and the communities.

Opium cultivation also has a strong impact on the security situation. Even though this economy dates back to pre-war times in Kandahar province, it started booming only in the late 1980s when the Soviet troops withdrew from Afghanistan. In 2005, nearly 13 percent of the Afghan land under poppy cultivation was situated in Kandahar province.[26] The opium economy dominates so strongly that it is almost impossible for elite families to maintain leading positions within their tribes without some involvement in the drug economy. The counter-narcotic strategy of the international community, which was initiated in 2004, pressures those elites loyal to the government to curb their poppy cultivation.[27] As a result, more and more farmers and traders who rely on the drug economy for their daily livelihood have shifted their loyalty to the Taliban. Today, the drug-trafficking networks make use of both the government and the Taliban, depending on which group controls a given area.

Summing up, in recent years the combination of insurgency, well-financed drug networks, and hierarchical tribal structures has restricted the influence of the Afghan government in Kandahar province but has favoured the emergence of strong warlords and the Taliban. The only difference between the former and the latter is that the Taliban still present a corporate identity to the outside world. It can be noted, however, that the Taliban are also becoming more and more an umbrella for heterogeneous actors such as militant Islamists, drug barons, tribal elders, warlords, and unemployed youth.[28] Furthermore, there are significant differences between the former Taliban and those operating under this label today. This is why many analysts are now using the term *neo-Taliban*.[29]

Kunduz: Fragmented Warlordism

Despite the long distance between the capital, Kabul, and Kunduz as well as the geographical barrier of the Hindu Kush mountain range, the Afghan state following its emergence at the end of the nineteenth century was quite influential in the northeastern province of Kunduz.[30] This territorial influence was a prerequisite for Pashtun colonization, which took place in several waves beginning in the early 1920s and encompassed stockbreeders, farmers, and the Pashtun aristocracy. While the aristocracy received large landholdings from the central government, the migration of stockbreeders was a greater source of tension with the indigenous population.[31] This colonization policy required a strong state to effectively control the distribution of land. Large, mainly Uzbek landholdings were confiscated, completely changing the power structure. All influential officials were Pashtuns, mostly related to the king's family. The language spoken in the provincial government was Pashtu, thus excluding the bulk of the population from direct access to the state.[32] Moreover, the ethnic diversity of Kunduz is enormous, often changing from village to village. Besides Pashtuns, there are Tajiks, Uzbeks, Hazara, Arabs, Baluchs, and Turkmen in Kunduz province.

The historical presence of the Afghan state in Kunduz significantly influences today's organization of power. Holding an official position in Kunduz province is regarded by the elites as a guarantee of power and as an important material as well as symbolic resource. The common practice of pursuing personal interests while holding a state position directly affects the security situation; for example, high-ranking officials in the highway, border, and provincial police have been accused of deploying police officers for their own personal interests. In fact, the local population view the police as private militias in uniform.[33] Public attention is repeatedly drawn to this practice by those warlords who do not hold an office, often by the use of violence against rivals who do hold an office. For example, in 2005 several clashes took place between the police on one side and the subcommanders of Mir Alam, a powerful strongman in Kunduz, on the other. This violent conflict stemmed from a long-standing rivalry between Mir Alam, who was pressing for an official position, and Mutalib Beg, then chief of police.

Because of migration and Pashtunization, the ethnic diversity within the province, and the frequently changing front lines during the war, there are no universally accepted communal forms of organization or institutions capable of checking and balancing the power of individuals. This has resulted in myriads of mini-fiefdoms as well as localized "rules of law" or "rules of the gun." Thus each village is headed by a "big man," who often held the position of a commander during the civil war. The reputations of these "big men" differ from place to place. While some are seen as good and honourable, others are described as killers and thieves. Smaller warlords can often act with impunity since they are backed by others. In the past, the territory under the control of each commander was sharply demarcated through the levying of taxes such as *ushr* or *zakat*.[34] But with the collapse of the Taliban and the presence of the Provincial Reconstruction Team in Kunduz, the commander system ended: the levying of taxes was disrupted and consequently the borders of the warlords' territories vanished. Nowadays, armed militias are not often seen; nonetheless, the relationship between commanders and militiamen remains significant. Given the hierarchical structure of the militias in Kunduz, the loyalty of a militiaman is directed primarily toward his immediate commander. Alliances among militias tend to be brokered on a broader scale and seldom rely exclusively on tribal, ethnic, or regional similarities. Communal or religious institutions no longer exist to control these small warlords and their militias.

The cities of the province (Kunduz, Khanabad, Imam Sahib) are today controlled by the police, which is composed of former militiamen. The rural areas are still controlled by numerous warlords. However, the security architecture varies from place to place, as illustrated by the two districts of Imam Sahib and Khanabad. Imam Sahib is situated on the border of Tajikistan. It is a fertile agrarian district and a key hub for the drug trade. Accordingly, both the district itself and the post of the chief of border police are strategically very significant. Imam Sahib is dominated by the Ibrahimis, a family belonging to the Uzbek clan.

In the course of war, the Ibrahimis rose from nothing to become the predominant family of that district and beyond. Ibrahim Abdul Latif became the governor of Kunduz province in 2002 and was appointed governor of Faryab in 2004. His brother Haji Raoof earned a reputation as a commander, headed the border police in Imam Sahib, and won a seat in the parliamentary elections. Finally, the locally strategic position of the *mirab bashi*, who controls the farmers' access to the important resource of water, is monopolized by Afiz, the brother-in-law of Haji Raoof, whereas in other districts this position is commonly exercised by members of different clans and usually varies from one irrigation canal to the next.[35] Thus the Ibrahimis rule the district in a quasi-feudalistic way and control access to economic resources. Most small warlords in Imam Sahib depend directly on this family.

While the means of violence in Imam Sahib are monopolized by one family, Khanabad provides a different picture. During the war the district was under the control of Commander Amir, the most influential commander of the Islamist Abdulrab Sayyaf in northeastern Afghanistan. After Amir's death, he was succeeded by his brother Ghulam, who lost several of his subcommanders in the upsurge of ethnic and political polarization following the collapse of the Taliban. Together with the lack of commonly shared institutions, these losses led to a fragmentation of violence and the emergence of many loosely connected small warlords who rarely control more than one village. Their actions are restricted only by competition with other warlords, and are not controlled or regulated by the local population or the government.

Summing up, a great variety of warlords, who differ widely in the scope of their influence and power, control the means of physical violence in Kunduz province. There are, moreover, no religious, ethnic-tribal, or modern institutions capable of constraining the arbitrary acts of the rulers. This has resulted in a strong localization of the "rules of the game" and in varying power structures from district to district and, as in Khanabad district, from village to village. Additionally, the rentier economy strengthens the position of the warlords, makes them independent of the population, and further weakens existing institutions.

Paktia: Rule of the Tribes

Paktia province is located in the eastern part of the so-called Pashtun belt and is more or less ethnically homogeneous. The state presence in Paktia has remained weak, despite its geographical proximity to Kabul, largely because of the strength of the tribal system. By the end of the 1970s, the state's influence did not extend beyond the provincial capital of Gardez. Similarly, the Taliban were present only in the provincial capital and had no control whatsoever of the countryside. Even today the power of the government is very limited: the Afghan National Army and the Afghan National Police are concentrated in Gardez and along the main roads.

The Pashtuns of Paktia are divided along tribal lines. Tribal identities are still perceived as the most important points of reference, incorporating ideas of honour and justice as well as daily behaviour.[36] The *pashtunwali,* the Pashtun tribal code of law and behaviour, is the commonly accepted "rule of the game," binding on everybody and providing strict guidelines as to how to deal with specific situations. Although the community values of the pashtunwali vary slightly from tribe to tribe, the main underlying notion influencing all interpretations of the pashtunwali in the east is that all Pashtuns have equal status: no one should possess more rights and power than others,[37] because all Pashtuns descend from the same ancestor. Furthermore, the Paktia tribes settle their problems by consensus building, meaning that tribal gatherings (*jirga*) are the place to mediate conflicts until a solution is found. In contrast to many other regions of the Pashtun tribal belt such as Kandahar, the tribal system in Paktia is still intact.

Due to this tribal structure and the underlying egalitarian understanding of society, the pursuit of political leadership is always hard fought.[38] The last two decades have been characterized by a continuous struggle between the tribes on the one hand and single warlords who challenged the tribal system on the other. Very often, strong men—first mujahidin, then warlords—sought power and status within their tribes. But as soon as they behaved contrary to the pashtunwali, conflicts arose between them and the tribes. This was especially the case after the collapse of the Taliban in the winter of 2001–02, when Bacha Khan of the Zadran tribe seized power in Paktia even without the support of his own tribe. Bacha Khan was initially backed by the Northern Alliance and the coalition forces in his operations against the Taliban. He was able to mobilize warriors from his Zadran tribe as well as small warlords such as Raz Mohammad and Wazir Khan. As a result of his pursuit of power in the province, disregarding the rules of the pashtunwali, most of the tribes regarded him as an illegitimate bandit or *jang salar.* Within a few days, the tribes reacted to Bacha Khan's seizure of power and managed to build up a counterforce across tribal boundaries. After several days of heavy fighting in Gardez, which left about a hundred people dead, the tribes were able to oust Bacha Khan from the town. The coalition forces took sides with the newly appointed governor of Paktia against him. Following this, the tribes established their power across the entire province.

Since that incident, policing in the tribal areas of Paktia has been carried out by the *arbakee,* a sort of traditional tribal police. According to the tribal system, the establishment of an arbakee becomes necessary if the decision of a jirga is not accepted by one of the persons affected by a dispute and if a ruling has already been passed. Hence, the arbakee implements the decisions of a jirga and is legitimized and controlled by tribal elders. However, the arbakee remains a spontaneous force that is in power only as long as the tribal jirga needs it. Since the force was first established in 2001, arbakee members have been installed in all districts of Paktia and today they far outnumber the regular police. They have taken over classic police tasks as well as the protection of tribal resources such as forests and pastures. That scope of operations sits very comfortably with the notion of community policing. The arbakee is controlled by a *wazir* (commander) who takes part in the tribal gatherings and receives his orders from the tribal elders. Since 2002 the arbakee has increasingly become an interface between the state and the tribes. Several security tasks, such as the protection of forests and road security, have been officially handed over from the provincial government to the arbakee. Moreover, the state has been financing forty to sixty members of the arbakee in each district since 2002 and has increased this number drastically during elections. Although paid by the state, arbakee members remain loyal to the tribes and are exclusively controlled by the tribal jirga. Consequently, arbakee officers experience a much broader acceptance by the local population than regular police officers, who are often regarded as corrupt and ineffective.

The tasks of the arbakee depend greatly on tribal norms and values, which in many cases are diametrically opposed to Western norms and values but are in full accordance with the pashtunwali. For example, the strictly obeyed exclusion of women from the public sphere in Paktia contradicts the Western idea of gender-equal communal participation but accords with tribal norms. The continuing legitimacy of blood feuds also undermines attempts to introduce modern conflict-resolution mechanisms. Finally, it must be stressed that the arbakee is not a neutral force but is time and again involved in tribal rivalries. For example, the long-lasting feud between the neighbouring Ahmadzai and Totakhel tribes was aggravated by the establishment of the arbakee.

Furthermore, socioeconomic differences challenge the egalitarian idea within each tribe. In particular, tribesmen receiving remittances from family members working in the Middle East or Pakistan are gaining a stronger influence on decision-making. This increasingly challenges the egalitarian character of the tribal system. Furthermore, in Paktia ex-commanders of the jihad have also succeeded in obtaining positions in the governmental system, and they use these positions to enforce their will. Especially in land conflicts, which occur regularly, official positions are used to pursue private interests. A recent example is a land conflict in Shana Zawar in which Matin, a serving officer in the Afghan National Army, has played a significant role. Moreover, he is supported by the governor of a neighbouring province to whom he is related.

The *pashtunwali* has, however, remained strong enough in Paktia that tribal leaders have to follow the egalitarian ideal in their rhetoric and behaviour. In other words, the tribal system in Paktia obstructs or at least constrains the emergence of warlordism.

Taliban as Context and Pretext

As we have shown, since 2001 the situation in southern Afghanistan, particularly in Kandahar, has been dominated by the struggle between the insurgents and the Taliban on the one side, and the international forces and the Afghan government on the other. In Kandahar, the local structures of violence have been strongly shaped for many years by the insurgency. Since 2006, a rise of insurgency has been observed across the country. This fresh wave of insurgency has also affected the provinces of Kunduz and Paktia. In both provinces, the insurgency cannot be separated from the local scene, and yet the political context varies greatly.

In Paktia, most of the tribes seek to stand apart from the conflict between the insurgents and the government and international troops. They followed more or less the same strategy during the Soviet occupation. The tribes allow the Taliban, the government, and the international actors to cross their tribal territories as long as they do not challenge the tribal order. While most of the tribal leaders endeavour to sit on the fence, they also maintain their networks with influential actors in the Afghan government, the International Security Assistance Force (ISAF), and the insurgent groups. In recent years, however, the Taliban have started to directly attack tribal elders who are collaborating with the government and the ISAF. On the other hand, in the southern district of Zurmat, where the tribal system is fragmented and tribal codes are weak, the insurgents have gained more support than in other parts of the province where tribal structures are more stable.[39] However, a pronounced rift between pro-government and pro-Taliban tribes and subtribes cannot yet be observed. If this were to materialize in the future, it would be defined by long-standing tribal rivalries rather than by political ideologies.

The situation in Kunduz is different. Here most of the recent conflicts have revolved around land disputes between returnees who had gone into exile in Pakistan during the war and others who had stayed in Kunduz. These conflicts are complicated by the fact that, depending on political constellations, land often changed hands in wartime. Moreover, this conflict about land tenure often coincides with the ethnic composition of the province. Most of the returnees are Pashtuns, who are now reclaiming their lands and feel sidelined by the administrative structures, which are dominated by non-Pashtun warlords who established and enlarged their power bases during the war. These land conflicts are—at least as viewed by large segments of the population and by international observers—strongly interwoven with the recent emergence of the Taliban. A popular rumour says that Pashtun communities, which are dissatisfied with the current balance of power and resource allocation, are harbouring and supporting Taliban fighters. This rumour is supported by the fact that most ambushes and roadside explosions occur along the roads to Pashtun settlements in the districts of Aliabad and Khanabad. The deterioration of the overall security situation and the mushrooming of the Taliban in recent years are used by many warlords to legitimize the rearming of their militias. Even the fact that the Afghan government is deploying auxiliary militia forces among the Pashtun tribes in southern Afghanistan to counter the insurgency is widely interpreted by non-Pashtuns in northern Afghanistan as a rearming of the Pashtun tribes in general. This policy is regarded by non-Pashtuns as part of an overall agenda of the Afghan government to re-establish Pashtun domination across the country. It is against this background that resistance to the appointment of Juma Khan Hamdard as governor, discussed earlier in this chapter, is to be understood. In Kunduz today, an ethnic antagonism that dates back to the Pashtun colonization in the first half of the twentieth century is used not only as the dominant explanation of violence but also as an argument for strengthening warlordism.

Security Architecture

After the fall of the Taliban, people "hated the commanders, but now they love them again," one informant told us. This statement reflects concerns about the return of the Taliban among many Afghans, especially in the north, as well as the inability of the international actors to establish a new political order. Moreover, it shows that, in the absence of a reliable state, many Afghans regard warlordism as a system of political life that is at least better than an unpredictable future.

This chapter has aimed to illustrate the diversity of security architectures in different Afghan provinces. As the case of Kunduz shows, one can find a variety of different security architectures even within a province, often changing from valley to valley and village to village. Because of this diversity, the term *warlord* does not inadequately characterize all the various forms of control of the means of violence, although it does apply to many of the influential actors currently found in Afghanistan. The term also fails to differentiate these actors from state security structures. The fundamental finding of our research is that context is the key to understanding different security architectures. The three cases discussed here show that the prime factors affecting local security structures are social structures, economic resources, and the presence of state and international actors.

Social structures play an eminently important role and, moreover, must always be viewed in a specific local context: the different social structures in Paktia and Kandahar make clear that a characterization such as "tribal Pashtuns" is too superficial to say anything meaningful about the tribal impact on the security architecture. In addition, the history of each region has to be considered: because of the colonization process in the twentieth century, the population of Kunduz is shaped by great heterogeneity and by a rift between the Pashtun latecomers on the one side and the indigenous inhabitants on the other. The difficulty of achieving a common ground of values and rules contributed in Kunduz to the fragmentation of warlordism. Here Paktia provides the opposite example: with its tradition of tribal culture accepted by the people at large, strong tribal institutions averted warlordism.

Similarly, local economies affect the security architecture. In regions such as Kandahar, which rely heavily on drug cultivation and the drug trade, one can observe the establishment of strong warlord structures. Apparently, the financial resources connected with the drug economy strengthen hierarchical structures. This argument is supported by the example of Kunduz, where a strong clan succeeded in establishing itself in the district of Imam Sahib, strategically important for the drug trade, while the district of Khanabad, which does not benefit from the drug economy, faces fragmentation of the control of power and violence.

The presence of the state also has a significant impact on the security architecture. In general, the aim of the state is to control the security sector and to establish a monopoly of violence. One might imagine that where the concept of state is more accepted, the dominance of the warlords would be easier to break. But as the examples of Kandahar and Kunduz reveal, warlordism is in fact prominent in exactly those regions where the state—at least to elites—is regarded as important. Warlords often perceive the state as a desirable resource to control and access. Thus it seems that Charles Tilly's argument—that warlordism is a concomitant phenomenon of the state-building process rather than being diametrically opposed to it—applies in the case of Afghanistan.[40] In contrast, the egalitarian tribal structures in Paktia, where the state is hardly recognized as such, prevent the consolidation of warlordism.

The role of the international community in suppressing warlordism is difficult to judge. Without a doubt the presence of international actors led to the disappearance of weapons from public display—warlords and militias are forced to keep a low profile. This trend is particularly evident in those Afghan provinces that are heavily funded by the international community for purposes of reconstruction (e.g., Kabul, Herat). For many warlords, a share in international reconstruction resources constitutes a vital economic incentive. Yet the international presence does not always have a taming influence on the structures of violence. Ultimately, it was the establishing and equipping of Afghan warlords and their militias by the US Army in its "war on terrorism" that caused the temporary emergence of warlordism with Bacha Khan in Paktia, and warlordism continues to shape security structures in Kandahar to this day.

This chapter aimed to make a contribution to understanding the complex and locally very heterogeneous security structures in Afghanistan by examining the adequacy of the term *warlord* to describe the structures of violence. Even though a broad definition of that term can be applied to many actors in Afghanistan, it fails to take into account the vast variety of local security architectures. In international media, the fashionable term *warlord* has been more and more replaced by the term *Taliban* to make sense of the highly dynamic political structures in Afghanistan. Many analysts, who aim to provide tidy models to understand the political situation, seek to redefine—again along a bipolar axis—what is in fact a highly differentiated political landscape. The recent trend is to blend the categories of Taliban, Pashtuns, insurgents, and drug dealers to construct a single, clear enemy. Thereby the debate on "warlords versus state" becomes more and more a side show, subordinate to the conflict between the Taliban and the state. However, a discourse that attempts to define the lines of conflict in Afghanistan reflects much more the concerns of the interventionists than it does the highly differentiated local realities: the Taliban phenomenon is locally contextualized in Paktia differently than in Kunduz. Instead of this polarized discourse, we argue that the security architecture is shaped primarily by local social and economic conditions. The presence of state and international actors also has a direct influence, but the concentration of power at the local level is so strong that even the core institutions of the state are under siege by local interests.

Notes

This chapter is based on an article entitled "Beyond Warlordism: The Security Architecture in Afghanistan" in *International Policy and Society* 2 (2007): 136-53. In this revised version we take into consideration the political dynamics since 2007, especially the re-emergence of the Taliban. Moreover, it should be mentioned that this paper is a result of the research project "Staatsverfall als friedens- und sicherheitspolitische Herausforderung," which was generously funded by Deutsche Stiftung Friedensforschung.

1.   Astri Suhrke, Kristian Berg Harpviken, and Arne Strand, "Conflictual Peacebuilding: Afghanistan Two Years after Bonn," Chr. Michelson Institute Report 2004:4 (Bergen, 2004), http://www.cmi.no/publications/2004/rep/r2004-4.pdf.

2.   Mark Sedra, *Challenging the Warlord Culture: Security Sector Reform in Post-Taliban Afghanistan* (Bonn: Bonn International Center for Conversion, 2002); Michael Ignatieff, *Empire Lite* (London: Vintage, 2003).

3.   Mark Sedra, "New Beginning or Return to Arms? The Disarmament, De-mobilization and Reintegration Process in Afghanistan" (paper presented at the State Reconstruction and International Engagement in Afghanistan symposium, organized by the Center for Development Research (ZEF) and the Development Research Centre, London School of Economics, Bonn, 30 May–1 June 2003).

4.   Antonio Giustozzi, "Respectable Warlords? The Transition from War of All against All to Peaceful Competition in Afghanistan" (Research seminar, 29 January 2003), http://www.crisisstates.com/download/others/Seminar AG29012003.pdf; Gordon Peake et al., *From Warlords to Peacelords: Local Leadership Capacity in Peace Processes* (London: INCORE, 2004); Sedra, "New Beginning or Return to Arms," 2003.

5.   William Reno, *Warlord Politics and African Society* (Boulder, CO: Lynne Rienner, 1998); John Mackinlay, "Defining Warlords," in *Peacekeeping and Conflict Resolution,* ed. Oliver Ramsbotham and Tom Woodhouse (London: Frank Cass, 2000), 48-61; Paul Collier, "Doing Well out of War: An Economic Perspective," in *Greed and Grievance: Economic Agendas in Civil Wars,* ed. Mats R. Berdal and David M. Malone (Boulder, CO: Lynne Rienner, 2000), 91-112.

6.   Giustozzi, "Respectable Warlords," 2003.

7.   Rahimullah Yusufzai, "Warlords Are Going to Remain a Fact of Life in Afghanistan," *Daily Jang Pakistan,* 7 March 2005, http://jang.com.pk/thenews/.

8.   Berdal and Malone, eds., *Greed and Grievance.*

9.   William Reno, "Welthandel, Warlords und die Wiedererfindung des Afrikanischen Staates," *Welttrends* 14 (1997): 8-29.

10.   Jennifer Milliken, *State Failure, Collapse and Reconstruction* (Malden: Blackwell, 2003); Robert I. Rotberg, *When States Fail: Causes and Consequences* (Princeton: Princeton University Press, 2004).

11.   Collier, "Doing Well out of War."

12.   François Jean and Jean-Christophe Rufin, *Ökonomie der Bürgerkriege* (Hamburg: Hamburger Edition, 1999); Phillipe Le Billon, "The Political Economy of War: What Relief Agencies Need to Know," Humanitarian Practice Network Paper 33 (London, 2000).

13.   Barnett R. Rubin and Helena Malikyar, "The Politics of Center-Periphery Relations in Afghanistan" (draft paper, Center on International Cooperation, New York University, March 2003), http://www.cic.nyu.edu/peacebuilding/oldpdfs/WBCPAfgh.pdf.

14.   Antonio Giustozzi, "Bureaucratic Façade and Political Realities of Disarmament and Demobilisation in Afghanistan," *Conflict, Security and Development* 8, no. 2 (2008): 169-92.

15.   See Conrad Schetter, "Grauzone der Macht: Warlords und Bürgerkriegökonomie in Afghanistan," in *Unterwegs in die Zukunft. Afghanistan drei Jahre nach dem Aufbruch vom Petersberg:Grundlagen und Perspektiven deutsch-afghanischer Sicherheitskooperation,* ed. Claudia Gomm-Ernsting and Annett Günther (Berlin: Berliner Wissenschafts-Verlag, 2005).

16. Schetter, "Talibanistan – der Anti-Staat," *Internationales Asienforum* (2007b): 233-57.

17. Christine Noelle, *State and Tribe in Nineteenth Century Afghanistan* (Richmond, UK: Curzon Press, 1997).

18. International Crisis Group (ICG), "Afghanistan: The Problem of Pashtun Alienation" (Kabul/Brussels, 2003a).

19. Findings of a survey undertaken in 2005–2006 by the Tribal Liaison Office on local leadership in Kandahar province. Information about Kandahar is based on field research if not indicated otherwise.

20. International Crisis Group, "Disarmament and Reintegration in Afghanistan," ICG Asia Report No. 65 (Kabul/Brussels, 2003b), 26.

21. Human Rights Watch, "The Rule of the Gun: Human Rights Abuses and Political Repression in the Run-up to Afghanistan's Presidential Election" (briefing paper, September 2004), http://www.hrw.org/backgrounder/asia/afghanistan0904/afghanistan0904.pdf.

22. Scott Baldauf, "Warlord Politics Heats Afghan Vote," *Christian Science Monitor*, 6 October 2004, http://www.csmonitor.com/2004/1006/p01s01-wosc.html; Carlotta Gall, "Afghan Poppy Growing Reaches Record Level, UN Says," *New York Times*, 19 November 2004.

23. International Crisis Group, "Disarmament and Reintegration."

24. Antonio Giustozzi, *Koran, Kalashnikov and Laptop: The Neo-Taliban Insurgency in Afghanistan* (London: Hurst Publishers, 2007).

25. Rainer Glassner, "Semi-Annual Risk Assessment June to November 2006" (FAST report, 2006), http://www.swisspeace.org/.

26. United Nations Office on Drugs and Crime, *Afghanistan: Opium Rapid Assessment Survey 2006* (February 2006), 39, www.unodc.org/pdf/research/Afg_RAS_2006.pdf.

27. Christopher M. Blanchard, "Afghanistan: Narcotics and U.S. Policy," CRS Report for Congress (Washington, 2005), 17-18.

28. Schetter, "Lokale Macht- und Gewaltstrukturen in Afghanistan," *Aus Politik und Zeitgeschichte* 39 (2007a): 3-10.

29. Giustozzi, *Koran, Kalashnikov and Laptop*.

30. Noelle, *State and Tribe*.

31. Erwin Grötzbach, *Afghanistan: eine geographische Landeskunde* (Darmstadt: Wissenschaftliche Buchgesellschaft, 1990); Audrey Shalinsky, "Islam and Ethnicity: The Northern Afghanistan Perspective," *Central Asian Survey* 1, no. 2/3 (1982): 71-83.

32. Mervyn Patterson, *The Shiwa Pastures, 1978–2003: Land Tenure Changes and Conflict in Northeastern Afghanistan* (Kabul: Afghanistan Research and Evaluation Unit, 2004).

33. In the context of projects funded by the German Peace Research Foundation and the Volkswagen Foundation, the authors carried out research in the Kunduz and Paktia provinces in the spring and summer of 2005.

34. Gilles Dorronsoro, "Afghanistan: von Solidaritätsnetzwerken zu regionalen Räumen," in *Ökonomie der Bürgerkriege*, ed. François Jean and Jean-Christophe

Rufin (Hamburg: Hamburger Edition, 1999), 121-54; Jonathan Goodhand, "From Holy War to Opium War? A Case Study of the Opium Economy in North-Eastern Afghanistan," in *Afghanistan: A Country without a State*, ed. Christine Noelle-Karimi et al. (Linz: IKO, 2002): 139-60.

35. Usman Shah, "Livelihoods in the Asqalan and Sufi-Qarayateem Canal Irrigation Systems in the Kunduz River Basin," Amu Darya Series 4 (January 2007), http://131.220.109.9/fileadmin/webfiles/downloads/projects/amudarya/publications/ZEF_Amu_Darya_Series_SMWA_4.pdf.

36. Willi Steul, *Paschtunwali: Ein Ehrenkodex und seine rechtliche Relevanz* (Wiesbaden: Franz Steiner Verlag, 1981); Bernd Glatzer, "The Pashtun Tribal System," in *Concept of Tribal Society*, ed. Georg Pfeffer and Deepak Kumar Behera (New Delhi: Concept Publishing, 2002), 265-82.

37. Alfred Janata and Reihanodin Hassas, "Ghairatman: Der gute Paschtune – Exkurs über die Grundlagen des Paschtunwali," *Afghanistan Journal* 2, no. 3 (1975): 83-97.

38. Jon W. Anderson, "Khan and Khel: Dialectics of Pakhtun Tribalism," in *The Conflict of Tribe and State in Iran and Afghanistan,* ed. Richard Tapper (New York: St Martin's Press, 1983), 119-49; Steul, *Paschtunwali*.

39. Sébastien Trives, "Afghanistan : réduire l'insurrection : le cas du sud-est," *Politique étrangère* 71, no. 1 (2006): 105-18.

40. Charles Tilly, "War Making and State Making as Organized Crime," in *Bringing the State Back In*, ed. Peter B. Evans, Dietrich Rueschmayer, and Theda Skocpol (Cambridge: Cambridge University Press, 1985), 169-91.

Chapter 4

Supporting the State, Depleting the State: Estranged State-Society Relations in Afghanistan

Florian P. Kühn

Introduction

The literature on state-building has, in recent years, accumulated many insights into the ideological and functional characteristics of this endeavour.[1] While the term itself implies at least some deficiencies in state capacity, which—in the eyes of the international interventionists—need to be fixed, its application in cases such as Bosnia and Herzegovina, Afghanistan, or Iraq has never overcome the implicit assumption of an already-existing connection between society and state. The frequently used term *nation-building* suggests even more the existence of a rather homogeneous social group with at least some affection towards its state. Both these mindsets, state centred and nation centred, assume that European history can serve as a template for the development of states worldwide.[2] While it is true that *statehood* on the international level is exercised by almost all states characterized by sovereignty and territoriality,[3] *stateness* is a feature mainly of Western states,[4] consisting of a wide array of interlocking mechanisms of public control of the use of violence.[5]

Post-conflict political spaces, however, provide for a state that finds itself in the unpromising situation of harsh, sometimes violent, competition with intra- and inter-societal structures, as well as with supra-societal relations where ethnic, tribal, or religious affiliations transcend the territories of post-colonial states.[6] In these cases, state-building means the pursuit of societal modernization, which raises multiple legitimacy problems. In Afghanistan, but also in other countries, these legitimacy problems can trigger religious and tribal mobilization against foreign engagement. In Western understanding, this opposition is often conflated with indigenous resistance to well-intended initiatives for stable development—underestimating the possibility that such resistance represents a rejection of Western approaches by categorically different forms of rule. These forms of rule, though, are hard to understand using the tools of Western political analysis. Hence, while governance structures remain largely obscure because they are interwoven with non-representative sources of power and influence, we also need to take a closer look at the structures that *parallel* local politics. In countries such as Afghanistan, where administrative capacities are hardly developed, and hence state finances originate mainly from external donors, a decoupling of the post-conflict state—that is, the ruling elite—and society is to be expected.

The external funding of states can become a special form of aid dependency, which we may capture by models of rent-seeking and rentier states. Developing societies are especially likely to grow these structures, which impede their very development process.[7] Development is often assumed to support post-conflict stabilization and state-building,[8] which means that quick aid inflows and sustainable development support would be the first choice for steering post-conflict countries clear of the conflict trap: "The conflict trap is a tendency, not an iron law. Middle-income countries have a lower probability of falling back into it."[9] The risk of regression into conflict appears to be directly linked to the poverty level of a country; the accrual of foreign money would have a decisive impact within the post-conflict space. Of course, as Stephan Klingebiel has shown for several countries, assuming that economic improvement leads directly to lower levels of violence falls short of reality.[10] In post-conflict situations, external donors decide in favour of one actor (the "government"), leading to high levels of aid flow. This influence can also have negative effects, including the encouragement of

> self-enriching and corrupt clientelist structures at national, regional and local levels. Some development cooperation projects and programmes helped to increase disparities (e.g., among ethnic groups) by supporting, for example, infrastructure measures which were being implemented by the partner government and entailed the resettlement of certain ethnic groups.[11]

While not aiming to explain "Afghan politics," this chapter shows how rentier structures in Afghanistan played a decisive role in state formation throughout much of the twentieth century. The first section outlines the general characteristics of rents and their influence on states and interpenetrated societies. Since the fall of the Taliban, rentier structures both within the state bureaucracies and the economic and political elites have been revived and strengthened, as described in the second section. As a result of international involvement since the termination of the Taliban's rule, the new state forms a buffer between society and intervention; it does so without being able to fulfill the tasks attributed to it by donors, such as the provision of security and social services. This lack of stateness is the focus of the third section, which shows how rentier-state and rent-seeking theories help to explain the paradoxes and shortfalls of international intervention. The final section moves beyond the state-centrist approach and proposes to shed light on the interplay between state and non-state actors, particularly drug traffickers, by conceptualizing the latter as beneficiaries of rents who behave accordingly. It turns out that the interventionists contribute significantly to the structures of dependency they claim to oppose. Security concerns appear to outweigh potentially destabilizing efforts to enhance democratization or political openness in the nascent political entity. The regime is a result of the international community's installation of a state through political reform, which in time will limit external influence. The rentier structures that characterized Afghanistan for decades before the Taliban's rise have proven to be remarkably stable; indeed, rentier-state structures are central to the political development of Afghanistan.

Rentier States and Rent-Seeking

An income with no corresponding investment or working activity is called rent.[12] While profits from capitalist activity require some reinvestment to secure future profits, rent flows allow for a substantially lower or non-existent circulation of resources. From a development point of view, it is significant that rents do not trigger a cycle of investment and subsequent reinvestment.

Of the different types of rents, what matters here are political rents, which are paid through money transfers. These are distinct from migration rents, where a part of (labour) income obtained in other countries is transferred to family or friends. Migration rents are difficult to quantify.[13] Remittances are an important source of income for many Afghans, as many families fled the country and are now in a position to support their kin.[14] This type of rent is nevertheless beyond the scope of this paper, as it is distributed widely and hence does not put a certain segment of the populace in a privileged position: it does not lead to the emergence of a politically influential rentier group.

A defining quality of rent is its independence from work or investment by the recipient; it can be disposed of freely. Not only can it be used for consumption, but also a significant share of the money tends to be used for cultivating relations with donors. These networks are not productive in a capitalist sense: although they help to secure future rent

flows, they do not feed an accumulative production circle. The recipients
of rents "invest" in socio-political networks, which tend to constitute a
form of corruption.[15] From this perspective, rents may be normatively
problematic for the global donor community. Even if one does not agree
that Western governments disregard their citizens' property rights when
financing aid, as Nozick and Bauer contend, the system still poses a
problem for Western governments who may have to justify financing
"bad practices."[16]

One effect of the recipient's investment in good donor relations is that
state administrations direct their efforts away from providing public
goods. In developed Western societies, the state is funded by the financial contributions of citizens; taxation provides for political control and
voter influence. The American independence movement's slogan "No
taxation without representation" means precisely that the legitimacy of
government decisions depends on participation rights. Paradoxically,
by funding rentier-state structures, international donors acquire participation rights that are being withheld from the Afghan people. State
agencies, being responsible to the donors, in turn develop better and
closer relations with outside actors than with their own constituencies.
Unless loyalty toward a political entity is based on ties such as kin or
charisma, its legitimacy tends to be procedural and functional (generally distributive and redistributive).[17] If these qualities are absent or in
decline, loyalty and legitimacy decrease accordingly.

While it is lamented that much funding bypasses Afghan government
organizations because of their presumed lack of institutional capacity,[18]
the amounts actually reaching the administration trigger rent-seeking
activities. Rent-seeking is an economic term, defined as "use of resources
in actually lowering total product although benefiting some minority."[19]
From the minority's or individual's point of view, though, rent-seeking
behaviour is rational: it aims to raise their share of a given amount
of funds at the cost of others, who might likewise try to participate.
Rent-seekers will try to monopolize their role as counterparts to the
international donors. If it is the state and its representatives who benefit
most from external relations, why is it that the bonds between state actors and international donors are comparatively weak? Different levels
of rent-seeking show why: as rents are not being used as productive
capital, there is little benefit to the public or to the economy when the
rent is first distributed to government officials. Individuals may profit
anyway by trying to acquire a share of the rent. Elites try to push into the
public sector to get their hands on money, which leads to the development of a structure of clienteles. The upper echelons of administration
will try to secure and reinforce their influence by keeping lower strata
dependent on them—personally, and through rent payments. Also,
people bribe themselves into positions that may give them a reliable

source of income in the form of bribes from others at lower levels. This constitutes a structural incentive for corruption, which can be viewed as a form of taxation.[20]

This rentier structure illustrates two points: First, rent-seekers need to invest in order to get access to funding, although this is not an investment in a capitalist cycle, and they may have to renew payments in order to keep a post or a licence. Second, while vaguely securing rule for an emerging state class, this system tends to develop vertical links rather than horizontal ones. Equivalent levels of ministries tend not to cooperate, in order to immunize themselves against (public) control, criticism, and charges of inefficiency, and to insulate themselves from cross-ministerial influence. This decreases the state's ability to effectively provide the public goods so urgently needed to bolster its legitimacy. The bureaucratic state class is increasingly able to monopolize financial inflows and at the same time avoid controls by other organized interest groups. The result is the maladministration of government funds.[21]

Historical Roots of Rentier Structures

Afghanistan has been influenced through rents from the earliest stages of state formation. Since taxation was limited, the strained connection between modern stateness and tribal rural society helped to develop rent dependencies. Often, taxation raids by central rulers disenfranchised tribes and rural populations. Also, competing imperial ambitions provided external sources of funding for rulers—after the British Empire ceased to be the leading power, the United States tried to strengthen its influence in Central Asia. In an environment of accelerating rivalry between the Soviet Union and the West, for the United States it seemed all the more important to forge "close political, economic and military ties with Pakistan, Iran and Turkey, which eventually led to these states being incorporated into western-sponsored regional alliances."[22] Despite the economic incentives, Afghanistan kept its distance for several reasons: First, since its government was not convinced of America's commitment, there was no reason to complicate relations with the Soviet Union. A second crucial factor was its tradition of neutrality in international relations. This was particularly important in relation to Pakistan and India because the Durand Line, which separates Afghanistan and Pakistan, has never gained international recognition and remains an unresolved issue.[23]

Mohammad Daoud, Afghanistan's prime minister from 1953 to 1963, driven by a strong Pashtunistan ideology, pressed for a strong centralized state and modernized society. Miscalculating the United States' policy of providing aid only to countries that shared its anti-communist stance, he failed to mobilize substantial support for his political ambitions in Washington. Instead, clinging to his modernization ambitions, he turned to Moscow for help: "While fearing US encirclement and the probability of Washington's establishing military bases in Iran and Pakistan, the Khrushchev leadership welcomed Afghanistan's request."[24] Soviet influence increased rapidly as the Afghan military became Soviet trained and equipped. Soviet influence was also vast in administrative, educational, and technical matters, even if it was not as pervasive as in the military. Over the years, Soviet influence gained firm ground on the basis of loans and assistance. These were, in turn, exploited as a source of rent for state structures, lowering Daoud's dependency "on administrative control or penetration of society."[25] Despite this apparent weakness in fiscal issues, "Daoud was the first Afghan leader ever who managed to elevate the state to the heights of a relatively autonomous institution capable of imposing its rules of behaviour on the bulk of the populace."[26] By leaning toward Moscow, he intended "to induce a reluctant Washington to attach greater importance to Afghanistan . . . to accord it substantial aid as it had requested."[27] This amounts to a clear rent-seeking strategy pursued at the highest levels of government.

During that time, a class of educated citizens emerged from foreign-funded schools; Afghan students joined schools and university faculties or received scholarships for education in foreign countries, including Germany, the United States, and Egypt. They were marginalized in their own society, being perceived as having culturally distanced themselves from Islamic values. A literacy rate as low as 10 percent (for women the figure was 2 percent)[28] curtailed domestic dialogue about social values. The newly educated elites were kept away from real participation in political processes. At the same time, in the absence of central rule, autonomous power structures emerged in the distant regions. These structures were strengthened by the trickling down of funds from the centre, as the state tried to solidify its stance against the tribes. Following Daoud's *coup d'état* in 1973, the educated class, together with the Soviet-trained military, tried to get a grip on the state.[29]

During the democratic phase in the 1960s, the state sector had swallowed the educated class who, with rent flow decreasing toward the end of the decade, feared a loss of benefits. At the same time, democratic procedures had degenerated into a mere façade, and the level of the state's legitimacy—in terms of both its procedural and functional aspects—was at its lowest. Daoud's programs after the coup, funded by foreign aid,[30] sought to restore legitimacy; consequently, he tried to diversify international support by strengthening ties with the oil-rich states of the Persian Gulf. By reducing his dependence on Moscow, he was able to sideline the communists, who had played a vital role in keeping his government in office. Finally, Daoud lost their support and started purges against them. Moscow, being forced to choose between losing its influence and a fair amount of money already invested in Afghanistan, opted to support the People's Democratic Party of Afghanistan against Daoud. He was removed from power in a bloody coup in 1978, in which the Soviets were not directly involved. Compared with leftist groups in other countries, the communists did have modest popular support; they sought to compensate for this by pressing ahead with Daoud's policy of quick and thorough modernization. Additionally, they found a functioning rentier system in Afghanistan.

Opposition to Daoud's elite-based coup had formed both in the country and in exile, when the political program of modernization was discerned as running counter to traditional values (garnished as Islamic values). This opposition, of course, did not change when the communists took over the government. Influenced by the Muslim Brotherhood and the writings of Sayyed Qutb, these forces saw Islam as the source of moral politics and as the only legitimate power base, but they could likewise make use of foreign funding. The events that followed have been well reported elsewhere, so there is no need to further elaborate on the history of the Afghan war(s). The important point here is that in Afghanistan, rentier structures were in existence long before the war crippled the country and many of its people—indeed, many of the rentier state structures recovered faster than administrative or political capacities.

Political Rentier Structures in Post-Taliban Afghanistan

In 2001, while the fighting that led the Taliban to abandon Kabul to the militias of the so-called Northern Alliance was going on, plans were already being drawn up for a postwar Afghanistan. In talks held in Bonn, Germany, and organized by the United Nations with strong German support, the participating groups—including diaspora and mujahidin formations of the victorious Northern Alliance[31]—agreed to appoint an interim government. Its main tasks would be to organize and hold a Loya Jirga,[32] a semitraditional "Great Council," which would legitimize this plan and elect an interim government. Following this, another Constitutional Loya Jirga would be held to finalize a draft constitution prepared by a Constitutional Council. The last steps in the state's reconstruction process would be presidential and parliamentary elections. By then Afghanistan would have a Western-style liberal political system.

This raised the question of dealing with an independent government. Unlike earlier interventions, such as in East Timor, Kosovo, or Bosnia-Herzegovina, where UN or other international missions were at least partially in charge of administrative tasks, in Afghanistan a sovereign government existed. The international community, recognizing the risk of losing popular support for the project if it appeared to be all too foreign, decided that "to be sustainable, institutions of good governance must be Afghan; a transitional administration run by Afghans will be 'far more credible, acceptable and legitimate' than one run by the UN."[33] Hence, the government should have led the reconstruction process from the very beginning. But the functional elite bore little legitimacy, because Afghans who were educated or who had lived in the West as refugees were still seen as foreigners in Afghanistan. Moreover, the "light footprint" approach, which aimed to minimize the number of expatriate personnel, was mere lip service: a coordinating body was supposed to be established to minimize conflict among organizational interests, but it would be designated as the sole disseminator of aid and development funds.[34] The inherent paradox of the international community's policy, namely, that it placed the responsibility for its own political aims in the hands of the Afghan government, remained unresolved.

The Afghan state constituted a political space that incorporated rent-seeking by the elites, counter-terrorism and stabilization policy by the international actors, and day-by-day struggles for survival by the people. Classical features of stateness,[35] like internal finances, monopoly of the use of force, and especially territoriality, were absent. Western donors still clung to the image of stateness as it had developed in Europe—at least as an ideal for a distant future. In this situation it did not seem appropriate to confront the warlords, who subsequently started adapting to the situation either by cooperating with the foreign forces in the fight against those labelled as "terrorists," or by using the politically volatile process to position themselves in the political landscape. Neither did the international community attempt to clear up the question of the stationing of foreign troops and their task in Afghanistan. Since the coalition had been involved with the Northern Alliance against the Taliban, these groups had a head start in the new Afghan state, in spite of the fact that their reputation was stained by human rights violations and war crimes similar to those of the regime they replaced.

The reservoir of able and educated personnel being small, a state class quickly formed as local capacity was urgently needed. Northern Alliance personnel largely filled the ranks, as they were the coalition's main partner during the first phase, but attempts were also made to involve broad-based groups to balance ethnic issues.[36] Among the state class were Afghans who had been educated abroad—either in the West or in neighbouring countries such as Iran, Pakistan, or India—and who supported the development of a Western-style state. Many had their salaries paid by the Afghanistan Reconstruction Trust Fund.[37] Also, members of the state class used elections to legitimize existing power structures by falling back on religious or tribal networks. The electoral system of single, non-transferable vote helped candidates who held traditional leading roles or who were closely affiliated with those who did.[38] In the absence of parties or other institutionalized political structures, some independent candidates did win seats, but in general they found it difficult to mobilize sufficient support, despite a voting system that in principle allowed independents to run against established power bases. This reproduced traditional societal structures in parliament. Perversely, parliamentarians were expected to spearhead political and societal modernization but proved hardly amenable to it, despite their dependence on aid.

Although the political landscape in parliament is fragmented,[39] political formations are being established. If these fairly volatile coalitions find their institutional weight, they might provide a power base for properly organized parliamentary groupings, although one must not forget that in the constitutional presidential system, the Afghan parliament's position is rather weak. Generally, the aim of creating a broad-based government was nominally achieved, as all ethnic groups and some organized interests are present in the governing elite. However, bonds between the governing and the governed are not very strong and, in the peripheral areas, hardly developed. All this constitutes a set of structural, ideological, and procedural impediments, putting the president in charge of reconciling Afghan and donor interests.

The president is the focal point for international funding, and Western sponsors will approach him whenever there are developments that run counter to their expectations. While they do not protest the weakness of democratic rule, public cases require him to act. One of the most visible of these was that of Abdul Rahman, an alleged convert to Christianity who in 2006 was in danger of being executed according to Sharia law.[40] In order to keep the donors happy, Rahman was sent to Italy where he was granted political asylum—the donors' political influence outweighing the nominally sovereign state's judiciary in the name of human rights.

The Afghan state depends on external resources, which means that its incumbents may act autonomously so long as vital interests of the donors are not ignored too obviously. According to the logic of rentier states, the Afghan state will try to behave in a way that ensures continuous external funding. Internally, the state class will try to form political and economic dependencies so as to stabilize its position. Externally, the international community demands an accessible governing elite, which tends to support its quest for greater autonomy.[41] The president represents the state on the international stage and in front of the donors. At the same time, his state apparatus is unable to rule the country effectively. On the whole, funding of certain interest groups secures consent. Groups that are organized and able to mobilize large constituencies are most likely to acquire shares of the rent. Consciously or not, groups in opposition to the state may also follow a rent seeking logic by fighting the state: unless they strive to eliminate the state entirely, they will start to develop some kind of relationship with it when rents become available. Meanwhile, the state class has an interest in depoliticizing groups by pampering them with money and posts. This policy is put into practice partly by systems of patronage, and partly through repression.[42] It works in various ways: the middle class will be incorporated into the public sector, and higher strata of society may obtain licences (e.g., for policing certain areas or for importing profitable goods) or be "awarded" development projects.[43] Being "well organized" as a condition for rent-seeking success means that individuals, especially those who are in the lowest classes and geographically distant from the power centres, have little chance to receive funds from such sources.[44]

Any transfer of funds to promote the political status quo qualifies as political rent in this regard. As has been shown, an emerging state class can be identified that will try to further consolidate its position;[45] it receives only 8 percent of its funding from domestic revenues. Somewhat paradoxically, Afghanistan is best defined as a rentier state with a high degree of autonomy. In the terminology of Rubin, the availability of foreign funding, weapons, and training leads to a state's "overdevelopment" in relation to society.[46] The apparent paradox of a "strong state" can be explained only in relation to the society it rules: it can act autonomously, as it does not owe the people any redistribution of taxes, and where there are several donors or donor groups, there is room to manoeuvre to avoid tight monitoring. In the specific Afghan context, this situation is affected by the state's competition with another group of rentiers: those benefiting from narcotics rents.

Drug Rentiers and the State

Competition for power and influence, and subsequently for securing resource inflow, does not lead to a fight for the dominant position within society but instead facilitates cooperation between both groups of beneficiaries—the political elite and the drug traders.[47] In the long term, this may lead to a merger of both "spheres" of rent recipients. Both recipient groups benefit from this cooperation because they attain legitimacy based on each other's existence. In other words, while the drug trade looms large, the necessity of a strong administration is apparent; at the same time the existence of state authority makes high prices for illicitly crossing borders plausible. But this mutual vindication hinders or even prevents political and economic development.

In Afghanistan, large parts of the population profit from the drug business, not just a criminal minority.[48] Other beneficiaries include farmers and their families, who make a living from the labour-intensive work of harvesting the opium poppy. Programs against the drug trade are themselves open for rent-seeking, as the only option available to farmers who wish to exclude their land from eradication is to pay those in charge of the program.[49] The burden is biggest for the poorest and least organized, as they are least able to secure their property and have few outside options in terms of land, capital, or know-how.[50] Other beneficiaries are involved in providing security for the poppy farms, as well as in transporting the raw and refined opium. Finally, some make money by organizing export to the final destination—mainly the streets of Europe.

Determining the dollar value of the drug trade is problematic: First, militias do not exist for the sole purpose of securing drugs. Second, profits are disparate, as much is earned by few and little by many. The relationship between the rich and influential and the farmers is at the same time a function of rule—either through clan structures or loans—because farmers are often subject to the exporters' decisions to either increase or decrease production. By doing so, traders can influence the market. Twenty to thirty families control the outside trade,[51] and they gain the most, since the closer trade comes to the borders the more the drug rent is valorized due to the risk of detection.[52] Market manipulations are common since opium is durable.[53] Market changes lead to price adjustments according to supply and demand mechanisms—although some actors are better able to manipulate these mechanisms than others. However, the supply and demand for the setting of prices is not a feature of rents.

The connection between producers and rents is shaped by the demand in downstream markets, in the consumers' countries. In effect, the connection is embodied in refining and export. For dealers who organize export, profits jump at each stage of refining—from raw opium to morphine to heroin—and when crossing borders.[54] Transport within and out of Afghanistan, and refining, both allow for higher capital accumulation than does production. The United Nations Office on Drugs and Crime (UNODC) notes that "while secure processing and transport of opium and heroin require investments in arms, laboratories, and vehicles, these capital expenditures are likely to be small relative to the revenue from trading, leaving processors and traffickers with substantial resources to invest in other productive or financial assets, domestic and foreign."[55] While drug rentiers might invest in domestic assets, they do not have to do so. When they do, they contribute further to the problems of the Afghan economy, one of which is a variant of the Dutch disease:

> By increasing demand for domestic goods and services, the drug economy contributes to higher consumer and asset prices. This is particularly marked for non-tradable goods and services such as rents [for housing, etc.], as their supply cannot adjust through imports. . . . By increasing demand for production factors, the drug economy also contributes to an increase in their rates of remuneration, raising production costs for other sectors. Given the labor-intensive nature of opium production, this translates primarily into an increase in wages.[56]

While dealers profit from these wage increases, producers do not. The fraction of the retail price in the consumers' countries that goes to the producers is about half a percent: while 1 kilogram of heroin sells for about US$110,000 in the United Kingdom, the opium needed to produce it is worth only US$640 at the farm gate. This huge increase stems mainly from the costs of trafficking, especially through industrialized countries where controls are tightest and seizures frequent.[57] Regardless of the price increases after heroin leaves Afghanistan, traders there still make profits of up to 90 percent of border prices; in any case in 2006 they were over 50 percent of export value.[58] Although it is impossible to quantify investment in chemicals for refining, securing transport, bribes, and the risk of loss (e.g., by confiscation), the remaining profits are still large enough to qualify as rent.[59] To appropriate the rent, it is not necessary for traders to have monopolies,[60] given that Afghanistan is the world's main exporter of opium. Drug traders can thus be analyzed as rentiers, and this raises the question as to how their influence translates into political power.

Intermingled Groups: Political Rentiers and Drug Rentiers

Apparently there are distinct categories of rentiers in Afghanistan: drug traders and political elites seem to compete for influence. To secure future rent flows, each group might be required to repress the other's influence, leading to violence. Competition might also be moderated by cooperation in selected fields. It can be assumed that cooperation depends on convergence of interests.

Competition over the expansion of the state's influence and its permeation of society, including the monopoly of the use of force, exists where the drug economy sets the rules. The newest data compiled by UNODC suggest that poppy cultivation decreases where resistance to the state-building project is scarce and where state structures develop step by step, such as in northern and central Afghanistan—despite higher poverty in those provinces. In the richer provinces, production soars. The case of the southern province of Helmand shows that a steep increase in opium production is possible in conditions of relative prosperity.[61] Widespread resistance to the state where there is also economic growth suggests a causal connection. However, it remains unclear whether insecurity and a lack of stateness facilitate poppy cultivation (in which case the resistance would be just a side product of the drug economy, not vice versa).

It is no secret that groups affiliated with the Taliban extort money from farmers to fight eradication.[62] They also exercise control over certain trade routes,[63] although it remains unclear whether they are able to appropriate a large share of the drug rent. The routes the opium trade takes—crossing the spheres of influence of ethnic and tribal groups without hindrance—indicate that the insurgents' disruptive potential on the opium trade is rather small.[64] In 2006, the Taliban were not a part of the exporter group. This group of twenty to thirty families disapproved of the Taliban because of their ban on the cultivation of opium in 2001.[65] The statistical correlation between drugs and the insurgency instead seems to indicate that the Taliban and other groups are trying to appropriate a share of the rent. This, in turn, might lead to increasingly violent competition between established traders and the Taliban, fostering cooperation between the former and state agencies. Over the last few years, the financial assets at the drug economy's disposal have already opened policy for debate within the Afghan state.[66] Traders and the state might henceforth find themselves jointly fighting the Taliban and the insurgents to reduce their access to these rents.

For the traders, production itself is of minor importance. Drug rentiers have a greater interest in the existence of some kind of state that controls trade routes and infrastructure. Such a state would allow higher profits than the Taliban did with their production ban.[67] Its existence becomes desirable if it sets up international rent to sustain itself and to reconstruct infrastructure. When civil servants do not adhere to a strict ethos (as did the Taliban), the state is easier to influence and more open to corruption. Also, the mobilization of social and religious networks is easier in a state that is only partially established throughout the country. Permeable politics allow for policy adjustments via paid-for parliamentarians, family members in influential positions, or bribes. Hence, on the individual level, drug rentiers may themselves become part of the state class while still remaining autonomous from the state. By influencing policy or using information from military and police sources, they may keep the drug rent flowing and at the same time participate in the political rent.[68]

Correspondingly, the drug economy provides the state class with an alternative rent. The security situation, combined with the inability to lower demand for illicit drugs in Western countries, allows the state class to portray its rent-seeking as promoting the donors' strategic goals. On the other hand, drug rentiers become donors too, for example by funding members of parliament or police, since state agencies are often unable to adequately pay employees, in particular the security forces. Employees then seek additional sources of income by not pursuing drug transports, by delivering information, or by keeping competitors of the drug rentiers at bay. This merger of private and public space obstructs the establishment of politically neutral state institutions. The most influential societal groups—such as formations of the state class or the economic elite of the drug trade—manage to distribute revenues among themselves, barring the majority of Afghans from participation. Intermingled interests prevent the identification of agency and political liability. Gradually or selectively merging interest groups thus monopolize appropriation of funds and state structures while limiting the development of stateness.

International intervention aims to help establish a political space of "modern" stateness in which the state monopolizes the use of violence and gains legitimacy. The legitimacy of the state stems from its distributive and redistributive obligations—although welfare-state politics is not the only source of legitimacy—which in this case the state is unable to deliver in the absence of sufficient political permeation of the post-conflict space. In the peripheral regions of Afghanistan, the state is hardly present with respect to monopolization of the use of force, regulation, or social interaction. Its rent dependency is continuously reproduced by its lack of administrative potential and taxation.[69]

The security-related argument that the existence of the Afghan state depends on the presence of foreign troops allows for the Afghan state class to secure steady inflows of political rent. The Afghan state has become an indispensable agent between Afghan politics and the international community. In order to elevate the state so that it sets the rules for conflict resolution itself rather than competing with local political forces, the international community directs know-how, legitimacy, and financial resources into the country. Through military engagement it secures the state and its incumbents. It provides an externally produced monopoly on the use of violence, which in Western countries is the state's own realm. In doing so, the international presence requires, supports, and perpetuates a form of stateness depleted of independence and internal sovereignty. Unless taxation is enforced, the legitimacy of the rent-dependent elites will remain close to nil. If aid dependency remains at its current level, the prospects are dim for successfully building a state that comes somewhere close to autonomous rule and the effective provision of security.

Notes

Field research for this article was conducted in Afghanistan during April–June 2006 with the kind support of the Konrad Adenauer Foundation's office in Kabul.

1. See, for example, Aidan Hehir and Neil Robinson, eds., *State-Building: Theory and Practice* (London: Routledge, 2007); Ulrich Schneckener, "Internationales Statebuilding. Dilemmata, Herausforderungen und Strategien für externe Akteure," in *Fragile Staatlichkeit: "States at Risk" zwischen Stabilität und Scheitern,* ed. Ulrich Schneckener (Baden-Baden: Nomos, 2006): 367-82; David Chandler, *Empire in Denial: The Politics of State-Building* (London: Pluto Press, 2006); Francis Fukuyama, *Staaten bauen: Die neue Herausforderung internationaler Politik* (Berlin: Propyläen Verlag, 2004); and as of 2007, the new *Journal of Intervention and Statebuilding,* among others.

2. But see John M. Hobson, *The State and International Relations* (Cambridge: Cambridge University Press, 2000); Klaus Schlichte, "Staatlichkeit als Ideologie. Zur politischen Soziologie der Weltgesellschaft," in *Ideologien in der Weltpolitik, ed. Klaus-Gerd Giesen* (Opladen: Leske u. Budrich, 2004), 149-66.

3. Jens Siegelberg, "Staat und internationales System – ein strukturgeschichtlicher Überblick," in *Strukturwandel Internationaler Beziehungen: Zum Verhaltnis*

Staat und Internationalem System seit dem Westfälischen Frieden, ed. Jens Siegelberg and Klaus Schlichte (Wiesbaden:Westdeutscher Verlag, 2000), 11-57.

4. *Statehood* here signifies a state's ability to play according to the rules of sovereign states, with ambassadors in the most important national capitals as well as membership in the UN and acceptance of the main regulations of international law. *Stateness* has to do with the state's relations with the individuals and groups that it presumably governs. In modern states the rulers are interchangeable, their rule is controlled by the people, governance is bound by moral and legal regulations, and the use of violence is legitimately monopolized within the institutions of the state; however, in many states this ideal is only partly put into practice.

5. Over the course of state formation, the use of violence has been placed with the state, which over time became depersonalized and, in a later development, subjected to procedural principles and, finally, democratized (see Norbert Elias, *Über den Prozess der Zivilisation,* vol. 2, *Band: Wandlungen der Gesellschaft. Entwurf zu einer Theorie der Zivilisation* (Frankfurt: Suhrkamp, 1976), 279-311). In this notion, the state is seen as a historical phenomenon, which over time developed different forms and depths of de facto societal embedding.

6. These differences illustrate why a dichotomous notion of state as opposed to society is not held here; also, Afghanistan has never been colonized in the classical sense. Still, the country owes its existence to the legacy of colonial India, parts of which turned into Pakistan, the Central Asian (now post-Soviet) states and, of course, Persia/Iran.

7. See Hartmut Elsenhans, *Globalization between a Convoy Model and an Under-Consumptionist Threat* (Berlin: LIT Verlag, 2006).

8. As expected, there is no definition or consensus on what "development" actually means. In the context of global interventionism, which has increasingly structured international politics over the last decade, it is understood as development of societal, political, economic, governance, and security structures. In the interventionist's view, these structures will at some point fulfil the duties that are attributed to modern statehood: monopolization of violence, self-sustaining financing of an impartial administration, and stable governance over a given territory. This notion of development is being augmented by aims of human development, including women's rights, education, and health care.

9. Paul Collier et al., "Breaking the Conflict Trap: Civil War and Development Policy" (World Bank Policy Research Report, Washington, 2003), 106.

10. Stephan Klingebiel, "Impact of Development Cooperation in Conflict Situations," Cross-Section Report on Evaluations of German Development Cooperation in Six Countries, Reports and Working Papers No. 6/1999 (German Development Institute, Bonn, 1999).

11. Ibid., vi.

12. See Martin Beck, *Friedensprozess im Nahen Osten: Rationalität, Kooperation und politische Rente im Vorderen Orient* (Wiesbaden: Westdeutscher Verlag, 2002), 103.

13. Most of the funds are presumably transferred through the *hawala* system, which facilitates quick money orders by paying a sum to a trustee in one country and having it paid to a remittee in another; often only one phone call is needed for the transaction, fees are low, and there are no records kept. Of course, there are no statistical data as to how much is being transferred. That is why illegal groups like to use *hawala* as well. See Loretta Napoleoni, *Die Ökonomie des Terrors* (München: Kunstmann, 2004), 205.

14. See Kevin Savage and Paul Harvey, eds., *Remittances during Crises: Implications for Humanitarian Response* (London: 2007), 10.

15. Beck, *Friedensprozess im Nahen Osten*, 109.

16. Robert Nozick, *Anarchy, the State, and Utopia* (New York: Basic Books, 1974); Peter T. Bauer, *Equality, the Third World, and Economic Delusion* (Cambridge: Harvard University Press, 1981).

17. Klaus Schlichte, *Der Staat in der Weltgesellschaft* (Frankfurt: Campus-Verlag 2005), 180.

18. See Florian Kühn, "Außer Balance: Militärische und politische Strategien zur Terrorismusbekämpfung in Afghanistan," *Schriftenreihe zur Internationalen Politik* (June 2005): 36.

19. Gordon Tullock, *The Economics of Special Privilege and Rent Seeking* (Boston: Kluwer, 1989), vii.

20. See, for example, Frank Flatters and Bentley Macleod, "Administrative Corruption and Taxation," *International Tax and Public Finance* 2, no. 3 (October 1995): 397-417.

21. Hartmut Elsenhans, *Abhängiger Kapitalismus oder bürokratische Entwicklungsgesellschaft: Versuch über den Staat in der Dritten Welt* (Frankfurt: Campus-Verlag, 1981), 24-25.

22. Amin Saikal, *Modern Afghanistan: A History of Struggle and Survival* (London: I.B. Tauris, 2004), 118.

23. See Boris Wilke, "Boundaries of State and Military in Pakistan," in *The Dynamics of States: The Formation and Crises of State Domination*, ed. Klaus Schlichte (Aldershot: Ashgate, 2005), 183-210.

24. Saikal, *Modern Afghanistan*, 123.

25. Barnett Rubin, *The Fragmentation of Afghanistan: State Formation and Collapse in the International System* (New Haven: Yale University Press, 2002), 75.

26. Saikal, *Modern Afghanistan*, 126.

27. Ibid., 127.

28. Rubin, *Fragmentation of Afghanistan*, 70.

29. Ibid, 74. While historically revolutionary movements have always consisted of an educated avant-garde, in Afghanistan this group, educated elsewhere and accustomed to requesting money from foreign sources, relied on foreign support more than on mobilizing a critical mass of domestic political actors.

As Rubin states, preconditioned by the "structure of opportunities," the "rentier state produced rentier revolutionaries" (81).

30. His development plan for the period of 1976–1983 was costed at US$3.85 million, two-thirds of which was to be financed by the Soviet Union; see Saikal, *Modern Afghanistan*, 177.

31. The United Front for the Liberation of Afghanistan, better known in the West as the Northern Alliance, in late 2001 was led by mujahidin commanders of the late Ahmad Shah Massoud; other parties to the interim agreement were the "Italian" group of the former king Zahir Shah and two smaller Pashtun groups; see Saikal, *Modern Afghanistan*, 236.

32. The Great Council historically had little relevance for the central state, and in this regard it would be an "invented tradition"; see Christine Noelle-Karimi, Conrad Schetter, and Reinhard Schlagintweit, eds., *Afghanistan: A Country without a State?* (Frankfurt: IKO, 2002).

33. Chris Johnson and Jolyon Leslie, *Afghanistan: The Mirage of Peace* (London: Zed Books, 2004), 199.

34. Ibid., 199-200.

35. Florian Kühn, "Das Engagement der Europäischen Union zur Demokratisierung Afghanistans," in *The EU as an External Democracy Promoter*, ed. Annette Jünemann and Michèle Knodt (Baden-Baden: Die externe Demokratieförderung der EU Schriftenreihe des Arbeitskreises Europäische Integration e.V, 2005).

36. Conrad Schetter, *Ethnizität und ethnische Konlikte in Afghanistan* (Berlin: Dietrich Reimer Verlag, 2003), 579ff.

37. US$1.4 billion had been administered through the Afghanistan Reconstruction Trust Fund by September 2006, of which US$860 million was channelled to the Afghan government to pay wages and to cover investments. See World Bank, "Afghanistan Reconstruction Trust Fund," http://web.worldbank.org/WBSITE/EXTERNAL/COUNTRIES/SOUTHASIAEXT/AFGHANISTANEXTN/0,,contentMDK:20152008~pagePK:141137~piPK:217854~theSitePK:305985,00.html.

38. The single, non-transferable vote allows only single candidates to run for office; for a given electoral district, seats are reserved for the first few candidates. That means, for example, that the first of three may have 90 percent of the votes, while the second and third might win seats with only 3 percent and 2 percent, respectively. Because candidates are not allowed to run on a party ticket, there is no incentive to organize politically. That, in turn, means that parliament is comparably weak, as it is made up of ad hoc coalitions rather than organized interest groups. See Thomas Ruttig, *Islamists, Leftists — and a Void in the Center: Afghanistan's Political Parties and Where They Come From. 1902–2006* (Berlin: Konrad Adenauer Stiftung, 2006), 11ff.

39. Ruttig, *Afghanistan's Political Parties*; Babk Khalatbari and Christian Ruck, "Fünf Jahre nach den Taliban: Aktuelle Entwicklungen am Hindukush," *KAS-Auslandsinformationen* 1 (2007): 73-91.

40. Ulrich Ladurner, "Wer ist Abdul Rahman?" *Die Zeit*, 30 March 2006.
41. Rubin, *Fragmentation of Afghanistan*, 12.
42. Beck, *Friedensprozess im Nahen Osten*, 122.
43. See International Crisis Group (ICG), "Countering Afghanistan's Insurgency: No Quick Fixes," Asia Report No. 123 (2 November 2006), 9.
44. This is not to say that the differences in the "peripheral" parts of society do not matter; of course the repercussions of societal change outside the "centre" are felt by elites and transform them and their behaviour into what Migdal calls a "melange"; see Joel S. Migdal, *State in Society: Studying How States and Societies Transform and Constitute One Another* (Cambridge: Cambridge University Press, 2001), 47-53.
45. For example, parliament might change the voting system, which is unfavourable for MPs because it makes re-election subject to short-term changes in voter support and prevents the evolution of a party system with reliable structures. Also, there might be a long delay before the next round of elections, as the voting system is too complex (and hence too expensive) for Afghanistan to support alone. By agreeing to this system, international donors had to accept the financial and logistical burden of supporting it following the first nationwide poll in 2005; otherwise, they would be responsible for these elections being a one-off event.
46. Rubin, *Fragmentation of Afghanistan*, 12. See Beck, *Friedensprozess im Nahen Osten*, 96ff, for a discussion of several types of classifications for "strong" and "weak" states. Afghanistan is not a strong state in a neo-Marxist sense, which requires a firm or even dominant position in the world system, nor by "effectively permeating its territory" (Beck, 97). Rubin's argument is confined to seeing a strong state solely on the grounds of whether it is able to act autonomously, regardless of any external dependencies. Migdal traces the debate over the term in *State in Society*, 59-60.
47. For example, by permeating societal structures more thoroughly or by mobilizing resources.
48. In 2007, 3.3 million persons were involved exclusively in opium cultivation—that is, 14.3 percent of the population. It becomes clear that the number living off drug revenues including traffickers, refiners, and militias consists of several millions; see United Nations Office on Drugs and Crime (UNODC), *Afghanistan Opium Survey* (Vienna, 2007), 10.
49. See UNODC, *Afghanistan Opium Survey* (Vienna, 2006), 6.
50. Ibid., 9.
51. Interview with an expert, Kabul, 26 May 2006.
52. UNODC, *2006 Survey*, 11.
53. In 2006, prices decreased in relative terms (by 9 percent for wet and 2 percent for dry opium), but since overall production increased by 34 percent, opium's total farm gate value was US$1 billion (UNODC, *2007 Survey*, 11-13). These numbers hint at the complexity of the opium production economy: In the south of Afghanistan, with resistance against foreign and state troops at a high, cultivation increased; while in the relatively stable north, where

alternative goods are easier to transport and trade, the number of poppy-free provinces more than doubled. The 2007 production of 8,200 metric tons of opium in Afghanistan was an all-time high (6,100 metric tons were produced in 2006). Afghanistan has practically monopolized the opium market, producing 93 percent of the world's total crop (see UNODC, *2007 Survey*, vi).

54. See Doris Buddenberg and William A. Byrd, eds., *Afghanistan's Drug Industry: Structure, Functioning, Dynamics, and Implications for Counter-Narcotics Policy* (Vienna/Kabul: UNODC and World Bank, 2006), 128.
55. Ibid., 31.
56. Ibid.
57. Ibid., 131.
58. Ibid., 136.
59. In 2001, when the Taliban banned opium production as against Islam, the profits of heroin traders amounted to only 7.5 percent of export revenues. Independently of the absolute profits realized by using up inventories, this points to investments being a lot lower than 50 percent; otherwise, traders would have gone out of business due to a lack of profitability (see UNODC 2006 Survey, 134-35).
60. See Elsenhans, *Abhängiger Kapitalismus*, 64.
61. UNODC, *2007 Survey*, vi.
62. See Conrad Schetter, "Talibanistan – der Anti-Staat," *Internationales Asien-forum* 38, no. 3/4 (2007): 236.
63. UNODC, *2007 Survey*, v.
64. See Janet Kursawe, "Afghanischer Teufelskreis," E+Z 48 (March 2007): 119.
65. Interview with a UNODC expert, Kabul, 24 May 2006; also Kursawe, "Afghanischer Teufelskreis," 119.
66. Interview with a UNODC expert, Kabul, 24 May 2006.
67. Although the Taliban did not ban the trade in opium, they endangered Afghanistan's leading position in the globalized drug market.
68. Paradoxically, the same applies to local power brokers and clan leaders close to the Taliban; see Schetter, "Talibanistan – der Anti-Staat," 248.
69. The border regions of Pakistan have a similar problem, in that the state also patronizes local elites to pursue its own ends. This likewise triggers rent-seeking activities and all of the undesirable economic side effects. One common practice to gain the support of local elites is to supply them with licences for cross-border trade, "resulting in a wide income and resource gap between those with access to the administration and those deprived of it" (ICG, "Countering Afghanistan's Insurgency," 9). While the borders are porous—either hardly controlled or disputed—this practice puts local elites in a privileged position while not hindering smuggling on the part of other actors, hence "causing significant revenue losses in uncollected duties and taxes" (ibid.). The usual role of borders in defining political spaces is significantly limited in this context.

Chapter 5

NGO Myths, Realities, and Advocacy on the International Strategy in Afghanistan

Lara Olson and Andrea Charron

Introduction

The scope of current international interventions in Afghanistan brings together a diverse and chaotic group of actors. Foreign military forces under the NATO-led International Security Assistance Force, US counter-insurgency forces, and a range of donor governments, private contractors, United Nations and non-governmental relief and development actors, and diplomatic missions are all in attendance. The overlap between active war-fighting, robust peace enforcement, and security stabilization with efforts to rebuild the physical, governmental, and socioeconomic infrastructure destroyed by thirty years of war has created unprecedented challenges but has done little to diminish the strength of the many insurgency groups operating in Afghanistan.[1]

The war-fighting and peace-building frameworks that simultaneously define the international strategy in Afghanistan have been less successful than hoped. International military and civilian, governmental and non-governmental efforts have lurched along on often separate paths for the past seven years since the overthrow of the Taliban. Only recently, however, have the deep flaws and strategic gaps in the strategy gained the attention of policy-makers as deteriorating security in Afghanistan becomes impossible to ignore.

The current scenario has given rise to a chorus of calls for greater, stronger, and tighter coordination of all international efforts. This implies that the strategies are sound but the execution is faulty. Naysayers who question some of the fundamental premises of the international strategy have been paid scant regard. Operational humanitarian and development

NGOs in Afghanistan have argued continuously for a rethink of some fundamental tenets of the international mission, yet with little impact to date. It is fair to say that concerted advocacy by NGO coalitions within Afghanistan and within donor countries has been largely marginalized by the strategists of the international mission.

This paper is divided into four parts. The first section reviews the unusual aid context in Afghanistan within which NGOs operate, marked by conflicting frameworks of peace-building versus war-fighting and by widespread experimentation with integrated civil-military approaches. The second section examines misconceptions about NGOs and their role in the international aid "system" that hamper constructive dialogue with other civilian and military state actors in Afghanistan. The third section describes the relief and development roles of NGOs in Afghanistan during the last thirty years, and particularly since 2001. The final section reviews the persistent NGO advocacy in Afghanistan and its minimal impact to date on the broader international strategy.

The non-governmental aid sector is not well understood; instead, NGO aid workers are often stereotyped as "missionaries, mercenaries, or misfits."[2] There are legitimate questions to be asked about the accountability of NGOs and whether they represent a fledgling global civil society, more narrow organizational interests, or simply repositories of technical expertise.[3] As well, the NGO sector, like any other, is populated not only with highly professional organizations that employ best practices and have outstanding reputations but also with mismanaged and wasteful organizations, and with everything in between. Because of the size and diversity of the NGO sector, the lack of vertical leadership structures within the community, and the deep commitment to independence from governments, NGOs and state actors have difficulty understanding each other. In the context of the international effort in Afghanistan—a confused war-and-peace context untethered from a strong UN peace-building framework and a strong civilian leadership—the relationship between NGOs and state donors has become very difficult.

NGOs do not have all the answers to Afghanistan's problems, nor do they expect to achieve reconstruction, development, and security in Afghanistan alone. Nevertheless, given their hands-on role working with Afghan communities and their long history in the country, taking their perspectives seriously could help all actors arrive at better overall strategies. The marginalization of NGO views to date on key strategic issues has weakened the ability of the international mission to effectively respond to Afghanistan's challenges.

War-Fighting and Peace-Building

Generally, one thinks of war-fighting and peace-building as occurring at different times within the lifetime of a conflict, or at least in separate theatres given the military-like nature of the former and the civilian-led, development-like nature of the latter. Increasingly, however, these two activities are occurring simultaneously in the same theatres. The complex and unwieldy architecture of the international mission in Afghanistan represents distinct—and sometimes unreconciled—agendas of the major actors involved. These conflicting agendas are reflected in how the effort is named: terms such as peace-building, state-building, complex peace operations, counter-insurgency, and nation-building are used almost synonymously to characterize the broad international effort.[4] The two basic paradigms at play in Afghanistan are summed up here as war-fighting versus peace-building. These terms reflect not mere semantic differences but a deep tension in the nature of the broader international engagement in Afghanistan that creates enormous challenges for NGOs.

The War-Fighting Agenda

In a "typical" conflict, the military would lead with war-fighting, a peace accord would be established, and then the United Nations and non-governmental organizations would follow to monitor the peace and begin reconstruction. In Afghanistan, the war-fighting has continued with the consent of an elected Afghan government, while no peace agreement has ever been reached.

After the terrorist attacks on US soil by al Qaeda on 11 September 2001, NATO and the Organization of American States (OAS) immediately identified the attacks as "acts of war."[5] The UN Security Council labelled the attacks as a "threat to international peace and security" and reiterated the inherent right of individual and collective self-defence,[6] providing the United States with a green light to begin planning for a "war on terror." A US-led coalition called Operation Enduring Freedom (OEF) launched wide-ranging military strikes against terrorist targets and Taliban positions in Afghanistan, ousting the predominantly ethnic Pashtun Taliban from power in early December 2001, thanks in part to the Northern Alliance—a coalition of Afghan anti-Taliban groups drawn from non-Pashtun ethnic groups. On 20 December 2001, the Security Council authorized the establishment of an International Security Assistance Force (ISAF) for an initial six months to aid the Afghan transitional authority in maintaining peace and security in Kabul, Afghanistan's capital city.[7] The force was authorized to take "all necessary measures." In 2003, the Security Council authorized the expansion of the ISAF to allow it, as resources permitted, to maintain security in areas of Afghanistan outside of Kabul and its environs.[8] As a result of the expansion of the mission, NATO (an organization whose purpose for nearly sixty years has been to defend collectively against an outside attacker[9]) took over the command and coordination of the ISAF but with a two-pronged approach: war-fighting through donor country battle units, and stabilization and reconstruction through Provincial Reconstruction Teams.

The United States, by far the biggest military and aid donor to Afghanistan, has always used the language of war-fighting in relation to Afghanistan: for US military and civilian policy-makers, the Afghan mission has been the centrepiece of the "war on terror," reframed in recent years as the "counter-insurgency war." This war-fighting agenda reflects the distinct interest represented by the US role in Afghanistan as a response to the 9/11 attacks on its soil, and its early rejection of a role in an expansive nation-building agenda in Afghanistan. Consistent with this underlying approach, US policy-makers openly talk of the role of development aid as a tool of counter-insurgency, and critics fault the Afghanistan Compact for being incoherent as a "war plan," calling for metrics to measure the things that will matter in "winning the conflict."[10]

Beyond the US position, the current military posture of the International Security Assistance Force in Afghanistan's southern and eastern provinces is also an explicitly war-fighting one. Canada, the Netherlands, and the United Kingdom have active battle units in these areas whose rules of operation are to engage the insurgency. The civil-military and counter-insurgency doctrine of the United States and other troop-contributing countries emphasizes the use of aid to civilian populations as a means of ensuring force protection, securing intelligence, and winning the "hearts and minds" of the people—all as explicit elements of a war-fighting strategy.

The Peace-Building Agenda

Peace-building, an umbrella term referring to the broad spectrum of efforts for post-conflict recovery in a given crisis, was defined by the Brahimi panel on UN peace operations in 2000 as the creation of conditions for more than just the absence of war.[11] Peace-building includes rebuilding basic infrastructures, reintegrating former combatants, strengthening the rule of law, improving respect for human rights, providing technical assistance for democratic development, and promoting economic sustainability, conflict resolution, and reconciliation. In Afghanistan, this broad range of efforts is currently funded by donor governments and international financial institutions, and implemented by fledgling Afghan government institutions, UN agencies, international and Afghan non-governmental organizations and, often, by foreign military forces. However, peace-building in Afghanistan has a unique flavour: these activities occur in the context of an ongoing armed conflict and in the absence of a peace accord.

Peace-building state actors in Afghanistan include donor countries, the United Nations, the European Union, and the World Bank, all of whom are involved in financing and/or delivering aid to Afghanistan. Donor countries from around the world have met on four occasions to pledge financial aid and to set benchmarks.[12] The conference held in London in 2006 endorsed the Afghanistan Compact—a five-year blueprint for Afghan-led recovery that identifies three critical and interdependent pillars: security; governance, rule of law, and human rights; and social and economic development.[13] The Compact represents the key framework for cooperation between the Government of Afghanistan, the United Nations, and the international community.

The United Nations has sent a (predominantly) political mission, the UN Assistance Mission in Afghanistan (UNAMA), in addition to its specialized agencies such as UNICEF, the World Food Programme, and the Refugee Agency (UNHCR). UNAMA coordinates all activities of the UN system in the country, has played a key supporting role in the post-Bonn political transition, and works for the establishment of strong and sustainable Afghan institutions. As a new type of "integrated" UN mission, UNAMA is directed and supported by the UN Department of Peacekeeping Operations—though it is not a classic peacekeeping mission. However, a key element of the integrated mission structure is that it unites the two key sectors of the mission—political affairs, and development and humanitarian affairs—under the same chain of command, an innovation that critics claim subordinates aid to the political goals of the mission in counterproductive ways.[14] The mission has some 1,300 staff, the vast majority of whom (around 80 percent) are Afghan nationals.[15]

The European Union is a major backer of Afghan reconstruction and of the political transition. Its member states collectively account for nearly 30 percent of the US$12.5 billion in grants pledged by the international community at conferences in Tokyo (2002) and Berlin (2004). At the London Conference in the spring of 2006, the European Commission and member states pledged a further US$2.4 billion for reconstruction assistance to Afghanistan over the coming years. The European Union provided substantial support for the presidential and parliamentary elections. In financial terms, the European Union's collective financial contribution (European Commission plus member states) accounted for around 50 percent of the cost of the presidential election and 40 percent of the cost of the parliamentary and provincial elections.[16]

The World Bank also plays a major role, managing key multi-donor trust funds that provide vital operating revenues for the government and financing for twenty-one projects. The World Bank has committed approximately US$1.13 billion, mainly through grants.[17] Bank-funded projects mostly support rural livelihoods by providing job opportunities, rebuilding infrastructure, and developing education and basic health services.

The Provincial Reconstruction Teams (PRTs) can also be seen as peace-building actors in that their goal is to establish stability and to enable conditions for recovery efforts—much like classic UN peacekeeping troops. PRTs are the main framework for international security assistance outside of Kabul: they are provincial bases established by "lead nations" that combine small numbers of troops and civilian aid personnel to promote stability and reconstruction in the area.[18] The PRT military contingents are not battle groups, but rather their purpose is to protect the PRT base, to facilitate the movement of civilian development specialists, and to promote stability in the area through their presence. PRTs have been criticized by many for being an unsuccessful attempt at "security on the cheap."[19] In fact, in terms of troop presence and volume of assistance per capita, the mission in Afghanistan is significantly under-resourced compared with other international missions in the 1990s.[20] To be fair, PRTs are recognized by NATO and donor countries as a less than an ideal solution to security in the provinces, but the only realistic one given constraints on troops available and the "light footprint" strategy decided for the mission early on. In the southern and eastern provinces, the coexistence of large battle groups and special forces doing the war-fighting and other soldiers deployed in the PRTs makes a confusing scenario. For the population and anti-government groups, it is easy to assume that all soldiers are combat soldiers and all military projects have a war-fighting aim.

Implications of These Conflicting Frameworks

The pervasive tensions between the peace-building and war-fighting mandates and mechanisms of international interveners are manifested, in concrete terms, in the deep conflation of military and civilian assistance roles inside Afghanistan.[21] Since security is seen as the necessary condition for development, and development is seen as the peace dividend that will give Afghans a stake in the new order, these two realms are tightly interlinked in theory and in practice. The PRTs are the practical expression of this thinking in Afghanistan and are often run as part of the lead nation's "whole of government" approach to aiding fragile states. Whole of government or "integrated" approaches aim to maximize the impact of efforts in a given crisis by bringing together all relevant arms of the donor government: typically the foreign ministry, the defence ministry, and the international development agency, along with other branches of government such as law enforcement or agriculture. These approaches promote coherence across all arms of government through mechanisms of joint planning, resource pooling, and joint decision-making at headquarters and in the field.[22]

However sensible in theory, recent reviews of the practical experience to date with the whole of government approach have revealed serious dilemmas and challenges, since the different agendas of the ministries toward fragile states mean that friction still abounds.[23] Each department views failed states through a separate lens: defence ministries and foreign ministries are concerned with home country interests and instability, while development ministries are primarily focused on fighting poverty and improving beneficiary welfare. Some critics argue that this approach, while well-intentioned, has directly contributed to adverse outcomes in Afghanistan—to aid being subordinated to political interests in counter-productive ways.[24]

Many analysts argue that these conditions are merely reality, a part of the new context of conflict to which all actors must respond with new approaches. The problem with this argument is twofold: first, the effectiveness of the whole of government approach is not clear, and the downward trend in security of late in Afghanistan suggests that the jury is still out. Second, the cost of this approach in terms of other core goals of the international assistance effort is, according to critics, unjustifiably high. The politicization and militarization of aid is seen, for a variety of reasons, as having undermined the effectiveness of the development effort on which long-term security presumably rests.

NGO Realities and Myths in International Aid

To understand current NGO perspectives on Afghanistan, it is important to clarify basic facts about the role of NGOs in the international aid system and to correct several common misperceptions.

NGO Realities

In the international response to natural and man-made disasters, NGOs have always played an important role. While historically there have been clear divisions between NGO activities and those of the United Nations and donor states, since the early 1990s a new operating environment for aid NGOs has arisen, marked by three basic realities:

- *Shared space:* In Afghanistan and elsewhere, NGO personnel work and live in the same areas as "joined up" donor-government project workers and military actors who may be implementing relief, reconstruction, and development programs that are similar to those of NGOs
- *Significant donor dependence on NGO implementing capacity:* NGOs have a crucial implementation role in the architecture of international aid, and a large amount of donor assistance is operationalized through NGOs. Donor-government development agencies, in general, have minimal direct implementing capacity and rely on the operational UN agencies, NGOs, and private sector contractors.
- *Significant NGO dependence on state donors:* Globally, significant amounts of funding for NGO work now come from governments, a fact that has dramatically increased the size of the major international

NGOs in recent years.[25] In Afghanistan, the same donor governments that are actively engaged in implementing whole of government approaches through Provincial Reconstruction Teams are major funders of many NGO programs. Some NGOs strictly limit funding from governments to protect their independence from government policies.

As a result of these factors, NGOs seem part and parcel of the "international mission" to the broader public, both in crisis zones and in donor countries. This perception poses an acute dilemma for NGO independence, particularly in Afghanistan where the international war-fighting element is not an impartial peacekeeping force but is the result of an invasion and militarily supports the central government. For NGOs whose work has historically been predicated on responding to human need rather than supporting political projects (however worthy) and on keeping a distance from the agendas of powerful states, this is a new situation fraught with dangers.

NGO Myths

Powerful myths and misconceptions about the role of NGOs in international aid complicate relations with other actors in these theatres. The most problematic are listed below.

Working Side by Side Means Working "Together." It is widely believed that since NGOs share a common space with international military forces and state aid agencies, NGO independence is no longer possible, or even desirable. NGOs that remain committed to independence are accused of naiveté, of living in the past and reifying independence to a religion that has lost practical relevance. Insistence on independence is suspected of damaging the broader effort and of being "futile," particularly in Afghanistan, because of the widespread misperception of NGOs as agents of "the West" regardless of their particular stance.

While many NGOs acknowledge that their mere presence in such theatres is not neutral,[26] they still see the necessity for independence of humanitarian and development efforts. In Afghanistan, many NGOs see the current erosion of humanitarian space as entirely preventable, and as possibly reversible. They cite specific actions and policies that have blurred distinctions between civilian and military aid providers, among them the early use of civilian dress by US special forces, Colin Powell's infamous remark about NGOs as "force multipliers," and the widespread use of aid for intelligence, force protection, and hearts-and-minds efforts.[27] However, even in Afghanistan NGO independence is still seen as possible. NGOs with decades of presence there report that the communities they work with still actively protect their programs and personnel, but these communities claim they cannot continue doing so if the NGO works with the foreign military forces.[28]

NGOs Normally Rely on Military Protection. It is widely assumed that explicit military protection enables relief and development work in dangerous environments, whether through armed escorts or military presence. In fact, the norm for most relief and development NGOs has been to reject the use of armed escorts unless in extreme circumstances. NGO security practices today involve a three-pronged approach: acceptance, deterrence, and protection, with explicit protection measures deemed a last resort for both practical and ethical reasons.[29] Instead, most NGOs rely for their security in conflict environments on belligerents' acceptance of their impartiality and, relatedly, on community acceptance, entailing the protection of agency personnel by the communities they work with. A key concern in Afghanistan is that with deteriorating security and reduced humanitarian access in many parts of the country, community acceptance approaches can no longer work—without long-term presence, NGOs cannot build those relationships of trust. Yet working closely with military actors engaged in active peace enforcement undermines an NGO's reputation as impartial, which in turn limits its ability to reach needy populations on all sides of the conflict with assistance.

NGOs Are "Subcontractors" to Their Donors. NGOs rarely engage in relationships where they are simply subcontractors to donors—whether states, multilateral organizations, corporations, or individuals. When these entities fund NGO programs, it is usually through "partnership agreements" that are based on a very different premise. In general, NGOs accept government funding when there is a clear confluence of what donors want to do and what NGOs want to do based on their independent assessment of community needs and capacities, and their own values and principles.[30] Almost all development aid programming delivered by NGOs (unlike private sector contractors) is driven by a grassroots, bottom-up approach emphasizing participatory assessment and planning with communities, rather than directive programming responding to top-down frameworks. Furthermore, NGOs have very different assets to offer than subcontractors expertise in working with communities in participatory, sustainable ways; clearly articulated ethics; a focus on relationships and capacity building; and their very reputation for independence from governments. When donors partner with NGOs, they are recruiting these assets and skills for their programming because they add significant value.

There Is a Single NGO Community (vs. Communities). Outside observers tend to lump NGOs together as the "NGO community," one presumably based entirely on a shared non-governmental identity. But it is more accurate to refer to an NGO *sector,* which like the business or government sectors, contains a great diversity of groups. Even the subset of NGOs involved in international crises has very diverse mandates (relief, development, human rights, and peace-building, to name a few) and sometimes conflicting priorities and approaches, though these NGOs may share similar values and principles. Over the last decade NGOs have established strong international coalitions and networks, created voluntary professional standards or codes of conduct, and engaged in joint advocacy. Those NGOs that align their activities and approaches through such mechanisms can be seen as a "community," but those who remain outside this framework cannot. In reality, there are many distinct NGO communities reflecting the diversity of civil society around the world.

The Role of NGOs in Afghanistan

Many of the biggest international and Afghan aid NGOs have been providing emergency relief and development support to Afghans for over thirty years. Even during the Soviet occupation, major international relief and development NGOs like Médecins Sans Frontières, CARE International, World Vision, and Oxfam worked from bases in Pakistan running cross-border programs in Afghanistan as well as assisting Afghans in refugee camps. Given this history, "many Afghans initially viewed all foreign aid providers as NGOs in the early years of the [current] international mission."[31]

Throughout the 1990s, there was a dramatic growth in the number of national Afghan NGOs. Their members received training, support, and funding from international NGOs. At the same time, international NGOs worked in the country providing a combination of emergency relief and "chronic emergency" development programming, including support to formal and informal education programs.[32] Under the Taliban regime, some NGOs expanded emergency activities and continued development support despite political restrictions, while others left Afghanistan to protest the regime's human rights policies.[33] In those years, the Taliban were ambivalent toward the humanitarian organizations, tacitly relying on their programs for social welfare. It has only been since the fall of the Taliban regime that their leaders have adopted a "with us or against us" attitude toward the aid community.[34] After 2001, when government donor agencies established offices in Afghanistan, it was often with the help of international NGOs long established in the country. Many NGOs that had left the country because of the Taliban's policies returned. As well, new NGOs arrived in response to the lifting of restrictions and the availability of funding.

As civil society actors, NGOs see their primary loyalty, accountability, and responsibility as being to the people of Afghanistan, and they aspire to develop their programming through approaches that involve Afghans in the conception, implementation, and evaluation of the projects and programs.[35] The majority of NGOs in the country are Afghan, and because NGOs place a major priority on capacity building, the international NGOs are staffed mostly by Afghan nationals. The biggest international NGOs employ a handful of expatriates and thousands of Afghans.

The Afghan government, international donors, and civil society actors all acknowledge that the NGO sector is critical to rebuilding Afghanistan and to providing vital services until the government can effectively assume these roles. To date, NGOs have provided emergency relief, infrastructure reconstruction, community development, civic education, and capacity-building programming in Afghanistan. They have played a major role in education, health, rural development, and mine clearance. They have provided food and shelter to refugees and internally displaced people. They have helped to improve water supply and sanitation. Some NGOs have focused on human rights and particularly women's rights. Furthermore, NGOs have supported community-level peace-building initiatives that have contributed significantly to local governance and dispute resolution.[36] NGOs have supported efforts in every sector of development, and they continue to provide critical employment and training opportunities for Afghans, as they have for decades. They work in partnership with other NGOs, the Afghan government, international donors, and Afghan communities. As well, NGOs help the government implement key national programs such as the National Solidarity Program focused on rural development, Basic Package Health Services, Rural Expansion of Afghanistan Community Health, and the Rural Agricultural Marketing Program.[37]

In short, NGOs have played and continue to play a vital role in Afghanistan's recovery. Recent studies show that NGOs receive 10–15 percent of all aid to Afghanistan, which seems relatively modest.[38] However, the importance of NGOs can be better understood by looking at specific sectors. Though hard to pin down, some estimates put the NGO share of service delivery in the health, education, and rural development sectors at 70–90 percent.[39] Furthermore, NGOs also play an essential role in the vital "software" side of development—capacity building and grassroots development.

The presence of NGOs in Afghan communities, however, has meant that since 2001 they have often borne the brunt of public frustration with waste, corruption, and the slow pace of recovery. While some critiques are valid, these negative public perceptions have also been fuelled by various "for-profit" and political actors who "misuse the NGO umbrella to promote their commercial or political interests,"[40] and by poor NGO legislation in the initial years after the US-led invasion. By 2005, the number of "NGOs" registered with the government was close to 2,500— most of whom were private contractors that Afghan law had failed to distinguish from non-profit organizations. The corruption, waste, and questionable practices associated with some of these contractors hurt the reputation of the aid community as a whole. As well, some Afghan government figures publicly blamed NGOs for misuse of funds and wastefulness, criticisms that the aid NGOs felt had some validity but that also seemed intended to deflect public frustration with the Afghan government over slow results to date.[41]

The response from the NGOs, led mainly by the Agency Coordinating Body for Afghan Relief (ACBAR), was fourfold: (i) to pressure the Afghan government to clarify NGO status, (ii) to develop a code of conduct with member NGOs, (iii) to take steps to improve accountability and performance, and (iv) to educate the public about NGOs. After concerted NGO lobbying, the government passed new NGO legislation in 2005 and undertook a re-registration process that separated the real non-profit organizations from other sorts. As of December 2006, 277 international and 891 national NGOs were registered with the government.[42]

ACBAR is one of four NGO coordinating bodies in Afghanistan, but the one that has pursued the highest-profile advocacy role.[43] ACBAR's one hundred members include the biggest international and Afghan NGOs, fifty of whom are active in its advocacy and policy group, which works closely with NGO networks in donor countries to develop common positions. ACBAR has played a key role in formulating the new NGO legislation, in feeding input from civil society into the Afghanistan National Development Strategy (ANDS), and in advocating for humanitarian space with civilian and military actors present in Afghanistan.

NGO coordination networks in some donor countries have also been very active. The United States' NGO coordination body, InterAction, has a long-standing Afghanistan Working Group composed of the major American NGOs working in the country. InterAction's participation in a US civil-military task force resulted in agreed-upon guidelines on relations between US military forces and NGOs, adopted in July 2007 by the US Department of Defense.[44] The guidelines seek to mitigate friction between NGO staff and military personnel. Among other provisions, the guidelines prohibit the military from wearing civilian clothing, from referring to NGOs as "force multipliers" or "partners," and from making unannounced visits to NGO sites—all of which had contributed to the blurring of the lines between military and civilian aid providers in Afghanistan. These guidelines have largely been respected, according to InterAction's vice-president, James Bishop. However, beyond this accomplishment, Bishop reports a "feeling of pessimism among US NGOs about influencing US policy regarding Afghanistan."[45]

In Canada, concerted NGO networking concerning Afghanistan has only recently emerged with the creation in September 2007 of the Afghanistan Reference Group. The group's energetic advocacy directed at political leaders and Canada's "Manley Commission" (officially named the Independent Panel on Canada's Future Role in Afghanistan[46]) has given aid issues more prominence. The government has welcomed the Afghanistan Reference Group as a vehicle to channel NGO views and has established dedicated liaisons with NGOs on Afghanistan policy. However, the group's advocacy efforts have not greatly influenced Canada's policy on Afghanistan; indeed, NGOs maintain that the Canadian government has largely ignored NGO views on its overall strategy in Afghanistan.

In Europe, the British and Irish Agencies in Afghanistan Group (originally called the British Agencies Afghanistan Group) was set up by British NGOs in 1987 to draw public attention to the humanitarian needs of Afghans. Since 2001, this group has tenaciously lobbied the British government on civil-military issues and the Provincial Reconstruction Teams.[47] A similar group, the European Network of Agencies in Afghanistan, was established in 2003.[48] Based in Brussels as a convening body for NGOs from Germany, the Netherlands, France, Sweden, and Norway, it works closely with the British and Irish Agencies group. The two recently collaborated on a major field study of Afghan perspectives on civil-military relations.[49]

NGO Advocacy: Is Anyone Listening?

Recent NGO advocacy has highlighted key gaps and strategic mistakes in the international engagement to date. This assertion of NGO perspectives represents a shift to a more forceful, evidence-driven strategy. In a recent series of reports, NGOs and NGO coalitions have presented a significant amount of field evidence on these issues. This evidence-based approach contrasts with that of earlier years when NGOs focused more on principled arguments about humanitarian space and aid priorities, with little effect on policy-makers who did not share these mandates or priorities. A review of these reports and country-specific advocacy campaigns on Afghanistan reveals broad agreement among NGOs in five areas: the militarization and politicization of aid, the neglect of agriculture and the rural economy, the neglect of a comprehensive peace process and community-level peace-building, an insufficient focus on civilian protection and human rights, and a top-down focus on national governance structures.

The Militarization and Politicization of Aid

In reports, news releases, and advocacy statements, the NGO sector has consistently condemned the deep conflation of military and aid roles in Afghanistan. NGOs are deeply concerned about the security of their personnel in the face of the deliberate killings of more than one hundred aid workers since 2003 by anti-government groups. Insecurity has led NGOs to sharply curtail operations, resulting in major gaps in urgently needed assistance to Afghans. According to these critiques, the confluence of roles has deeply compromised the operating environment for humanitarian and development NGOs, while current trends show it has not produced the security and political dividends expected.

Much of the debate on NGO insecurity and reduced access has focused on the alleged "blurring of the lines" caused by the presence of the Provincial Reconstruction Teams and the widespread use of aid to win "hearts and minds," gather intelligence, and ensure force protection by the combat arms of the two foreign military missions (OEF and ISAF). This militarization of aid has not only undermined the perceived impartiality of NGOs but has also "reduced the areas in which NGOs can safely undertake development and humanitarian activities."[50] As Canadian NGOs noted in the fall of 2007, "NGOs on the ground in Afghanistan have emphasized, again and again, that this practice turns aid workers and Afghans into war targets, and often has no long-term security or development benefit."[51] Local NGOs, especially, fear that if they accept funding for development work from the Provincial Reconstruction Teams, they will be accused of being partners with the military, or "spies."[52]

NGOs' critique of the militarization of aid is often mischaracterized as rooted in their anti-military orientation. Instead, according to CARE Canada's president Kevin McCort, it stems from NGOs' concerns about the dangers of getting too close to governments and becoming instrumentalized as arms of government foreign policy.[53] In Afghanistan, the foreign military forces are there at the behest of their governments and at the invitation of the Karzai government, and therefore most NGOs fault the politicization of aid in Afghanistan as the root problem. Many NGO critiques centre on the notion that the whole Afghan recovery process is led by political concerns rather than by the needs of Afghans or the principles of effective relief and development practice. In a recent article tracing the evolution of Provincial Reconstruction Teams since their inception, Barbara Stapleton argues that PRTs were in fact "oversold" as tools to impact security and reconstruction, when essentially their main contributions to date have been largely political. In her analysis, the PRTs more than anything have helped maintain the momentum of the political transition and state-building process, kept donors engaged, and "enabled the appearance of progress."[54]

Putting such political goals first may be justifiable for the state actors involved in the recovery effort, but creates serious dilemmas for NGOs as civil society actors. As CARE Canada's advocacy director Stephen Cornish argues, putting the welfare of Afghans tomorrow ahead of the needs of Afghans today is a highly political calculation that many NGOs feel their ethics cannot support.[55] As well, many aid agencies claim they are pushed by donors to initiate work where their PRTs are based so that the donor countries can show home audiences that "their" NGOs are engaged. This politicization of aid is also evident in the fact that dramatically more government assistance is allocated to the insecure areas of the south and east, and to areas of high poppy cultivation, instead of responding to needs and capacities across the country.[56] In the eyes of many NGOs, all of these trends diminish their ability to effect real progress on development—an anchor of the recovery process—and so these policies are seen as ultimately counterproductive for the whole mission.

The UN Assistance Mission in Afghanistan (UNAMA) led advocacy efforts in the early post-invasion years to redirect PRT activities toward security sector reform and away from a direct role in aid distribution. However, despite some initial success in influencing the PRT models of some nations, in general the trend has gone the other way, with PRTs (especially the US-led ones) disbursing large amounts of aid for reconstruction and development. Of this aid, a large portion goes to quick impact projects intended to advance force protection rather than long-term development goals. NGOs raise many concerns about the effectiveness of PRTs as reconstruction and development mechanisms, citing the numerous small projects designed primarily for political impact and the use of expensive private contractors that pay scant attention to sustainable development practices and that lack sensitivity to local conflict dynamics and other important goals such as capacity building and Afghan ownership.[57]

Although most operational NGOs are pragmatic and forge working relationships with the PRTs simply because "they are there," the NGO position remains that PRTS should not have a development role.[58] The March 2008 ACBAR report on aid effectiveness reiterated previous calls for a change of emphasis for PRT activities from development to security, and for adherence to previous UN guidelines and agreements on military roles in aid provision that have been largely ignored in Afghanistan. The report went further in urging that the PRTs be closed down in the secure areas of the country and funding be channelled through the government instead.[59]

NGOs have also called for the UN mission to play a stronger role but point out that the development and humanitarian coordinator within UNAMA lacks the resources and capacity to do so; moreover, they see this unit's subordination to the political dictates of the UN's role in Afghanistan as problematic. In April 2008, nineteen of the largest humanitarian NGOs in Afghanistan signed a letter to the UN calling for an independent UN Office for the Coordination of Humanitarian Affairs (OCHA) operation in Afghanistan. The reason for such a call was to address major problems with how humanitarian issues are positioned within UNAMA. Such a change would improve the quality of the humanitarian space, NGOs argued, by promoting a clearer separation of humanitarian coordination from the proposed closer integration between UNAMA and the international military forces.[60] However, such a major change to the UN's structure in Afghanistan is widely viewed as unlikely.

Neglect of Agriculture and the Rural Economy

The NGO sector has repeatedly and urgently called for massive, strategic, and long-term programming to support rural agriculture and sustainable livelihoods. Agriculture is the mainstay of 80 percent of the Afghan population and yet, inexplicably, it has not been prioritized to date, leaving the vast majority of Afghans unable to sustain themselves through any licit economy in rural areas.[61] According to an Oxfam report, "urgent action is required to promote comprehensive rural development, where progress has been slow. . . . A multi-stakeholder strategy should be developed to ensure the provision of agricultural support at the local level, covering arable and livestock farming, rural trades, and improved land and water management."[62] NGOs have been vocal advocates for this shift in priorities in recent years, along with other development actors. They also urge action on sustainable rural development programs and support for licit agriculture across Afghanistan as the only viable way to reduce opium production.[63]

Neglect of a Comprehensive Peace Process and Community-Level Peace-Building

Many Afghan and international NGOs have called for priority attention to be given to specific peace efforts as the crucial basis for Afghan recovery. At the national level, there are calls to work for a political settlement to the ongoing conflict through an Afghan-led comprehensive peace process. NGOs suggest that the process should engage the Taliban and other anti-government groups in order to address the conflicts and grievances left unsettled in the absence of a peace accord.[64] Characterizing the current situation as an "unresolved civil war" between the Taliban-Hekmatyar factions and the former Northern Alliance (now United Front),[65] such proposals call on governments to recognize that the insurgency cannot be solved militarily, and that a truly inclusive peace process led by the United Nations and including regional actors is the only path to a durable solution.[66] As Gerry Barr, president and CEO of the Canadian Council for International Cooperation (a coalition of almost one hundred Canadian NGOs) explains, "A peace process aimed at reconciliation and creating and building trust in institutions of governance, justice and human rights is the key to security for Afghans, and for our troops."[67] This proposition, however, is highly contentious not only with governments but also with some NGOs who reject any openings to the Taliban because of their dire record on human rights (and women's rights), and who worry that recent gains could be rolled back by a future Taliban-influenced government. While peace initiatives are currently being carried out by the Afghan government and civil society organizations, they are reportedly underresourced, disconnected, and often based on competing visions.[68]

Some NGOs argue strongly for a community-level peace-building focus for the international mission, as the larger conflict dynamics intersect with and are exacerbated by local disputes. A recent security survey of five hundred people in six provinces conducted by Oxfam showed that poverty is an underlying source of insecurity, and that local disputes are often related to resources, particularly land and water, and also to family, ethnic, and tribal differences. According to an Oxfam research report, "the resulting insecurity not only destroys quality of life and impedes development work, but is exploited by criminal or anti-government groups to strengthen their positions in the wider conflict."[69] The report, endorsed by fifteen of the biggest Afghan peace-building NGOs, calls for an expansion of current small-scale peace-building programming into a nationwide strategy to be led by civil society groups.[70]

Insufficient Focus on Civilian Protection and Human Rights

Another consistent critique of the international mission from the NGO sector is the neglect of a sufficiently strong human rights orientation—including on issues of protection of civilians and respect for international humanitarian law, rule of law, and women's rights. With the deterioration in the security situation overall and the rise in violence in recent years, the level of security of Afghan civilians has worsened. The "economy of force" and tactics employed by the US military have at times put civilians at risk and, at a minimum, have failed to provide the population with a basic level of security.[71] The PRT mechanism in turn has not afforded adequate protection to Afghan civilians or to development actors, although in fairness PRTs were not mandated to protect civilians directly.[72] A November 2007 report by Oxfam documented that at least 1,200 civilians were killed in 2007, half of them by international or Afghan government forces. A significant number of these deaths were due to the heavy use of air strikes by international forces.[73] According to a coalition of Canadian NGOs, "all of the actors—Afghan security forces and armed groups as well as the various international forces—have committed abuses including indiscriminate attacks and/or failed to distinguish between civilians and military targets. . . . On the contrary there are instances where their actions have put civilians at risk."[74] Furthermore, there is a "troubling lack of accountability" by Afghan security forces and armed groups as well as by international forces, and an unwilling-ness to investigate abuses.[75] NGO groups have documented torture and ill-treatment of detainees by Afghan institutions, widespread violations of human rights and particularly women's rights (including high levels of domestic and sexual violence, and lack of access to basic services, education, employment), corruption and lack of capacity in the courts and police, and violent reprisals against human rights defenders.[76]

Top-Down Focus of National Governance Structures

NGOs fault the international strategy in Afghanistan for an overly nar-row focus on legitimating the national government while neglecting the importance of civil society and local/subnational governance structures. NGO advocacy statements and recent field reports criticize the notion of state-building in Afghanistan as being about supporting the formal mechanisms of the central government. According to a 2007 Oxfam report, the development process to date has been "too centralized, and top heavy." The report recommends building local governance and chan-nelling more resources directly to communities.[77] Currently, officials at the provincial and district levels are unelected, and the elected village-level Community Development Councils that determine development spending through the government's National Solidarity Program face uncertain legal status. This lack of attention to subnational issues and to the non-governmental sector may have serious effects. According to American analyst Anthony Cordesman, the quality of local government and its ability to provide services may be the key to the legitimacy of the national government, as the majority of Afghans contact their govern-ment at the local level.[78]

Impacts to Date

Interviews with NGO leaders show that ongoing NGO advocacy has had some impact, albeit limited, on donor policies in Afghanistan. For example, James Bishop, vice-president of the American NGO network InterAction, cited the guidelines on relations between NGOs and military forces agreed to by InterAction and the US Department of Defense, and the US government's continued provision of funding for humanitarian assistance and refugee assistance in Afghanistan after concerted lobbying by InterAction.[79] In Canada, NGOs saw some of the extensive input from the Afghanistan Reference Group reflected in the Manley Commission's final report, though many NGOs were very disappointed that their core messages on the militarization of aid, peacemaking, and gender were not in the final report.

NGO critiques of the Provincial Reconstruction Teams and the co-opting of aid for political and military ends have been largely ignored by the major players, though some countries have modified their PRT policies. According to ACBAR's director, Anja de Beer,

> Some nations consult regularly with their own national NGOs and ACBAR on these issues, and UK, Dutch, and Scandinavian PRTS exhibit stronger separation of civil-military issues in response and take measures recommended by the NGO sector such as not naming NGOs that work with them, and avoiding public ceremonies for aid projects.[80]

Inside Afghanistan, the impact of NGO advocacy and coordination with the government and donors has been strong in those sectors where NGOs play major roles, notably health, rural development, and education. As well, ongoing advocacy by ACBAR has had some impact on the formulation of the Afghanistan National Development Strategy. However, all NGO coalitions acknowledge that despite spending a lot of time in dialogue with their home governments, with the United Nations, and with NATO, they do not believe that they are having much influence on these sectors. Some question whether a spirit of "tokenism" drives donor states and NATO to engage with the NGO sector. As de Beer observes, "often we are invited to high-level consultations but the feeling is that this is so that they can 'tick off' civil society involvement. We have the feeling that if we say something that supports an agenda, we are listened to, but if not, we are ignored."[81] As well, states and international organizations reportedly engage NGO coalitions in unhelpful ways that reflect a lack of understanding of the nature of the NGO sector. For example, often ACBAR is invited into consultations at the last minute, with no expectation that time is needed for internal consultation across the diverse NGO sector to enable the representative to bring some substantive input to the table. The expectation is that civil society should speak with one voice, though for leaders of NGO networks the notion that they can "represent" the diversity of civil society is extremely problematic.

Other explanations for the limited NGO impact centre on shortcomings and problems within the NGO sector itself. Interagency competition, dependence on government funding, and the very diversity of the NGO communities have hampered effective NGO advocacy. Some NGO personnel note that many NGOs have a narrow self image as "service providers" rather than development actors, and do not feel comfortable participating in policy debates. In general, broad recognition is lacking across the NGO sector of the importance of advocacy and developing common platforms. Other observers note that discussions within NGO coordination bodies and with other actors are too often marked by a lack of preparation and a clear understanding of the issues, which speaks to the limited capacity of many operational NGOs to engage in policy issues. Some question the very inclusiveness of the NGO world, noting the lack of criteria for involvement in such discussions, and the fact that sometimes very vocal NGOs with no operational presence dominate while those "on the ground" find their views marginalized among NGOs.

Funding constraints further limit effective advocacy. Advocacy work requires time and dedicated resources, and it is no surprise that only the largest international NGOs can afford to hire full-time advocacy staff. These NGOs are consequently the most active in advocacy work. Even these larger networks, including ACBAR, face a constant struggle to maintain basic funding, and this uncertainty about their own survival severely constrains their ability to be strategic and to devise long-term plans. Currently, much of the funding for NGO coalitions comes from the donor governments that they critique, which is ironic but unavoidable as NGOs are highly dependent on government funding for all their programming. Across the board, the NGO leaders interviewed agreed that reliable independent funding is needed for NGO networks to provide a flexible, open space for dialogue within the NGO sector and a platform to engage other actors.

Conclusion

Afghanistan represents an incredibly challenging scenario for NGOs. The tensions between the peace-building and the war-fighting agendas of the international mission present them with more acute ethical and operational challenges than ever before. In the north, NGOs often see themselves as partners in the peace-building strategy of the international mission, while in the south, NGOs are unwilling to be partners in the parallel war-fighting strategy. As well, fundamental dilemmas emerge from the way international civilian and military resources have been integrated as part of a top-down state-building agenda in Afghanistan. State-building is often a very conflictual process that produces clear winners and losers. Though a strong state may be necessary for people's stability and welfare in the long term, historically the state-building process has not put the basic needs and security of individual citizens first and foremost. The NGO sector, whose values and operating modes are to work directly with citizens and communities to collaboratively define and address pressing needs, is often a "strange bedfellow" in the state-building enterprise. In recent years, rights-based programming has become a mainstay of much NGO development programming, emphasizing the needs of populations who may be marginalized and powerless in the current political system. Yet in Afghanistan, NGOs are under constant pressure to work as integral parts of a top-down state-building process because of direct pressure from donors and because of the design of the mission overall.

NGOs have had to reconcile their commitment to support needy Afghan communities with an operating environment created by international strategies that they often directly oppose. However, they have not done so quietly. The recent high-profile NGO advocacy on these key issues represents a concerted, re-energized effort to engage policy-makers on a series of essential policy changes. Given the diversity of NGO mandates and perspectives, there are widely differing views over which of these issues is the most important, and which must be addressed first. While these multiple perspectives may frustrate other actors, the expectation that NGOs as civil society actors should speak with one voice is unrealistic in the first place. Especially in Afghanistan, where there are few accountable mechanisms for local governance, NGOs should be viewed as reflecting and representing the views and dilemmas of communities and individual citizens, and they should be engaged in ways that respect their diversity and independence as assets, not liabilities.

NGOs are an indispensable element of the international aid system globally and in Afghanistan. Furthermore, the concentration of international and national NGOs with deep ties to Afghan communities is a major resource for the country's recovery. Though not without problems, the NGO sector makes a huge contribution to the welfare of Afghans and, indirectly, to the success of the international mission. No one suggests that NGOs have all the answers. However, for the best possible strategies for Afghan recovery to emerge, the views of the NGO sector—and those of the communities they work with—must be given more than a token voice in the policy dialogue.

Notes

1. According to Seth Jones of the RAND corporation, there are six major insurgent groups in Afghanistan: (1) the Taliban, which is headquartered in northwest Pakistan and represents the largest of the groups; (2) Jalaluddin Haqqani Network; (3) Hezb-i-Islami; (4) al Qaeda and foreign fighters operating out of Pakistan tribal areas (especially Libyans, Egyptians, Saudis, and Uzbeks who have since become entrenched in the tribal areas); and, within al Qaeda, (5) Pakistani and Afghan Pashtun tribes; and (6) criminal groups, especially drug-trafficking groups. Within al Qaeda are two more rings consisting of central affiliated groups, and loose networks of affiliated individuals and other individuals inspired to take independent action. See Seth Jones, "Counterinsurgency in Afghanistan," *RAND Corporation*, 7 November 2007, http://web.mit.edu/ssp/seminars/wed_archives_07fall/jones.htm; and Seth Jones, "Averting Failure in Afghanistan," *Survival* 48, no. 1 (Spring 2006): 111-28.

2. NGOs poke fun at themselves and this notion with T shirts emblazoned with "3 Ms."

3. Kenneth Anderson and David Rieff, "'Global Civil Society': A Skeptical View," in *Global Civil Society 2004/5*, ed. Helmut Anheier, Marlies Glasius,

and Mary Kaldor (London: Sage, 2004), 26-39; Alan Fowler, "Civil Society, NGOs, and Social Development: Changing the Rules of the Game," Geneva Occasional Paper No. 1 (January 2000).

4. See Roland Paris, *At War's End: Building Peace after Civil Conflict* (New York: 2004), 38. Whether or not these terms should be used interchangeably is an important point to consider but beyond the scope of this paper.

5. North Atlantic Treaty Organization (NATO), "Statement by the North Atlantic Council September 12, 2001," Press Release No. 124, http://www.nato.int/docu/pr/2001/p01-124e.htm; Organization of American States, "Terrorist Threat to the Americas," 24th Meeting of Consultation of Ministers of Foreign Affairs, Resolution 1, OEA/Ser.F/II.24/RES.1/01 (21 September 2001).

6. UN Security Council, S/RES/1368 (12 September 2001).

7. UN Security Council, S/RES/1386 (2001). Initially, individual countries volunteered to lead the ISAF until NATO took command.

8. UN Security Council, S/RES/1510 (2003).

9. The Afghanistan mission is NATO's first (and to date only) mission on the ground in a fighting capacity outside of Europe.

10. Anthony H. Cordesman, "The Missing Metrics of 'Progress' in Afghanistan (and Pakistan)" (working draft presented at the Conference on Peacebuilding in Afghanistan: Taking Stock and Looking Ahead, Ottawa, Canada, 10-11 December 2007).

11. *Report of the Panel on United Nations Peace Operations* (Brahimi Report), A/55/305-S/2000/809, 3, http://www.un.org/peace/reports/peace_operations/.

12. Donor conferences took place in Bonn in 2001, Tokyo in 2002, Berlin in 2004, and London in 2006.

13. See the Afghanistan Compact, http://www.unama-afg.org/news/_londonConf/_docs/06jan30-AfghanistanCompact-Final.pdf.

14. Espen Barth Eide et al., "Report on Integrated Missions: Practical Perspectives and Recommendations" (an independent study for the Expanded UN ECHA Core Group, May 2005).

15. See UN Assistance Mission in Afghanistan (UNAMA), "Mandate," http://www.unama-afg.org/about/overview.htm (accessed 30 April 2008).

16. See "The EU's Relations with Afghanistan," http://ec.europa.eu/external_relations/afghanistan/intro/index.htm (accessed 30 April 2008).

17. World Bank, "Afghanistan: Data, Projects and Research," http://web.worldbank.org/WBSITE/EXTERNAL/COUNTRIES/SOUTHASIAEXT/AFGHANISTANEXTN/0,,menuPK:305990~pagePK:141159~piPK:141110~theSitePK:305985,00.html.

18. Provincial Reconstruction Teams (PRTs) are led by a number of lead countries in various cities including Canada in Kandahar City; Hungary in Pol-e-Khomri; Italy in Herat; Lithuania in Chaghcharan; the Netherlands in Tarin Kowt; New Zealand in Bamyan; Norway in Meymana; Spain in Qala-e-Naw; Sweden in Mazar-e-Sharif; Turkey in Wardak; UK in Lashkar

Gah; Czech Republic in Pole-Alam; Germany, with two PRTS in Feyzabad and Konduz; and the US with twelve PRTS primarily situated in southeastern Afghanistan. There are twenty-six PRTs in total with two hundred civilians deployed alongside military personnel. The number of civilian personnel deployed to each team varies dramatically.

19. Nancy Lindborg, executive vice-president, Mercy Corps, in a statement to the Senate Foreign Relations Committee Hearing on "Afghanistan: In Pursuit of Security and Democracy," 23 October 2003, quoted in Barbara Stapleton, "A Means to What End? Why PRTs Are Peripheral to the Bigger Political Challenges in Afghanistan," *Journal of Military and Strategic Studies* 10, no. 1 (Fall 2007).

20. Barnett Rubin et al., "Afghanistan 2005 and Beyond: Prospects for Improved Stability Reference Document" (Clingendael – Netherlands Institute of International Relations, Conflict Research Unit, April 2005), 54.

21. Carrie Vandewint, "A Better Helping Hand" (submission to the Manley Panel, Afghanistan Reference Group, 1 December 2007).

22. "Whole of government approaches" and "integrated approaches" are the terms used by the Organisation for Economic Co-operation and Development. Other synonyms include "joined up" government, or "3Ds"— referring to the key ministries of defence, development, and diplomacy.

23. Stewart Patrick and Kaysie Brown, *Greater Than the Sum of Its Parts: Assessing Whole of Government Approaches to Fragile States* (New York: International Peace Academy, 2007).

24. Stephen Cornish, "No Room for Humanitarianism in 3D Policies," *Journal of Military and Strategic Studies* 10, no. 1 (Fall 2007).

25. The operational budgets of some NGOs exceed that of many small states, and the eight largest international NGOs are all relief and development NGOs. The "big eight" are World Vision, Save the Children, Catholic Relief Services, CARE, Doctors Without Borders, Oxfam, International Rescue Committee, and Mercy Corps). Their annual budgets range from US$2.1 billion to US$185 million a year. See Risto Karajkov, "The Power of N.G.O.'s: They're Big, but How Big?" *World Press*, 16 July 2007.

26. See Mary Anderson, *Do No Harm* (Boulder, CO: Lynne Rienner, 1999).

27. For a review of these and other incidents that in the early years defined the civil-military landscape in Afghanistan, see Lara Olson, "Fighting for Humanitarian Space: NGOs in Afghanistan," *Journal of Military and Strategic Studies* 9, no. 1 (Fall 2006).

28. Kevin McCort (CEO, CARE Canada), interview with author, March 2008.

29. For more on NGO approaches to security, see Koenraad Van Brabant, "Operational Security Management in Violent Environments" (Overseas Development Institute, 2000); Tony Vaux et al., "Humanitarian Action and Private Security Companies: Opening the Debate," *International Alert* (2002), http://www.international-alert.org/publications/88.php (accessed April 2008).

30. McCort, interview, March 2008.
31. Moh Hashim Mayar (deputy director, Agency Coordinating Body for Afghan Relief), interview with author, 12 September 2006.
32. NGOs engaged in direct provision of primary education and capacity building, teacher training, and support for the education sector during the Taliban rule. Hassan Mohammed (CARE) and American Institutes for Research, "Education and the Role of NGOs in Emergencies: Afghanistan 1978–2002" (EQUIPS – Educational Quality Improvement Program, August 2006), http://www.eldis.org/vfile/upload/1/document/0708/DOC22953.pdf.
33. Agency Coordinating Body for Afghan Relief (ACBAR), "History of NGOs in Afghanistan," *A Handbook for Understanding NGOs* (Kabul: ACBAR, 2007), 7, http://www.acbar.org/downloads/Information%20Booklet%20(29%20Mar%2007).pdf (accessed 20 March 2008).
34. Conor Foley, "Caught in the Crossfire," *The Guardian*, 7 May 2004, http://www.guardian.co.uk/world/2004/may/07/usa.afghanistan.
35. ACBAR, *Handbook for Understanding* NGOs..
36. Matt Waldman, "Community Peace-Building in Afghanistan: The Case for a National Strategy" (Oxfam Research Report, February 2008).
37. ACBAR, *Handbook for Understanding NGOs*.
38. Waldman, "Falling Short: Aid Effectiveness in Afghanistan," ACBAR Advocacy Series (March 2008), 11.
39. World Bank, "Service Delivery and Governance at the Sub-National Level in Afghanistan" (July 2007), 26.
40. ACBAR, *Handbook for Understanding NGOs*, 4.
41. Aunohita Mojumdar, "Fighting NGOism," *Hindu Business Line*, 13 January 2006, posted on the Global Policy Forum website, http://www.globalpolicy.org/ngos/aid/2006/0113fighting.htm.
42. ACBAR, *Handbook for Understanding NGOs*, 1.
43. Other NGO coordinating bodies include the Afghan NGOs Coordination Bureau, the Islamic Coordination Council, and the South West Afghanistan and Baluchistan Association for Coordination. Of these, only ACBAR has a formalized collaboration with UNAMA; the others have established links with the Afghan Transitional Authorities or with local authorities.
44. InterAction, US Institute of Peace, and US Department of Defense, "Guidelines for Relations between U.S. Armed Forces and Non-Governmental Humanitarian Organizations in Hostile or Potentially Hostile Environments," http://www.interaction.org/files.cgi/5896_InterAction_US_Mil_CivMil_Guidelines_July_07_flat.pdf.
45. James Bishop (vice-president, InterAction), interview with author, 5 May 2008.
46. See the panel's website at http://www.independent-panel-independant.ca/main-eng.html for more information.
47. See the British and Irish Agencies Afghanistan Group website, http://www.baag.org.uk/index.htm.

48. For more details see "European Network of NGOs in Afghanistan (ENNA) and British and Irish Agencies in Afghanistan (BAAG) Position on Civil-Military Relations," http://www.baag.org.uk/downloads/baag%20 enna%20civ-mil%20statement%2029%20nov%2006.pdf.

49. Sippi Azarbaijani-Moghaddam and Mirwais Wardak, "Afghan Hearts, Afghan Minds: Exploring Afghan Perceptions of Civil-Military Relations" (British and Irish Agencies Afghanistan Group, June 2008).

50. Waldman, "Falling Short," 13.

51. Canadian Council on International Co-operation, "Manley Panel: Heavy on Combat, Light on Diplomacy, Development and Peace-Building," News release, 22 January 2008.

52. Surendrini Wijeyaratne (peace and conflict policy analyst, Canadian Council for International Cooperation), interview with author, April 2008.

53. McCort, interview, March 2008.

54. Barbara J. Stapleton, "A Means to What End? Why PRTs Are Peripheral to the Bigger Political Challenges in Afghanistan," *Journal of Military and Strategic Studies* 10, no. 1 (Fall 2007), 4.

55. Cornish, "No Room for Humanitarianism."

56. Waldman, "Falling Short," 12.

57. Ibid., 3.

58. Anja de Beer (director, ACBAR), interview with author, April 2008.

59. Waldman, "Falling Short," 24.

60. Nineteen NGOs in a letter to the Deputy Special Representative of the Secretary General (SRSG), Bo Asplund, "The Need for an Independent OCHA in Afghanistan," 4 April 2008.

61. Waldman, "Falling Short," 11.

62. Oxfam, "Development Assistance in Insecure Environments: Afghanistan" (submission to the UK House of Commons International Development Committee Inquiry, November 2007), 2.

63. Oxfam, "Development Assistance: Afghanistan," 2.

64. Gerry Ohlsen, "Peace and Security: New Directions in Afghanistan" (paper submitted to the Manley Panel, 1 December 2007); Surendrini Wijeyaratne, "Afghanistan: A Study on the Prospects for Peace," Canadian Council for International Cooperation Discussion Paper (March 2008); "No Exit Strategy for Canada without Negotiations: Group of 78, the Canadian Peace-Building Coordinating Committee, and the World Federalist Movement   Canada Responds to the Manley Panel Report," News release, 22 January 2008.

65. Ohlsen, "Peace and Security," 2-3.

66. "No Exit Strategy for Canada," News release, 22 January 2008.

67. Canadian Council on International Co-operation, "Manley Panel: Heavy on Combat," News release, 22 January 2008.

68. Wijeyaratne, "Afghanistan: Prospects for Peace," 2.

69. Waldman, "Community Peace-Building," 3.

70. Ibid.

71. Mike Capstick, "The Civil-Military Effort in Afghanistan: A Strategic Perspective," *Journal of Military and Strategic Studies* 10, no. 1 (Fall 2007): 2.
72. Stapleton, "A Means to What End," 11.
73. Oxfam, "Development Assistance in Insecure Environments," 16.
74. Hilary Holmes, "Human Rights, Gender and Governance: Building the Future through the Present" (submission to the Manley Panel from the Afghanistan Reference Group, 1 December 2007).
75. Holmes, "Human Rights," 1.
76. Waldman, "Falling Short"; Holmes, "Human Rights."
77. Oxfam, "Development Assistance in Insecure Environments," 2.
78. Cordesman, "Missing Metrics," 25.
79. James Bishop, interview, 5 May 2008.
80. Anja de Beer, interview, April 2008.
81. Ibid.

Chapter 6

Building Stability in Afghanistan

MIHAI P. CARP

Introduction

Six years into NATO's engagement in Afghanistan, there are growing concerns that the country may slide back into chaos and instability. With a Taliban-led insurgency and allied casualties on the rise, questions are being asked among the media and the general public about the international community's strategy, and NATO's strategy in particular. And while the news from Afghanistan has indeed been discouraging on some fronts, continued progress in many areas is often overlooked. This chapter reviews progress to date and delineates the challenges that must be met if the NATO-led mission is to be successful. Long-term success will depend not only on the implementation of a comprehensive strategy but also on tangible Afghan ownership.

In April 2008, NATO heads of state and government and other world leaders met in Bucharest on the margins of a NATO Summit to reconfirm their strong commitment to Afghanistan. A follow-up conference in Paris pledged billions of dollars in additional aid. While encouraging in themselves, such high-level strategic commitments must now make a tangible difference on the ground. Together with the important gains achieved in Afghanistan over the last few years, there is room for optimism that the broader international community's efforts to make Afghanistan a more secure, stable, and prosperous country can yet succeed.

For NATO in particular, prospects for the longer-term success of the alliance's first out of area mission remain contingent on a number of factors. While the alliance will continue to play a key role in assisting with security matters, it will remain in a supporting role in many other areas, notably civilian matters where the Afghan government itself and other organizations will have to increase their effectiveness and visibility, lest they lose the support of the Afghan population. Pitched against an increasingly fragile security environment in some areas of the country and in light of multiple challenges hitherto never experienced by many NATO nations, NATO will continue to be tested in Afghanistan from a political and an operational point of view. Ensuing developments will also be an indication to what extent the alliance has been able to adapt to the new security challenges of the twenty-first century.

For the time being, the strong formal political commitment by all allies and their partners in the International Security Assistance Force (ISAF) has ensured continuity of the mission. However, issues related to continued solidarity, force generation, more equal "burden sharing," public support at home, and the question of how to manage the complex civil-military interface in theatre were high on the agenda in Brussels. Failure of the mission would have dire consequences for regional and international security. Ensuring success in Afghanistan is thus not only a matter for NATO; it is imperative for the well-being of the Afghans and the international community at large.

Not All That Bleak

With frequent reports about growing violence and armed confrontation between international forces and the growing Taliban insurgency shaping public opinion about developments in Afghanistan, it may seem difficult to remain optimistic and to discern the progress that has been achieved in the once war-torn country. From impressive improvements in health care and infrastructure, to targeted development aid and the establishment of new institutions, Afghanistan has been able to embark on a gradual—albeit imperfect—process of reconstruction since the overthrow of the Taliban in late 2001. The broad international consensus to continue to assist Afghanistan in all areas—from security to development—provides the country with both a comparative advantage and opportunities to move forward. Moreover, while the average Afghan expects the national government to do much more, public support within Afghanistan toward the international community and the presence of international forces remains encouragingly high. Few favour a return of the Taliban, and most appreciate ongoing efforts to help the country and its people.

Much of this would not have been possible without the UN-mandated, NATO-led assistance force, the ISAF, which has been present in Afghanistan since 2003. Initially a modest force based in Kabul, the ISAF has grown in size and capability and today counts almost 50,000 troops from twenty-six NATO nations and fifteen non-NATO partners. Participation in the ISAF by nations as diverse as Canada and Singapore attests to the broad international consensus that exists to keep Afghanistan on track. The ISAF has not only become NATO's largest mission: new commitments and ongoing deployments of forces by nations since the Bucharest Summit have reinforced the positive trend. The growing number of forces and contributing nations has steadily increased the ISAF's overall strength. Within its assistance mandate, the ISAF is also a NATO operation like no other, carrying out tasks spanning a wide operational spectrum from training to traditional peacekeeping and combat. And while the ISAF's operational tempo has increased significantly, the strategic objectives have remained the same: to extend the authority of the Government of Afghanistan; to assist with the development of Afghan institutions necessary to maintain security across the country; and to establish a stable and secure environment in which sustainable reconstruction and development can take place. Looking ahead, the emphasis will clearly lie in allowing the Afghans to take more ownership over security matters.

From a military perspective, the ISAF has successfully fended off Taliban forces. Despite serious challenges posed by ruthless insurgents in some parts of the country, both the ISAF and the Afghan National Security Forces have consistently retained the operational initiative and impeded militant forces from gaining the upper hand. Such tactical successes have been crucial in restoring confidence among the population, and have allowed affected areas to benefit from reconstruction and development. While this progress is encouraging, it is well understood that the battle for Afghanistan will not be won through tactical military successes alone but through a comprehensive approach applied equally across security, governance, and development efforts and between local and international players in support of the Afghan government. Under such a scenario, both military and civilian efforts must continue to play complementary roles while at the same time strengthening Afghan ownership across the board.

Key Challenges – Not All for NATO to Solve

From a NATO perspective, a few areas will be crucial in moving forward the international community agenda, with a direct impact on the context in which the ISAF will continue to operate: (i) the strengthening of the Afghan National Security Forces, notably the police; (ii) the continued fight against the narcotics industry and its links to the insurgency; (iii) resolute action by the Afghan government to fight corruption and promote good governance countrywide; (iv) the establishment of a coherent and well-coordinated information policy; and (v) the development of a more proactive engagement policy with neighbouring Pakistan.

Success will first and foremost require a renewed emphasis on the mentoring and building up of Afghanistan's fledgling security forces. While much money and effort has already been invested both multilaterally and bilaterally in this field (with US assistance by far exceeding that of all other donors combined), there is still a long way to go before the Afghan forces will be fully capable of ensuring countrywide stability and carrying out local policing functions. As a first step, NATO/ISAF handed over authority for the security of Kabul in late August 2008. While the ISAF will still retain its headquarter presence in the Afghan capital and provide much-needed specialized support, this is a step in the right direction. More broadly, however, both the US-led Combined Security Transition Command in Afghanistan, which falls under Operation Enduring Freedom, and the ISAF will continue to carry out important mentoring and training roles for the Afghan National Security Forces in the years to come.

On the positive side, the Afghan National Army (ANA) has made respectable progress and is gradually maturing into a capable force with a visible presence across most provinces. ANA participation in both ISAF and US coalition operations is now a constant feature. Both US and NATO efforts to train the ANA through Operational Mentoring and Liaison Teams have provided the necessary know-how and field experience for ANA units to become operationally more effective. With current plans to increase the ANA force ceiling to 120,000 men, this institution should increasingly be able to take over responsibilities from international forces; however, it is understood that the ANA will remain largely dependent on direct support, especially in logistics and deployment, for quite some time to come. Continued success in training and mentoring will also depend largely on NATO nations' willingness to provide additional personnel for the mentoring and liaison teams. At the time of writing, it is projected that by the end of 2008 forty-five out of sixty-four liaison teams will have been sourced by national contributions.

In contrast, the efforts to stand up a credible and operationally capable police force have been perhaps one of the most evident deficiencies in post-Taliban Afghanistan. The weak presence of the Afghan National Police (ANP), notably at provincial and local levels, has not only left communities vulnerable to insurgent attacks; its negative performance record and reputation has also reinforced the notion of a corrupt and inefficient institution that has yet to show its worth. Alarmed by the large gap in performance between the ANP and the ANA and against the background of a growing insurgency, the international community has renewed its attention to police reform. However, reform has been hampered by differing views—at the national level in Kabul and at strategic levels among the different international actors—about the nature of the training needed. "Fit for purpose training," which encompasses both traditional policing and more *gendarmerie*-type training (for the more unstable areas), is seen as a possible way forward. Focused district police mentoring and training has also begun under US leadership. A rather modest EU police-mentoring mission, dispatched to Afghanistan in 2007, remains largely undersourced despite ministerial commitments to double the size of its personnel. Overall, police training efforts will remain of limited value if they are not matched by visible progress on improving the rule of law, extending the fight against corruption, and reforming the justice system.

A second challenge is that Afghanistan's insurgency cannot be successfully fought without also addressing the narcotics problem. In its *Afghanistan Opium Survey* released in August 2008, the UN Office on Drugs and Crime (UNODC) offered slightly more encouraging figures than in the previous year but also underscored the strong link between poppy cultivation and security. According to the survey, while opium cultivation had decreased, production in key poppy-growing areas had dropped less than expected. Although eighteen of Afghanistan's thirty-four provinces are now poppy-free, 98 percent of poppy cultivation is concentrated in seven provinces in the south and west.[1] In a point also argued by NATO's military authorities, UNODC thus makes a compelling case that there is a geographic overlap between regions where the drug industry is thriving and those where the insurgency has been most active. Against this troubling background, the question to what extent the ISAF should be involved in counter-narcotics is once again on the agenda for political review by NATO nations. So far, counter-narcotics tasks by the ISAF have been limited to providing support to Afghan-led forces, and interdiction operations by the ISAF against specific narcotics-related targets and linked to ongoing security operations did not meet with consensus in Brussels. Fighting the narcotics plague will also require determined action on the part of the Afghan leadership to break the vicious cycle of interdependency of warlords, corrupt officials, criminals, and insurgent leaders who have been financing many of their operations with drug money.

Third, efforts toward establishing a more efficient justice system and the rule of law are linked to the wider problem of good governance. While there has been a renewed commitment at the highest levels of the Afghan government to root out corruption, many elements of Afghanistan's government and institutions at national and subnational levels continue to be plagued by unacceptable degrees of corruption, inefficiency, and incapacity. A newly created Independent Directorate of Local Governance, responsible for the supervision of provincial governors, district administrators, and municipalities, may yet improve accountability. Its work, however, will be hampered by political deal-making and the protection of vested interests, of which President Karzai himself has been accused. Equally, the evolving security situation in individual provinces will continue to restrict the ability of national and local authorities to deliver badly needed services. In his report to the UN Secretary General in the spring of 2008, the head of the UN Mission in Afghanistan pointed out that provinces not affected by anti-government violence have demonstrated an increasing capacity for delivering governance and economic development. In turn, in unstable areas where the Taliban are active, it is not the latter but the government that is blamed for continued insecurity.

A fourth concern is how to spread the message about the mission and counter Taliban propaganda. As has become strikingly evident, Afghanistan's insurgents use an effective propaganda mechanism to gain the initiative even if their forces are regularly beaten on the battlefield. High-profile, asymmetric attacks as witnessed on occasion in Kabul, while perhaps of little tactical value, not only serve the purpose of undermining the Afghan government but also draw the attention of governments and publics in distant capitals like Berlin and Madrid with the aim of weakening international commitments in Afghanistan. In the country's unstable provinces, Taliban information tactics seek to exploit the weaknesses of the national government and to undermine the presence of international forces, despite ongoing efforts, especially by the latter, to counter with targeted information campaigns. "Winning hearts and minds" will thus remain a major challenge for the alliance and a determining factor in Afghanistan.

In this regard, the issue of civilian casualties inflicted inadvertently by international forces, whether under ISAF or US coalition command, has affected the credibility of international forces present on the ground and has recently forced the Afghan government to go on the offensive for domestic political reasons. Meanwhile, civilian deaths caused by insurgents who deliberately use indiscriminate tactics such as suicide bombings and IEDs (improvised explosive devices) are not widely reported. While operational circumstances might not make it easy to avoid civilian casualties, the fact that these casualties tarnish the image of the international forces and could undermine the mission as a whole cannot be denied. In order to retain credibility, NATO will thus have to continue to show convincingly that every effort is being made to avoid civilian casualties and, most importantly, that targeting civilians is not a policy pursued by international forces in Afghanistan. The Afghan people will also have to distance themselves from uncorroborated reports, which often exaggerate or falsify specific incidents, that quickly hit local and international media outlets. At the same time, international forces must ensure that existing operational procedures—set up with the intent of avoiding civilian casualties to the extent possible—are being followed and that reported incidents are investigated thoroughly and in a timely manner. Reassuring the Afghan government and the wider public that proper procedures regarding detentions are also being followed in line with international conventions and norms remains equally important. Ever closer coordination among key players—the ISAF, the US-led coalition, and the Afghan government—will remain a top priority for NATO.

Finally, as reflected in the ISAF Strategic Vision endorsed by heads of state and government at the Bucharest NATO Summit,[2] support by Afghanistan's neighbours, notably Pakistan, will remain crucial if stability in Afghanistan and in the wider region is to be achieved. With growing cross-border incursions challenging the ISAF troops in Afghanistan's eastern and southern provinces, the situation in Pakistan—notably the impact of safe havens for insurgents in its border areas with Afghanistan—have become a major concern for the alliance. Nevertheless, within NATO, there is agreement that Pakistan must be part of the solution if wider regional issues are to be addressed effectively.

To further develop its relations with Pakistan, NATO can build on positive experiences, including the NATO earthquake relief operation of 2005 in Pakistan and the cooperation mechanisms that have been put in place in recent years. With a new government and president in Islamabad, additional opportunities now exist to enhance the military-to-military relationship and to establish a more regular political dialogue. On the military side, efforts are underway to make the work of the Tripartite Commission (bringing together Afghanistan, Pakistan, and ISAF military officials at different levels) more substantive with a view to genuinely enhancing cooperation and border security along the 2,400 kilometre frontier between Afghanistan and Pakistan. Unfortunately, the strained state of Afghan-Pakistan relations will continue to limit the degree of cooperation between Pakistani and Afghan military officials. In addition to the difficult historic relationship, there are concerns in allied capitals about the ability and strategy of the new government in Islamabad to deal with its own internal extremist threat and its relationship vis-à-vis its powerful national military and intelligence establishment. Despite these serious obstacles, both countries must be encouraged to refrain from mutual accusations and to pursue avenues of cooperation.

NATO "Internal Business" Regarding Afghanistan

At the Bucharest Summit, NATO allies and troop-contributing countries in the ISAF endorsed a far-reaching internal document, the Comprehensive Strategic Political-Military Plan, to guide the future of NATO's engagement in Afghanistan with clear benchmarks and timelines.[3] This development, coupled with existing broader frameworks such as the Afghanistan Compact, suggests that devising new strategies for NATO at this time would be counterproductive.

The Comprehensive Plan is being regularly reviewed by nations. The document makes important references as to how NATO/ISAF is to interact with other key players in theatre to maximize coordination. Relations with the UN Mission in Afghanistan (UNAMA), for instance, are given particular importance in order to enhance the military-civilian interface in theatre. Given the mission's strengthened mandate to take the lead in coordinating international support for governance and development, much hope now rests with the new head of UNAMA, veteran Norwegian diplomat Kai Eide, not only to re-energize the UN mission in Afghanistan but also to help expand the mission's field presence across Afghanistan.

Optimizing the work of ISAF's Provincial Reconstruction Teams (PRTs) has been identified as another priority. At the Bucharest Summit, NATO nations pledged to "provide all the PRTs needed, enhance their unity of effort, strengthen their civilian component and further align their development strategies with Afghan Government priorities until such time as Afghan Government institutions are strong enough to render PRTs unnecessary."[4] With the military elements already under the ISAF chain of command, efforts are now underway to provide more coherence and coordination among the different civilian elements throughout the country without infringing upon national prerogatives or subordinating the latter to the military chain of command. Following this line, in 2008 NATO nations agreed on a broad set of PRT guidelines that focus on the need for enhanced information sharing, including with Afghan authorities at all levels, and that call for adjustments in PRT composition and structures in accordance with requirements in each province. While plans for PRT transitions and their eventual disappearance may be premature at this time, it is hoped that individual civilian PRT components throughout Afghanistan will eventually outnumber their military colleagues, as a sign of an improved security situation and strengthened local Afghan ownership.

Discussions will also continue within NATO over continuing shortfalls and the need to fill all operational requirements to allow the commander of the ISAF maximum flexibility in carrying out the mission. With recent arrival of additional force contributions by several nations, notably the United States and France, the ISAF has been able to increase its profile in key provinces. However, such contributions have not alleviated the urgent need to fill specific mission-critical shortfalls (for instance, in intelligence and lift capability). In addition, NATO will continue to grapple with the issue of longer-term force rotations, interoperability, and national caveats. On the last point, some progress is at hand with several nations having lifted their restrictions, but still more needs to be done. Combining the efforts of twenty-six allies and several partners that each bring their own security culture and experience to a complex theatre such as Afghanistan remains a fact of life that has to be taken into account. In this regard, the relationship between the ISAF and the US-led coalition, Operation Enduring Freedom, will continue to be subject to regular review. While still operating under different UN Security Council mandates and commands, both operations have been working toward the same goal of assisting the Afghans. In fighting the insurgency, coordination of specific operations by the two commands as well as close coordination with Afghan security forces will remain equally important.

The Way Ahead

With Afghanistan at a defining moment in its post-Taliban development, negative perceptions of imminent failure must be countered at both the local and the strategic level. For its part, NATO/ISAF needs to continue to play a crucial role, in close cooperation with other international actors. NATO's strategy in Afghanistan, as expressed by its Comprehensive Strategic Political-Military Plan, remains valid. But if the insurgency is not to gain an upper hand and increase its popular support, implementation is crucial across four key pillars: a firm and shared long-term commitment; support for enhanced Afghan leadership and responsibility; a comprehensive approach by the international community; and increased cooperation and engagement with Afghanistan's neighbours, notably Pakistan. In applying such a multifaceted strategy, NATO nations must continue to demonstrate their full commitment and solidarity by, for instance, addressing continued shortfalls in a meaningful way. On the Afghan side, increased capacity, ownership, and accountability are critical.

More broadly, NATO's Afghanistan agenda will also continue to be driven by realities on the ground and by the wider geopolitical context, thereby moving the alliance's all-encompassing transformation process decisively forward—for it is in Afghanistan that the broader international efforts in defence of common objectives are being put to the test. With leading organizations such as the United Nations, NATO, and the European Union all engaged in assisting the Afghans, the job cannot be left half done.

The elections expected in 2009 will be another milestone and will require all concerned players, most importantly the Afghan authorities, to help solidify the democracy that Afghans have rarely enjoyed throughout their violent history. Achieving such a goal may seem difficult, especially given the current security environment in some parts of the country. But no efforts should be spared, as the elections also have the potential to turn around public perceptions about the ability of the Afghan government and the international community to change things for the better. In preparation, the ISAF is assisting the Afghan authorities with the voter registration process and has committed itself to providing third-tier support during the election period.

Overall success in Afghanistan must not be judged solely by a halfway peaceful and credible election process. The tasks at hand—building institutions, carrying forward reconstruction and development and, most importantly, providing better perspectives and opportunities for the average Afghan with respect to security—will remain part and parcel of a longer-term joint commitment of the international community, the people of Afghanistan, and their elected government. This commitment and its rationale cannot be taken for granted. It must be continuously renewed and explained, including in our own countries. With the Taliban not being able to win in Afghanistan outright but capable of preventing further progress, the stakes are high, not only for Afghanistan but for the region and indeed for global security.

Notes

An expanded version of this chapter appears in the *Georgetown Journal of International Affairs* 10, no.1 (Winter/Spring 2008).

1. United Nations Office on Drugs and Crime, *Afghanistan Opium Survey 2008* (Vienna, 2008), 3
2. NATO, "ISAF's Strategic Vision: Declaration by the Heads of State and Government of the Nations Contributing to the UN-Mandated NATO-Led International Security Assistance Force." News Release 052, 3 April 2008.
3. For a summary of the main points of the plan, see NATO, Meeting of the North Atlantic Council at the Level of Foreign Ministers, held at NATO Headquarters, Brussels, "Final Communiqué," Press Release 153, 3 December 2008, para 5.
4. NATO, "ISAF's Strategic Vision," para 7.

Chapter 7

Pakistan's Afghanistan Policy in the Shadow of India

Christian Wagner

Introduction

A National Intelligence Estimate published by American intelligence services in July 2007 concluded that Pakistan's border area with Afghanistan, the Federally Administered Tribal Areas (FATA), had developed into a safe haven for the Taliban and al Qaeda. In the FATA they had renewed their capabilities to launch attacks both in Afghanistan and globally.[1] The Taliban's ongoing campaign in Afghanistan, where they fight against both the government in Kabul and the International Security Assistance Force (ISAF) troops, has in recent years led to a clear deterioration in relations with Pakistan. Since 2004 the Pakistani army has been waging a campaign against Islamist groups in the FATA, losing more than one thousand soldiers, while these Taliban-affiliated groups managed to expand their activities within Pakistan. They no longer operate only in the FATA but also in certain districts of the adjacent northwestern border province (the North West Frontier Province). Spectacles like the occupation of the Red Mosque in the first half of 2007 demonstrate that these groups' radius of operation, at least in part, reaches even to the capital city, Islamabad.

The Pakistani army's costly battles in the tribal areas, the deterioration of Islamabad's bilateral relationship with Kabul, and international criticism of the Pakistani military's advances against Islamist extremists (which are often seen as half-hearted) have all helped shift Pakistan's foreign policy focus, traditionally centred on India, more strongly toward Afghanistan. However, relations with Afghanistan will remain just a dependent variable relative to India. Pakistan's interest in Afghanistan since the 1990s can only be understood within the context of its conflict with India over Kashmir and the military's domestic dominance. That said, there was hardly any connection between Pakistan's conflicts with India over Kashmir and with Afghanistan until the end of the 1980s. Only then did the Pakistani military leadership begin to more strongly link the two conflict fields. Yet this strategy has come under increasing pressure since the attacks of 11 September 2001. To make clear the complexities of this situation, this chapter will first discuss the army's role in Pakistan and then the relationships between Pakistan, India, and Afghanistan. It ends with a brief discussion of future prospects.

Pakistan's Foreign Policy: The Military's Omnipresence

Pakistan's independence on 14 August 1947 gave birth to a separate state for the Muslims of the Indian subcontinent after the decolonization of British India. As early as 1940 the Muslim League had employed its Two Nations Theory to make a claim for an independent Muslim state. This theory regarded Hindus and Muslims as two distinct nations due to their different religions and customs and asserted that each nation had a right to its own state. Against a background of violent riots between the two religious groups, the Muslim League feared that the Muslim minority in an independent but unified state would be dominated by the Hindus. Using this argument, Mohammed Ali Jinnah, the leader of the Muslim League, was able to prevail in negotiations with the British colonial power against the Indian National Congress led by Mahatma Gandhi and Jawaharlal Nehru, who had called for a unified state for all religious groups. The areas of British India with Muslim majorities were combined into the new state. It consisted of two regions, East and West Pakistan, which were separated from each other by more than 1,500 kilometres of Indian territory. British India's independence and the establishment of India and Pakistan triggered one of the largest migrations in modern times. About 15 million Hindus, Sikhs, and Muslims left their homes to settle in one of the two new states. This relocation was overshadowed by bloody riots and massacres by religious fanatics in which approximately five hundred thousand people were killed.[2]

Afghanistan was skeptical about the establishment of Pakistan and made territorial claims on the Pashtun-majority areas of the North West Frontier Province (NWFP). The Afghan government therefore refused to acknowledge the British-drawn Durand Line, which runs directly through the Pashtun areas, as the border with the new state of Pakistan. Yet in a referendum in July 1947 the Pashtun tribes in the NWFP clearly supported their regions joining Pakistan. The government in Kabul did not accept their decision.[3] Afghanistan was hence the only country to vote against Pakistan's acceptance into the United Nations.

The difficult process of state-building—given the two separate parts of the country as well as the territorial conflicts with neighbouring states, such as Afghanistan's territorial claims and the dispute with India over possession of Kashmir—all hampered Pakistan's democratic development. The Muslim League elite saw the western half of the country as the political centre, yet the majority of Pakistanis lived in the characteristically Bengali eastern half. Bengalis were thus heavily under-represented in the army and administration of the new state even though East Pakistan accounted for a larger portion of the new nation's economic development. Bengali demands for greater economic, political, and cultural participation constituted one of the central areas of domestic conflict from the very start.

While in India a democratic system was established under the leadership of the Nehru-Gandhi dynasty and the Congress Party, which had emerged out of the independence movement, developments in Pakistan took a different direction.[4] The Muslim League was unable to assume a leadership role comparable to that of the Congress Party in India. The early death of modern Pakistan's founder, Mohammed Ali Jinnah, in September 1948 robbed the country of the one leader recognized by all political camps. By contrast, in India Nehru developed into precisely such a leader in the 1950s. Pakistan's first constitution was adopted in 1956, but the parliamentary elections scheduled for February 1959 never took place. The continuous tension between East and West Pakistan led to the first military coup (by General Ayub Khan) in October 1958, after which Pakistan began to develop into a "garrison state."[5]

The first free elections were held in 1970. They brought a clear victory for East Pakistan's Awami League, which had campaigned for greater autonomy for the eastern half of the country. Yet the political and military elite in West Pakistan were unprepared to give up power to the elected newcomers from the east. In early 1971 negotiations over the formation of the new government failed and the Pakistani army advanced against the opposition in East Pakistan. The resulting civil war triggered a flood of refugees into India, which supported the East Pakistani rebels and actually intervened militarily in December 1971. This short war was a military, political, and ideological defeat for Pakistan. The army was crushed, with over ninety thousand soldiers becoming POWs in India. The political experiment of one state comprising two geographically separate parts failed because of the ruling military's unwillingness to compromise. The experiment was also an ideological defeat, as Jinnah's dream of obtaining a state specifically for the Muslims of South Asia failed with the war. The ethnic identity of the majority Bengali citizenry of East Pakistan proved a stronger political idea than a foundation of shared religion.

Yet even the crushing military defeat in the 1971 war did not permanently end the military's domestic power. After the country divided,

Prime Minister Bhutto propagated the concept of Islamic Socialism in order to strengthen Pakistan's national identity. Yet a series of insurgencies emerged among the Baluchis, Sindhis, and Pashtuns, all of which were directed against Punjabi dominance in the new Pakistan.[6] In the mid-1970s the army suppressed an uprising by the Baluchis, thereby strengthening its image as the guardian of national unity. After manipulations in the 1977 elections, the army conducted a *coup d'état* under General Zia-ul Haq. To increase the legitimacy of his government, the general then amended the constitution, not only concentrating the power of the presidency but also forcing a policy of Islamization.[7] Following the Soviet invasion of Afghanistan in 1979 and with considerable military aid from the United States, the Pakistani secret service—Inter-Services Intelligence (ISI)—trained the Islamic mujahidin to fight against the Soviet Union. This involvement further abetted Zia-ul Haq's efforts at Islamization.

The ongoing conflict with India over Kashmir likewise promoted the military's dominance. Kashmir became a central, identity-forming bond for Pakistani society, bringing together the various ethnic groups of the country. In reaction to the 1971 military defeat as well as to India's progress in the field of atomic energy, in the 1970s Pakistan began developing a nuclear program that continues to this day. As India, which had conducted its first nuclear test in 1974, did not join the Nuclear Non-Proliferation Treaty, Pakistan also dared to adopt this same position. Despite a series of sanctions, Pakistan managed to implement a military nuclear program. The alleged threat from India also justified continually high military spending, which in 2002 comprised 4.5 percent of the gross domestic product.[8] The defence budget was not subject to parliamentary oversight. This money was not available for any spending on health or education; hence Pakistan now ranks 134th on the United Nations' Human Development Index.

In addition to slowing the country's social development, in the 1990s the military hindered a political rapprochement with India. In the spring of 1999 Pakistani prime minister Nawaz Sharif and Indian prime minister A.B. Vajpayee signed the Lahore Declaration introducing a new phase of rapprochement, a new start after the 1998 nuclear tests. Yet at the beginning of 1999 the army leadership under General Musharraf had begun a large-scale infiltration of Kashmir, which led to the Kargil War of May–June 1999. The war abruptly ended the rapprochement. Under pressure from the United States, Nawaz Sharif pulled back the Pakistani units. In October, General Musharraf came to power in a *coup d'état*.

Since then the military has further extended its political and economic power. Today it occupies nearly all points on the social spectrum. Over and above their basic mission of ensuring external security, the armed forces institutionalized their political say by establishing a national security council in 2004. Economically, the army has developed into a "state within a state." It is, *inter alia*, the largest transportation firm and landowner in the country. A number of officers hold leading positions in public companies.[9] Musharraf himself has long simultaneously held the offices of president and commander-in-chief of the army, which is unconstitutional in Pakistan. With his concept of "enlightened moderation," he even claims moral leadership in questions of identity such as the significance of religion in Pakistan, which has been argued over since independence.[10]

A further characteristic of Pakistan's relations with India and Afghanistan has long been the military's use of violent non-state actors to achieve its foreign policy objectives. As early as the lead-up to the first war with India over Kashmir, in 1947–48, officers from the Pakistani army had helped tribal warriors infiltrate Kashmir to aid the revolts there. Leading up to the second war in 1965, Pakistan channelled armed civilian guerrilla fighters into the Indian part of Kashmir to ignite an uprising there. Since the Islamization policy under Zia-ul Haq and Pakistan's support of the mujahidin in Afghanistan in the 1980s, the military and the ISI have employed primarily Islamist groups to achieve their foreign policy goals—as demonstrated by the uprising in Kashmir at the end of the 1980s and the Taliban's triumphant conquest in Afghanistan in the 1990s. Of course, India and Afghanistan have also used violent non-state actors in their conflicts with Pakistan, but this strategy has a longer tradition in Pakistan due to the military's dominance. The military uses religion domestically to strengthen the legitimacy of its leadership and externally to counter the competing nationalistic visions of the Pashtuns and Kashmiris. Thus even today the Pakistani army, which has been understood as the guarantor of national unity since the *coup d'état* of 1958, determines the country's foreign and security policy discourse.

Relations between Pakistan, India, and Afghanistan
from 1947 to 1989

After 1947, one topic in particular dominated Pakistan's foreign policy: Kashmir, and relations with India in general. After British India gained independence, small kingdoms like Kashmir were able to keep their autonomous status. Kashmir symbolized for Pakistan the achievement of its national identity as a country for South Asian Muslims. By contrast, as a majority Muslim province, Kashmir symbolized for India the achievement of an Indian secular state.[11] The revolt in Kashmir in the autumn of 1947 induced the Maharajah of Kashmir to join the Indian Union that October. In return, the Indian government dispatched troops to suppress the rebellion. The first India-Pakistan War developed from these battles and ended only in 1949. Since then the former kingdom has been divided into two regions, one controlled by India and one by Pakistan. As early as December 1947, India had brought the issue before the United Nations; Nehru had even suggested a referendum on Kashmir's future status.

Although India's attempt to internationally denounce Pakistan's alleged aggression did fail, its call for a referendum in Kashmir was included in the UN resolution. Yet this inclusion was in fact a political victory for Pakistan, since it successfully internationalized the Kashmir question precisely as successive Pakistani governments increasingly demanded. The referendum, however, has still not been conducted because neither Pakistan nor India has met the relevant preconditions.

In the mid-1950s the conflict with India prompted Pakistan's leadership to join Western defence alliances such as the South East Asia Treaty Organization (SEATO) and the Central Treaty Organization (CENTO). Parallel to these multilateral alliances, Pakistan strengthened its military and economic relationships with the United States. While containing communism held primary importance for the Americans, Pakistan's strongest interests remained the Kashmir question and concerns over possible further conflict with India. After Indian prime minister Nehru's death in 1964, the Pakistani leadership believed they could profit from India's supposed weak phase to resolve the Kashmir question. They arranged for civilian guerrilla fighters to infiltrate the Indian part of Kashmir in 1965 to trigger a revolt against India, which would be facilitated by an intervention by the Pakistani army. The strategy backfired, though, as the insurgents found hardly any support among the Kashmiris. The second India-Pakistan war ended in September 1965 after a UN resolution and an arms embargo by the United States against the warring parties.

The third war with India, in 1971, was sparked by the civil war in East Pakistan. This conflict let loose a wave of refugees into India, which supported the East Pakistani rebels. The Indian army intervened in December 1971 and defeated the Pakistani army after a few short battles. Yet Pakistan's new prime minister, Zulfikar Ali Bhutto, achieved political rather than military success when in the peace negotiations with India he was able to prevent a permanent settlement of the Kashmir conflict.[12] In the Simla Treaty of 2 July 1972, Indian prime minister Indira Gandhi, under pressure from Bhutto, agreed not to transform the line of control in Kashmir into an international border. Such a definite border would have been an end to the Kashmir issue clearly detrimental to Pakistan's interests.[13]

The next military escalation developed in the mid-1980s.[14] At the beginning of the decade, India had accused Pakistan of supporting militant Sikhs fighting for their own state in the Indian Punjab province. Although the Simla Treaty had indeed newly established the line of control in Kashmir, a permanent line at Siachen-Gletscher had not been clearly demarcated due to the inhospitable natural environment. In April 1984, Indian and then Pakistani troops occupied a part of Gletscher, which has since held the record as the highest battlefield in the world. A further deterioration of bilateral relations followed with India's "Brasstacks" military manoeuvre in the winter of 1986–87. Pakistan saw this comprehensive military manoeuvre as preparation for an attack and responded by mobilizing troops on the border with India. The two armed forces faced one another on combat-ready status for over a week. During the crisis A.Q. Khan, father of Pakistan's nuclear program, revealed in media interviews that his country already possessed nuclear weapons. For the first time there was a danger of nuclear escalation between India and Pakistan.[15]

Although Pakistan was indeed founded as a state for the Muslims of the subcontinent, there were still numerous tensions in relations with its most important Muslim neighbour, Afghanistan. Because of its own territorial claims, the Afghan monarchy had only grudgingly accepted Pakistan's independence. In particular Prince Mohammed Daoud, prime minister from 1954 to 1963 and, after the *coup d'état*, president from 1973 to 1978, continually called for greater autonomy for the Pashtuns in Pakistan. His demands put a definite strain on bilateral relations. Pakistan supported the Afghan opposition against Daoud and granted asylum to his cousin, King Zahir, after the 1973 *coup d'état*.[16] In the 1970s, Prime Minister Bhutto played the religion card in order to counter the Pashtun nationalism coming from Afghanistan. His government supported small revolts in eastern Afghanistan.[17] In the fight against the Soviet invasion of Afghanistan in the 1980s, Pakistan refined this religious strategy with support from the United States and Saudi Arabia. The country had already begun a more intense Islamization under General Zia-ul Haq after the 1977 *coup d'état*. The resistance against the Soviet Union was built under Islamic auspices. The Pakistani secret service, the ISI, trained fighters in the majority Pashtun areas along the inaccessible mountain regions on the border with Afghanistan. A number of foreign fighters from Muslim countries, who had pledged holy war against the Soviet Union, trained alongside the Afghans in the opposition.

Relations between Pakistan, India, and Afghanistan
from 1989 to 2001

Pakistan's relations with India and Afghanistan remained largely independent from one another until 1989. The India-Pakistan conflict led India to improve its relationship with Afghanistan. In the 1950s, India had occasionally even supported Afghanistan against Pakistan in its calls for a Pashtun state,[18] but later India's close relationship with the Soviet Union ensured that it did not openly criticize the invasion of Afghanistan in December 1979. After the Soviet Union's final retreat in 1989, the network of relationships between Pakistan, Afghanistan, and India changed fundamentally.

Pakistan renewed its fear of a nationalist Pashtun government in Kabul, whose traditionally good relationship with India raised the danger that Pakistan could be encircled. Aslam Beg, who had taken over the office of commander-in-chief of the army after Zia-ul Haq's death in 1988, outlined the main features of a new strategy in which Afghanistan would act as Pakistan's strategic rear. Given the possibility of a conflict with India, a "friendly" (controlled by Pakistan) government in Kabul would allow Pakistan to gain a better strategic position. Afghanistan was also to serve as a training camp and safe haven for militant groups from Kashmir.[19]

Pakistan's strategy of employing militant Islamic groups to further its foreign policy interests regarding India and Afghanistan reached its peak in the 1990s. In Muslim-majority Kashmir a new opposition movement had arisen from the rigged parliamentary elections in the spring of 1987. Violent resistance was first propagated by the Jammu and Kashmir Liberation Front (JKLF), which supported a Kashmir independent from both India and Pakistan. The JKLF operated only in Jammu and Kashmir, and profited from the ISI's training and support. The JKLF's goal, however—national independence for Kashmir—caused problems for cooperation. The ISI therefore began to promote groups that agreed with Pakistan's request that Kashmir join Pakistan. It thus supported Islamist groups such as Hizb-ul-Muhahideen, which sought both a union with Pakistan and a more intense Islamization of Kashmir.[20] In addition, the ISI recruited armed foreign fighters from Afghanistan and some Arab countries for deployment in Jammu and Kashmir. India began a military suppression of the uprising and at times stationed more than 600,000 soldiers in Kashmir. In the 1990s the attacks by militant groups and the security forces' encroachment on the civilian population led to an escalation of violence and a clear deterioration of the human rights situation.

India's and Pakistan's nuclear tests in May 1998 seemed to raise the danger that the conflict over Kashmir would acquire a nuclear dimension. In February 1999 the Lahore Declaration did initiate a short-lived rapprochement that briefly lessened the danger of escalation, but after only a few months the Pakistani infiltration of Kargil and the subsequent India-Pakistan war brought the reconciliation to an abrupt end. The nuclear balance was not a true deterrence situation, as the use of non-state actors allowed armed conflicts between the two states to continue. Politically, Pakistan hoped its non-state actor strategy would internationalize the Kashmir conflict, a development that India continued to absolutely repudiate.

After the Soviet Union's retreat, civil war broke out in Afghanistan between feuding ethnic groups and various warlords. Starting in the mid-1990s Pakistan began to support the Taliban, which recruited primarily among the Pashtuns. Many recruits had been educated in madrassas in Pakistan that were under the control of religious parties such as the Jamiat-i-Ulama-i-Pakistan.[21] The Taliban's religious orientation was to function as a balance against any renewed rise of Pashtun nationalism, which was seen in Pakistan as a threat. The Taliban was the most successful group in the civil war, finally seizing power in Kabul in 1996.

Pakistan was one of the few countries to recognize Afghanistan's new government.

The Consequences of 11 September 2001

The Pakistani military's strategy of supporting Islamist groups in order to achieve its foreign policy objectives regarding India and Afghanistan suffered a clear setback from the attacks of 11 September 2001. Within a few days of the attack Pakistan decided, under massive pressure from the United States, to participate in the "war on terror." Consequently, Pakistan once again became one of America's most important allies and a "front-line state" in its foreign policy. Yet General Musharraf's government at first continued to support militant groups in Kashmir. In November 2001, General Musharraf declared that renouncing the Taliban had saved Pakistan's core interests—nuclear weapons and Kashmir.[22]

Pakistan initially sought to brand the human rights violations by the Indian armed forces in Kashmir as "state terrorism" within the newly arisen discussion over international terrorism. India, in turn, pointed to the ISI's support of Islamist groups and criticized Pakistan's involvement in the US alliance. On 13 December 2001, members of Lashkar-e-Toiba and Jaish-e-Mohammed, two terrorist groups operating out of Pakistan, failed in an attempted attack on the parliament in New Delhi. In reaction to this attack, the Indian government threatened a military strike to destroy the groups' infrastructure in the Pakistani part of Kashmir and to put an end to their continuous infiltration over the line of control. This troop mobilization led in the summer of 2002 to a further crisis with Pakistan that renewed the risk of war. Because of the threat of nuclear escalation, the United States and Great Britain intervened to settle the crisis diplomatically.

Musharraf's government strengthened the religious parties' domestic position by manipulating the 2002 elections. These parties can be considered ideological sponsors of the Taliban in Afghanistan. They have heavily criticized the international community's military approach in Afghanistan. In the 2002 elections, they won 11 percent of the national vote for the first time. Their success was doubly useful to Musharraf: First, he was able to present himself to the West as the last bastion against the Islamist powers.[23] Second, he needed the religious parties for his domestic reforms, which in 2003 further strengthened both his power as president and the role of the military.

The 2003 discussion sparked by the Iraq war, in which the United States justified military action against states that supported terrorism and/or the proliferation of weapons of mass destruction, was attentively followed in Islamabad. India had increasingly criticized Pakistan's support of terrorist groups, even expressing this criticism directly to the United

States. Furthermore, at the end of 2003 the network led by A.Q. Khan, which had delivered nuclear technology to states such as Iran and Libya, was discovered. Khan, who is revered as a national hero, was described as the sole person responsible for the network. However, he was "pardoned" by General Musharraf for his prominent service to the Pakistani nuclear program before a trial and possible conviction could uncover further details about the network. Given the strategic importance of the Pakistani nuclear program, it is difficult to imagine that the propagation of and trade in nuclear technology—which in part used planes from the Air Force—would have been carried out without the knowledge of the responsible military authority.

While the international situation deteriorated for Pakistan due to the Iraq war and the discovery of the Khan network, the regional environment improved considerably. In April 2003 at a speech in Srinagar, the capital of the Indian part of Kashmir, Indian prime minister Vajpayee unexpectedly offered to renew talks to improve bilateral relations. In August 2003 the two sides agreed on a ceasefire that eased the situation in Kashmir. At their meeting in the beginning of January 2004, President Musharraf and Prime Minister Vajpayee agreed on the organization of a composite dialogue. In the dialogue, which began in February, Pakistan reconsidered the question of Kashmir, and India that of terrorism. In the resulting joint statement, Musharraf pledged that no more terrorist attacks would come from Pakistani territory.[24] A series of attacks in India by militant Islamist groups—such as in Delhi in 2005, in Mumbai and Varanasi in 2006, and on the train line connecting with Pakistan in 2007—aimed to sabotage the rapprochement process. Yet, although a short interruption did occur after these attacks, the dialogue process did not end. At their summit meeting in New Delhi in April 2005, Indian prime minister Manmohan Singh and President Musharraf declared the peace process to be "irreversible." They also agreed on the main features of a possible resolution of the Kashmir conflict: each half's internal autonomy could be expanded according to the Indian and Pakistani national constitutions, respectively. In this way, the Kashmiris would gain more self-rule in comparison to the Indian states or Pakistani provinces.[25]

The October 2005 earthquake in Kashmir further strengthened the process of rapprochement. India and Pakistan came to an agreement on the organization of border crossings for civilians at the line of control in Kashmir—the first time the border had been opened. This agreement was an important step toward the establishment of the soft border that had been envisioned by the spring 2005 declaration. Trade between the two parts of Kashmir over the line of control began in August 2007, further improving bilateral relations.

Up to the end of 2007 there were a total of four rounds of negotiations within the dialogue process. The process included confidence-building measures such as new transportation connections to facilitate travel in Kashmir and Punjab, among other places, and improved economic, cultural, and academic cooperation. Although there has thus far been no breakthrough in the "Kashmir question" itself, through background negotiations the two sides have brought their opposing stands on Kashmir closer together.[26] Furthermore, President Musharraf introduced a variety of initiatives and in June 2007 even raised the idea of withdrawing Pakistani troops from Kashmir for the first time.[27] In July 2007, Prime Minister Singh argued for shared use of land and water resources in Kashmir.

The rapprochement between India and Pakistan since 2003 has led Musharraf to essentially reverse Pakistan's policy on the Kashmir question, a move that is not uncontested domestically. He has shifted Pakistan's original position from an international level, which insisted on a referendum in the context of the UN resolution, to a bilateral level, where an agreement with India and the Kashmiris is coming within reach. Infiltration over the line of control has lessened appreciably, although attacks by Islamist groups in Kashmir continue to occur.

Given the importance Kashmir has had in Pakistan's domestic politics for so many years, this change of course is proving difficult. The government has therefore stressed that it will at least continue to politically and morally support Kashmir's request for a referendum. However, it appears that contrary to official assurances the Pakistani army is continuing to directly support militant groups. Sayed Salahuddin, leader of the Hizbul-Muhahideen and chairman of the United Jihad Council, a consortium of militant groups, admitted in a televised interview in March 2008 that these groups had received direct support from the Pakistani army.[28]

In addition to the motives discussed above, Musharraf's rapprochement with India was likely also facilitated by the international community's growing pressure on Pakistan with regard to Afghanistan. Although the Pakistani security services have indeed eliminated numerous al Qaeda members and arrested a series of high-ranking leaders of terrorist networks in Pakistan since 2001, they have achieved only limited successes in the fight against the Taliban. In the course of the Taliban's military comeback in southern Afghanistan, it became clear that its most important safe haven, supply, and training areas lay in the self-ruling tribal areas of the FATA. In the spring of 2004 the Pakistani armed forces began military action against the militant groups in the FATA. It thus became apparent that during the fight against the Soviets in the 1980s the influence of religious groups had increasingly Islamicized the traditional tribal structures. Moderate tribal leaders who had cooperated with the government were killed, and Islamist groups, particularly in the tribal areas of North and South Waziristan and the districts bordering the North West Frontier Province, advanced a policy of "Talibanization." As the armed forces were unable to militarily defeat the tribes, in order to stop the infiltration into Afghanistan the government changed tactics and began to sign peace treaties with individual tribal groups, for example with the tribes in North Waziristan in September 2006.[29]

Given the growing problems in the FATA, Pakistan is now implementing a political, economic, and military strategy toward the rebellious groups. Politically, the government is aiming to cooperate with moderate tribal groups in order to strengthen the traditional leaders, the Maliks, against the Mullahs. Economically, it is working on a Sustainable Development Plan for FATA, 2006–2015, to improve infrastructure in the region, which is even today among the least developed in Pakistan. The United States has promised financial support for this strategy amounting to approximately US$750 million in the next five years. The Pakistani government has announced it will considerably expand its development efforts and pledged to invest up to US$1 billion in the region over the next few years. Militarily, the government is planning to more closely involve the paramilitary units of the Frontier Corps in the fight against terrorism. These units, founded by the British, are recruited from the tribes themselves. Implementing these strategies will shift the main burden of the fight to the tribes, who will be supported by the army. As early as the spring of 2007, heavy combat took place in which tribal groups loyal to the government and supported by the armed forces advanced against foreign Uzbek fighters in the FATA. Shifting combat operations to the tribal groups will most likely soften the growing resentment of the Pashtuns in the army, where they comprise 20 percent of the total troops, since the military approach causes not only high losses among soldiers but also many victims among the Pashtun civilians in the region.

Both the Afghan government and NATO criticize the obviously continuing support of the Taliban in Pakistan, even though the Pakistani armed forces have stationed more than eighty thousand soldiers in the FATA and thus far have suffered more than one thousand deaths. These criticisms reflect the fundamental dilemma in Pakistan's policy toward Afghanistan. Afghanistan remains of great importance to the Pakistani military. If it withdrew, whether due to a further escalation of the civil war or the pacification of the country, the Pakistani military fears that Kabul would renew its traditionally good relations with New Delhi. This reconciliation would bring a threat of "encirclement" by India. Indeed, India is already quite actively engaged in reconstructing Afghanistan. Pakistan views this engagement very skeptically and is suspicious of the Indian consulates along the Pakistani border. It especially suspects them of supporting rebellions in Baluchistan. The Pakistani military is seeking to secure continuing influence in Afghanistan by tolerating and supporting Taliban groups. It is simultaneously trying to fulfil US demands that it show success in the fight against terrorism by combatting al Qaeda cadres and foreign militant groups. This double-stranded approach can be understood as Pakistan's attempt to secure its political and military interests in Afghanistan.[30] Against this background, one of Pakistan's interests is to portray itself as the guardian of Pashtun interests in Afghanistan. The Pashtuns represent the majority of the population in Afghanistan and only a minority (about 15 percent of the population) in Pakistan. In absolute terms, however, more Pashtuns live in Pakistan than in Afghanistan.

Prospects

The past two years have demonstrated that pacifying Afghanistan without including Pakistan in the process is virtually impossible. From Pakistan's perspective, however, Afghanistan remains only one variable in a strategic context that continues to be dominated by relations with India. Problematically, Pakistan's foreign policy discourse is decided almost exclusively by the military's geo-strategic perspective. An alternative approach would be, for example, closer economic cooperation between Afghanistan, Pakistan, and India, all of which are members of the South Asian Association for Regional Cooperation. The South Asia Free Trade Agreement (SAFTA), which came into effect in 2006, offers a basis for such cooperation. Due to bilateral problems with India, however, Pakistan has only partially implemented the SAFTA. The new Pakistani government elected in February 2008 has shown that it wants to continue the process of political and economic rapprochement with India.[31] Since the military will for the foreseeable future continue to determine Pakistan's foreign and security interests, it would behoove the neighbouring countries to accommodate these interests. If India and Pakistan came to a solution on Kashmir that allowed Pakistan to save face, and Afghanistan recognized the Durand Line in exchange for Pakistan ending its support of militant groups, an important contribution would be made to the success of the international engagements in Afghanistan and to regional stability.

Notes

1. See Mark Mazetti and David E. Sanger, "Al Qaeda Threatens; U.S. Frets," *New York Times*, 22 July 2007.
2. See Hermann Kulke and Dietmar Rothermund, *Geschichte Indiens: Von der Induskultur bis heute* (Munich: C.H. Beck, 1998).
3. S.M. Burke and Lawrence Ziring, *Pakistan's Foreign Policy: An Historical Analysis* (Oxford: Oxford University Press, 1994), 70.
4. For an overview of the historical developments see Stephen P. Cohen, *The Idea of Pakistan* (Washington: Brookings Institution, 2005); Christophe Jaffrelot, ed., *Pakistan: Nationalism without a Nation?* (London: Zed Books, 2002); Ian Talbot, *Pakistan: A Modern History* (London: C. Hurst, 1999).
5. See Robert Laporte Jr., "Succession in Pakistan: Continuity and Change in a Garrison State," *Asian Survey* 9, no. 11 (November 1969): 842-61.

6.   See Tahir Amin, *Ethno-National Movements of Pakistan: Domestic and International Factors* (Islamabad: Institute of Policy Studies, 1988).

7.   See Louis D. Hayes, *The Struggle for Legitimacy in Pakistan* (Lahore: Vanguard Books, 1986).

8.   See International Institute for Strategic Studies, *The Military Balance 2002–2003* (London: 2003).

9.   See Ayesha Siddiqa, *Military Inc.: Inside Pakistan's Military Economy* (London: Pluto Press, 2007).

10. See "Enlightened Moderation," http://www.presidentofpakistan.gov.pk/ EnlightenedModeration.aspx (accessed 11 July 2007).

11. On the development of the Kashmir conflict see Alastair Lamb, *Birth of a Tragedy: Kashmir 1947* (Hertingfordbury, UK: Roxford Books, 1994); Robert G. Wirsing, *Kashmir: In the Shadow of War – Regional Rivalries in a Nuclear Age* (New York: Spring Books, 2003); Sumantra Bose, *Kashmir: Roots of Conflict, Paths to Peace* (Cambridge: Harvard University Press, 2003).

12. Stanley Wolpert, *Zulfi Bhutto of Pakistan: His Life and Times* (New York: Oxford University Press, 1993), 191-92.

13. See Amitabh Matoo, "Next Steps in Kashmir," in *Kashmir: How Far Can Vajpayjee and Musharraf Go?* ed. Karan R. Sawhny (New Delhi: Peace, 2001), 27-44.

14. See Hasan Askari Rizvi, "Pakistan-India Relations in the Eighties," *Regional Studies* 13 (Summer 1990): 3-31.

15. See Kanti P. Bajpai, P.R. Chari, Pervaiz Iqbal Cheema, Stephen P. Cohen, and Sumit Ganguly, *Brasstacks and Beyond* (New Delhi: Manohar Publishers, 1995).

16. Olivier Roy, "The Taliban: A Strategic Tool for Pakistan," in *Pakistan: Nationalism without a Nation?* ed. Christophe Jaffrelot (London: Zed Books, 2002), 150.

17. Marvin Weinbaum, *Pakistan and Afghanistan: Resistance and Reconstruction* (Lahore: Pak Book Corp, 1994), 5.

18. Burke and Ziring, *Pakistan's Foreign Policy*, 75.

19. Aslam Beg, quoted in Rifaat Hussein, "Pakistan's Relation with Afghanistan: Continuity and Change," *Strategic Studies* 22 (Winter 2002): 43-75.

20. Bose, *Kashmir: Roots of Conflict*, 106.

21. Roy, "The Taliban: A Strategic Tool," 154.

22. "We've Saved Our Core Interests: Afghan Policy Based on Principles: CE," *Dawn*, 20 November 2001.

23. Frederic Grare, *Pakistan: The Myth of an Islamist Peril*, Carnegie Endowment Brief No. 45 (Washington, 2006). Not for nothing did Musharraf give his autobiography the same title as the Hollywood film *In the Line of Fire*.

24. "Text of PM, Musharraf Statement," *The Hindu*, 7 January 2004.

25. See Christian Wagner, *Eine Roadmap für Kaschmir?* SWP-Aktuelle 2005/18 (Berlin 2005).

26. "Governments of both countries now have to decide on a time to disclose solution . . .," Pakistani Foreign Minister Khurshid Kasuri, interview in *The Friday Times*, 1–7 June 2007, 6.

27. "Musharraf Offers Troop Withdrawal," *The Hindu*, 6 June 2007.

28. "Hizbul Chief Admits to Pak Military Support in Kashmir," *The Tribune*, 19 March 2008.

29. See Christian Wagner and Citha D. Maass, *Frieden in Waziristan: Erfolg oder Rückschlag im Kampf gegen den Terrorismus in Afghanistan and Pakistan?* SWP-Aktuelle 2006/A 46 (Berlin, 2006).

30. See Daniel Markey, "A False Choice in Pakistan," *Foreign Affairs* (July–August 2007).

31. "India, Pak Should Focus on Trade Ties: Zardari," *The Hindu*, 1 March 2008.

Chapter 8

Iran's Influence in Afghanistan

JANET KURSAWE

Introduction

Iran lies between Iraq and Afghanistan in a key geographical location at the junction of the Asian continent and the low, mostly desert areas of the Arab Middle East. Throughout its history Iran has consistently exerted a powerful influence over neighbouring countries. Persian rule and language once extended all the way into Central Asia, and a strong cultural influence remains there today. Modern Dari, the Afghan Persian, is a major language spoken in the northern and western parts of Afghanistan as well as in the capital, Kabul, located in the east. Furthermore, neighbouring countries are influenced by Iranian religious traditions. In the Hazarajat region of central and northern Afghanistan, members of a Shiite minority, the Hazara, form approximately 20 percent of the country's population. Historically, Iran has frequently interacted with its neighbours vis-à-vis the ethnic group Hazara and the Dari-speaking population.

Moreover, throughout history parts of Afghanistan have belonged to various Iranian empires. The western part in particular has traditionally been under Iran's influence. During the Soviet occupation, Iran took a strong position against the United States, since it was alarmed by the growing American and Saudi Arabian involvement in Afghanistan. Iran sought to strengthen the Shiite minority and lent support to resistance parties within the Shia communities of Afghanistan, encouraging most of them to unite under a single party (Hezb-e Wahdat) to oppose the Soviets. Eight Iran-based, Shia mujahidin groups existed during the Afghan jihad against the Soviets. Iran supported the Afghan resistance by providing financial and military assistance to mujahidin leaders who subscribed to the Iranian version of Islamic ideology.

The Afghanistan Challenge: Hard Realities and Strategic Choices, ed. H.-G. Ehrhart and C.C. Pentland. Montreal and Kingston: McGill-Queen's University Press, Queen's Policy Studies Series. © 2009 The School of Policy Studies, Queen's University at Kingston. All rights reserved.

Iran also played a very active role in mediating between other different factions, including the Taliban in the mid-1990s. After the Taliban takeover of Kabul, tensions were mounting between Iran and the Taliban when the Taliban massacred thousands of Shiites in the Hazarajat region. Tehran came close to war with the Taliban when its leaders ordered the execution of eight Iranian diplomats in Mazar-e Sharif in 1997. The Taliban accused Iran of providing support to resistance forces in western Afghanistan and of strengthening efforts of the Northern Alliance to withstand Taliban attacks in northern and central Afghanistan. As a matter of fact, throughout the Taliban period of rule, Iran was a principal backer of the Northern Alliance (United Islamic Front for the Salvation of Afghanistan). Even today the Afghan bazaar is inundated with Iranian weapons that were supplied to Northern Alliance groups during the anti-Taliban resistance in the late 1990s.[1]

In opposition to the Taliban, Iran supported at least two prominent Afghan figures, Ismail Khan and Gulbuddin Hekmatyar. Ismail Khan had created a semi-independent emirate in the western Afghan provinces, based in Herat, and he was building an uneasy alliance of mutual self-interest with Iran. In cooperation with Ahmad Shah Massoud, he successfully defended his province against the Taliban in 1995. When his former ally, Uzbek general Abdul Rashid Dostum, changed sides and attacked his emirate, the Taliban took over Herat. Ismail Khan was forced to flee with his men to Iran where he found sanctuary. During the US intervention he fought against the Taliban within the Northern Alliance and was able to regain his position as governor of Herat. Iran welcomed the stability Ismail Khan brought to western Afghanistan and the opportunity this provided to facilitate the repatriation of the three million Afghan refugees in Iran.[2]

Gulbuddin Hekmatyar, the founder and leader of the Hezb-e Eslami, lived for six years in exile in Iran (from 1996 to 2002). The Iranian government gave him refuge because of common interests. At that time Hekmatyar shared Iran's opposition to both the Taliban and al Qaeda. Further, Iran supported his opposition to the return of the former Afghan king, Zahir Shah. The Iranian government opposed the revival of the Afghan monarchy in order to prevent a regional precedent that might pave the way for a return of the Pahlevis to Iran. Furthermore, Iran welcomed Hekmatyar's joining hands with the Iranian-backed Hezb-e Wahdat. This move gave him the opportunity to cultivate his ties with Iran. It has also been reported that Hekmatyar sold Iran sixteen Stinger missiles that had been supplied by the United States to mujahidin groups to support their fight against the Soviet army. In the end, Iran was forced to expel Hekmatyar from its territory after the Bonn Accord in 2001, since his growing anti-Karzai and anti-American campaign thwarted endeavours of the Iranian leaders to convince the international community of the constructive role they wished to play in rebuilding Afghanistan. It seemed that Hekmatyar had overstepped his mandate by embarrassing the Iranian government just when it was trying to claim that it was not destabilizing Karzai's interim government.[3]

After the expulsion of Hekmatyar, however, some Hezb-e Eslami leaders left behind in Iran were reported to have established a supply line for those fighting the US-led forces and targeting the coalition troops in Afghanistan. In northwestern Afghanistan, the Hezb-e Eslami was believed to be in contact with Ismail Khan, governor of Herat. It became clear that Tehran's decision to expel Hekmatyar from Iran was limited to getting rid of him physically from Iranian territory.[4] Worried about the possibility of a Western-leaning Afghanistan on its borders—a situation that could leave it sandwiched between two potential regional allies of the United States (Afghanistan and Iraq)—Iran also continued busily cultivating two other Afghan proxies, namely, Ismail Khan and General Dostum.

In the last two decades, Iran's approach to Afghanistan has been influenced by a large number of factors, beyond its opposition to US dominance and US sanctions against the Islamic Republic. First, Iran's Afghanistan policy has been driven by its concerns over the increase in drug trafficking, the flow of Afghan refugees and labour migrants, the water supply, and the arms trade. Second, Iran's assertion of Shia leadership and its duty to protect Shia minorities has influenced its approach to Afghanistan, particularly since the Taliban takeover of Kabul and their ensuing harassment and persecution of the Hazara minorities. Consequently, the Iranian government followed a policy of opposition to virulently anti-Shia Sunni Islamism such as that of the Taliban and their patrons in Pakistan and the Persian Gulf. Third, regardless of their resistance to US dominance in the region, at times Iranian leaders attempted to find some common ground for cooperation with the United States as well as with Pakistan and Russia. Fourth, the regional policy of Iran's leaders is based on their ambition to carve out an area of Persian cultural influence through northern Afghanistan to Tajikistan.[5] This chapter enlarges on the multiple factors influencing Iran's Afghanistan policy. By focusing on Iran's contemporary interests in Afghanistan, the chapter shows how Iran's approach has been shaped by numerous regional and international factors and reveals the kind of involvement and the strategies Iran is pursuing.

A Matter of Stability?
The Crux of Iran-Afghanistan Relations

Since the fall of the Taliban in the winter of 2001–02, Iran has had cordial relations with Afghanistan, even as its relations with the United States have grown strained over the issue of Iran's nuclear agenda. Although there are some strains, Iranian leaders are highly motivated to foster better relations with Afghanistan since they pursue multiple objectives there. Given concerns about increased drug-trafficking and the flow of Afghan refugees and labour migrants, Iranian leaders see a stable Afghanistan to be in their vital interests. Iranian politicians portray their government's activities as good neighbourly aid. As Iran's ambassador Mohammad Reza Bahrami depicted it, Iran's strategy in Afghanistan is based on "security, stability and developing a strong central government."[6] The Iranian leadership justifies its approach first and foremost by the tragedy of the Afghan people. It aims to avoid the calamities of recent decades, when more than two million Afghans took refuge in Iran. Consequently, Iran wants an Afghanistan that is stable enough to permit the remaining refugees in Iran to return home.

But here a dilemma arises for the theocratic leadership in Tehran, complicating its policy toward Kabul. On the one hand, stabilization and security in Afghanistan would mean success for the United States and its Western allies. On the other, ongoing insurgencies and further destabilization of Afghanistan would mean that the US occupation would continue for years, if not decades. From an Iranian perspective, neither the formation of a pro-Western democratic Afghanistan nor a continued US occupation is in its interests. Whereas Iranian leaders strictly disapprove of a continued US presence in their neighbourhood, Afghanistan's long-term stability is of utmost concern. A stable Afghanistan is the precondition for Iran's achieving all its other long-term goals in that country.

If Afghanistan were to stabilize one day, it would certainly play a key role in the regional energy and transit trade in the medium term and beyond. It could also act as a pivotal country in the regional gas-transit trade.[7] The Iranian leadership has plans to build oil and gas pipelines to Pakistan and India via Baluchistan, a region that covers southwest Pakistan, southwest Afghanistan, and southeast Iran. The Iran-Pakistan-India pipeline will compete directly with a proposed pipeline from Turkmenistan (Turkmenistan-Afghanistan-Pakistan-India). Although both prospects are still uncertain, Norling et al. argue that the prospective Iran-Pakistan-India (IPI) pipeline is more likely to be realized.[8] In fact, all states concerned with the IPI pipeline project resumed negotiations in fall 2008, a step that has led to the optimistic belief that the IPI could be in place by 2018.[9] But obstacles still hinder the project. First is the opposition of the US government, which wants to prevent Iran—which has the world's second-largest natural gas deposits—from breaking into new markets in Asia. This would undermine efforts of the US government to further isolate Iran. Second are the price disputes and economic concerns that have delayed the IPI pipeline project in recent years. Beyond the total costs, calculated to reach US$7.5 billion, controversial issues include gas prices and transit charges.[10] Finally, both pipeline projects are considered risky due to regional tensions and the volatile security situation in areas though which the pipelines must pass.[11]

Moreover, Iran is interested in scouting new Afghan markets. Since the Taliban were ousted in 2001, Iran has emerged as one of the major investors in Afghanistan, mainly in western parts of the country. Trade between the two countries has reached US$600 million and is expected to rise further. With Herat situated just 120 kilometres from the Iranian border, a nexus of trade routes between Central and South Asia could evolve in coming years. Since most Afghan trading centres are located along the east-west corridor to Iran, the current Iranian leadership is seeking to press ahead with construction of the east-west route.[12]

In sum, Iran's contemporary interests in Afghanistan are based on multiple factors, both regional and international. At the regional level, the current Iranian leadership wants to prevent other regional powers, including Russia, Pakistan, and Turkey, from dominating Central Asia and its resources. Although Iran's main security concerns since the end of the Iran-Iraq war in 1988 have derived from its conflict with the United States, a competition among regional players in Afghanistan had developed in the post-Cold War period. Suffice it to mention Pakistan's influence in Afghanistan, Iran's concern with the United States as Pakistan's supporter and sponsor, Russia's influence in Central Asia and its dominance in the energy sector, and Turkey's participation in the International Security Assistance Force (ISAF) in Afghanistan as well as its ambitions to exert influence in the five new Turkic states in the Caucasus and in Central Asia. Furthermore, Turkish commandos took part in the US-led Operation Enduring Freedom. All these factors converge in a competition that cannot be resolved solely in the immediate vicinity of Afghanistan.[13]

At both the regional and global levels, the theocratic leaders of the Islamic Republic of Iran want to ensure that the United States will not be a dominant player in whatever new order emerges in the region. Iran shares that objective with other regional powers, including Russia and China. Before the launch of Operation Enduring Freedom, Iran had found itself sandwiched uncomfortably between two ideological and material threats: the Taliban in Afghanistan and Saddam Hussein in Iraq. With the military intervention in Afghanistan in 2001 and the overthrow of the Baath regime in Iraq just eighteen months later, the United States removed both of these substantial threats. The position of the theocratic state remained ambivalent, however, as Iran worried about the effects of American presence on its borders, particularly after it was included in the "axis of evil" by President George W. Bush. The threat of a US military intervention in Iran increased, while the debate about Iran's nuclear program escalated. On the whole, both interventions provoked a permanent feeling of encirclement within Iran's leadership. In this new situation, Iran's leaders have followed a foreign policy that can be best described as "a combination of defensive caution and limited containment of the United States on its borders."[14] Both elements, caution and realism, have always been major determinants of Iran's foreign policy—particularly toward Central Asia—partly as a consequence of Iran's close relationship with Russia. Thus Iran has seldom interfered in Russia's policy on Central Asia. With regard to Afghanistan, Iran is playing an active role while following a policy of containing US influence on its eastern border. Since Iran is in a defensive position, it is pursuing a policy that ensures its influence in Afghanistan. Obviously, Iran's interests contradict those of the US administration.[15]

Signs of Influence: Iran's Strategies in Afghanistan

The Iranian leadership has followed a twofold strategy to achieve its multiple objectives in Afghanistan. At the diplomatic level, Iran collaborated closely with the United States and with the international community in seeking a political alternative to the Taliban during the Bonn process and after. But behind the scenes, Iran is seeking to undermine US efforts in Afghanistan. On the cooperative stage, Iran is a significant donor to reconstruction in Afghanistan. It has, however, taken advantage of the weakness of the Afghan government to pursue a more nuanced strategy that consists of part reconstruction, part education, and part propaganda.[16]

Reconstruction

Since the fall of the Taliban, Iran's contribution to the Afghan reconstruction process has been close to US$1 billion. Iran has been contributing in particular to prosperity in western Afghanistan. There one can find 24-hour electricity, largely provided by Iran. As mentioned above, trade between the two countries has reached US$600 million and is expected to rise further. Herat is emerging as a nexus of trade routes between Central and South Asia. Since Iran seeks Afghan and Central Asian markets for its non-oil exports, it is also actively interested in developing transport infrastructure in Central Asia that will enable it to take advantage of its strategic location between Turkey and the Arab states to the west; South Asia, the Caucasus, Caspian, and Central Asia region to the north; and the Persian Gulf to the south. For this reason, Iran has focused on the construction of roads. Since most Afghan trading centres are located along the east-west corridor to Iran, the theocratic leadership in Tehran is pressing ahead with construction of the east-west route.[17] Recently, Iran has been engaged in road-building projects in northwest Afghanistan, providing new routes to Uzbekistan and Tajikistan. Another major project has involved upgrading roads linking Afghanistan with the Iranian port of Chabahar, situated on the Gulf of Oman. Additionally, Iran has constructed a 60 kilometre road between Herat and Faryab province in the north of Afghanistan, and the 122 kilometre highway,

Dogharoun-Herat. These projects were funded by the Iranian Support Fund for Afghan Reconstruction.[18]

Railroads are another important element of Iran's transportation strategy. The Iranian leadership plans to extend railways to the western Afghan border town of Islam Qaleh. Moreover, the link between Iran's railroads and Herat is under construction. With the completion of this project, Afghanistan's first railroad will be linked to the Persian Gulf.[19] Altogether, it is obvious that through building roads, railways, and pipelines, Iran aims to make Afghanistan its door to Central Asia.[20]

Iran has contributed mainly to the reconstruction process in west Afghanistan, but signs of Iranian involvement can also be found in the capital, Kabul. Here, Iran's projects include a new medical centre and a water-testing laboratory.[21] Moreover, the Iranian leadership presents itself as a cooperative partner in Afghanistan's security sector reform. Since 2004, Iranian officials have been training Afghan counter-narcotics police officers and Afghan border guards. Furthermore, Iran set up twenty-four border posts in Afghanistan against the narcotics trade and equipped them with test kits, search equipment, and motorcycles. In total, Iran has spent more than US$900 million to secure the frontier with Afghanistan and Pakistan.[22]

With all these efforts, Iran is keen to present itself as a constructive force for stabilization in the region. To this end the Iranian leaders use Afghan diplomacy as a springboard and follow a pragmatic approach with Pakistan and, at times, with the United States.

Culture, and Education

Considering themselves defenders of the Muslim faith, especially the Shiite version, against US President George W. Bush's "crusade," part two of the Iranian leaders nuanced strategy has been to gain influence in the Afghan cultural and education sector. In general, the Iranian conception of regional culture forms the basis for cooperation. Accordingly, the theocratic leadership in Tehran attempts to cultivate closer ties with Afghanistan and Tajikistan. An Iranian initiative led to a tripartite summit in Dushanbe in July 2006. The leaders of the three states signed several economic treaties and agreed to establish a "cultural cooperation commission" to promote closer economic and security ties between the three Farsi-speaking countries. According to Iran's president, Mahmoud Ahmadinejad, the commission will convene twice annually, with the inaugural gathering in the fall of 2006 in the Afghan capital.[23] In addition, the president advocated the creation of a television network that would "broadcast the Persian language and culture to the world"[24] and promoted the expansion of educational exchanges. During the Tehran summit in August 2008, the three presidents highlighted the significance of establishing a common television network in expanding trilateral communications.[25] Further, Iran seeks to extend its cultural influence by setting up TV and radio stations.

In recent years, Iran has been seeking to increase its cultural influence in Afghanistan in different ways. It has built libraries that push the ideology of the Islamic Republic of Iran. Furthermore, it inaugurated a huge cultural centre in Kabul, which works to promote Iranian culture by organizing workshops and literary exchange programs. In addition, Iranian experts have trained more than 1,200 Afghan teachers, librarians, and diplomats. In 2005 the Iranian embassy in Kabul opened an Iranian corner in the main library of Kabul University and supplied it with computers, books, and magazines promoting Iran's theocratic culture.[26]

Propaganda

In its drive to become a bigger player in Afghanistan, Iran is exploiting new opportunities to spread its influence and ideas. To this end, the Iranian government has extended its influence by promoting clerics, mainly in western Afghanistan, who preach a pro-Iranian position and stir up feelings against foreign forces.[27] Furthermore, Iranian radio stations broadcast anti-US propaganda. There are also reports that the leadership in Tehran channels money to conservative Shiite religious authorities and schools. Beyond this, Iran encourages students who have graduated from Iranian universities to establish religious schools in Afghanistan and to strengthen Afghan-Iran ties.[28] Since 2001, Iran has funnelled millions of dollars to Shiite religious schools and charities in Afghanistan. In sum, the theocratic government in Tehran is very active in its efforts to spread Shiite fundamentalism in Afghanistan. Iran's leaders have realized that providing assistance for religious and cultural activities in Afghanistan can be an easy way to spread official propaganda. In fact, there are signs that an increasing number of Afghans are celebrating Shiite religious holidays, particularly in western Afghanistan. This is not the only indication of a Shiite revival in Afghanistan: in western provinces, Shiites now serve as governors. In total, four of Afghanistan's thirty-four provinces, including Herat, are ruled by Shiite governors.[29]

Support of Anti-Government Forces

In contrast to its endeavours in reconstruction, Iran is suspected of being a supporter of anti-government forces in Afghanistan. Since the beginning of 2006, numerous reports indicate that Iran has been increasing its operations in Afghanistan to gain influence with the contending insurgent factions there and to hasten the departure of US troops. According to various reports from western provinces, Iranian officials are secretly active in Afghanistan.

As mentioned earlier, the Iranian government has long-standing relations with many of the local and regional commanders and small-time warlords in western and northern Afghanistan. Although there is no proof that Iran is cooperating with militant forces, such cooperation could conceivably be part of its strategy. Iran is playing all sides in the Afghan conflict. The difference between its past and present Afghanistan policy is that the Iranian leadership now wants to cooperate with and support any group, regardless of its ethnicity, religion, or language. Therefore, Pashtuns and non-Pashtuns are both active in western Afghanistan and are being funded by Iran. In this way, the Iranian government provides financial support for local and regional commanders as well as for armed groups who have been sidelined or feel ignored by the Afghan government. Here Iran can find potential forces to harness and with which to influence the Afghan political sphere. Consequently, Iran keeps its aid money flowing steadily and continues to back its proxies in Afghanistan.[30]

Besides its financial support, Iran is accused by the US government of sending sophisticated weapons and Iranian-produced assault rifles, mortars, and plastic explosives to the so-called Neo-Taliban. The Iranian government has always denied such claims, although it is known that Iran sent weapons shipments to Ismail Khan and provided weapons and training to a junior commander loyal to him. Similarly, Iran has funnelled money and arms to General Dostum, who controls strategic northern areas around Mazar-e-Sharif. However, President Karzai has also insisted that there is no proof the Iranian-marked weapons are being provided by Iran's officials. He has even stressed that "Iran and Afghanistan have never been as friendly as they are today."[31] The only hint to the contrary that Karzai has given was in April 2007 when he said that information suggested "foreign embassies" were involved in the formation of a potentially powerful new opposition party.[32] Nevertheless, the US government insists that Iran is feeding weapons to Taliban insurgents. But why would Iran send readily identifiable Iranian-made weapons to Afghanistan? The Iranian government could sidestep any finger pointing by buying Russian weapons on the black market to arm the rebels. The fact that Iran is not following this strategy could mean either that other forces (foreign or unofficial forces in Iran) are sending Iranian weapons to Afghanistan or that the Iranian government is trying to make a statement with the weapons. It could simply be a message for the targeted rivals telling them of Iran's capabilities and suggesting that Iran could turn western Afghanistan into a nightmare for the Western troops deployed in Afghanistan.[33] Both scenarios are plausible since the Iranian leadership sees the presence of US troops in Afghanistan as a threat to its national security.

Moreover, details have emerged that US intelligence has been providing arms and training to an Iranian Sunni militant group called the

Jundollah, which means "army of God," in camps inside Afghanistan. The Jundollah is based in Pakistan's Baluchistan province and is said to have ties to the terrorist network of al Qaeda. The group is fighting for an independent Baluchistan in Iran's and Pakistan's Baluchistan provinces. In Iran the group has reportedly killed a number of Iranian soldiers. If the Iranians are convinced that the US government is undermining them by supporting the Jundollah in western Afghanistan, then it is very likely that its agents have been activated.

Conclusion

Afghanistan is one example of the Iranian way of increasingly spending its oil income in a variety of countries to realize its self-image as an aspiring regional power. Obviously, the Iranian government is playing a two-pronged game in Afghanistan. On the one hand, it is staging a friendly relations show with Afghanistan and supporting the current Afghan government. On the other hand, its armed forces (mainly the revolutionary guards) and its intelligence are suspected of supporting political opponents of the Afghan government. The aim is in part to put pressure on the United States, which is leading the drive to shut down Iran's nuclear program. Iran is boosting tribal, ethnic, and sectarian religious rivalries in Afghanistan to keep the country weak and to try to ensure US and NATO failure. Activities of the Iranian government in Afghanistan appear to be part of a calculated plan to safeguard its regime and regional aspirations.

After years of good will, Iran's involvement in Afghanistan has changed gradually into a multilayered policy that aims to hasten the withdrawal of US troops, to prevent the Taliban from regaining power, and to keep the Afghan west firmly under Iran's sway. Iranian leaders want to keep western Afghanistan stable and friendly toward them, while making it difficult for outsiders to operate there. Contrary to US accusations concerning Iran's support of anti-government elements, its involvement in Afghanistan is by no means limited to clandestine support of militant forces.[34]

The crucial point of Iran's Afghanistan policy is and will be its relations with the United States. The two countries are bitter opponents on a host of issues of great importance. Iran's pursuit of nuclear technology has recently dominated its relations with the Western powers and has aggravated its relations with the US government. But Tehran and Washington also have strong common interests on a number of key issues. Neither is willing to see the Taliban return or regain its former strength. Both vow to eliminate or to stem Afghanistan's flourishing drug economy, and both favour political and economic stability in Afghanistan. But the claim of US president George W. Bush that Iran was "not a force for good" hindered any form of cooperation with Iran in rebuilding the political and economic infrastructure in Afghanistan. Beyond this, the antagonism between these powers destroyed the potential for fruitful cooperation on a matter of strong mutual interest: the fight against the Sunni terrorist network, al Qaeda.[35] In sum, the war in Afghanistan (as well as the war in Iraq) has strengthened Iran's position in the region. The US-driven agenda for confronting Iran is compromised by the ease with which the latter can operate both openly and secretly in this region.

Notes

1. Victoria Schofield, *Afghan Frontier: Feuding and Fighting in Central Asia.* (London: I.B. Tauris, 2003); Ahmad Rashid, *Taliban: Islam, Oil and the New Great Game in Central Asia* (London: I.B. Tauris, 2001), 196-204.

2. Julien Bousac, "Reconstructing States. Afghanistan: Emirate of Heart," *Le Monde Diplomatique,* December 2003, http://mondediplo.com/2003/12/08Bousac (accessed 18 March 2006); Arne Strand, Astri Suhrke, and Kristian Berg Harpviken, "Afghan Refugees in Iran: From Refugee Emergency to Migration Management" (Policy brief, International Peace Research Institute and Chr. Michelsen Institute, Oslo and Bergen, Norway, 16 June 2004), http://www.cmi.no/pdf/?file=/afghanistan/doc/CMI-PRIO-AfghanRefugeesInIran.pdf.

3. Ishtiaq Ahmad, *Gulbuddin Hekmatyar: An Afghan Trail from Jihad to Terrorism* (Islamabad: Pan-Graphics, 2004), 55-57.

4. Ibid., 57-63.

5. Barnett R. Rubin, "US and Iranian Policy in Afghanistan," in *Iran and Its Neighbours: Diverging Views on a Strategic Region,* ed. Eugene Whitlock (Berlin: German Institute for International and Security Affairs, July 2003), 29-34.

6. David Rohde, "Iran Is Seeking More Influence in Afghanistan," *New York Times,* 27 December 2006.

7. Nicklas Norling, Ingolf Kiesow, Karlis Neretnieks, and Svante E. Cornell, "Southwest Asia," in *Asia 2018–2028: Development Scenarios,* ed. Niklas Swanström (Stockholm: Institute for Security and Development Policy, 2008), 129.

8. Ibid., 129-130.

9. Ariel Cohen, Lisa Curtis, and Owen Graham, "The Proposed Iran Pakistan India Gas Pipeline: An Unacceptable Risk to Regional Security," Backgrounder 2139 (Heritage Foundation, Washington, 2008).

10. Shiv Kumar Vermer, "Energy Geopolitics and Iran-Pakistan-India Gas Pipeline," *Energy Policy* 35 (2008): 3280-301.

11. Norling et al., "Southwest Asia," 129-130.

12. Rohde, "Iran Is Seeking More Influence."

13. Svante Cornell, "Regional Politics in Central Asia: The Changing Roles of Iran, Turkey, Pakistan and China," in *India and Central Asia: Building Linkages*

in an Age of Turbulence, ed. Indranil Banerjee (Middlesex: Brunel Academic Publishers, 2004).

14. Cornell, "Regional Politics"; Robert Lowe and Claire Spencer, *Iran, Its Neighbours and the Regional Crises: A Middle East Programme Report* (London: Royal Institute of International Affairs, 2006).

15. Lowe and Spencer, *Iran, Its Neighbours and the Regional Crises*.

16. Rohde, "Iran Is Seeking More Influence."

17. Abbas Maleki, "Iran," in *The New Silk Roads: Transport and Trade in Greater Central Asia*, ed. Frederick Starr (Uppsala: Central Asia-Caucasus Institute and Silk Road Studies Program, 2007), 167-92.

18. Ibid.

19. Ibid.

20. Guli Yuldasheva, "Geopolitics of Central Asia in the Context of the Iranian Factor," *Caucasian Review of International Affairs* 2, no. 3 (Summer 2008), http://cria-online.org/Journal/4/GEOPOLITICS_OF_CENTRAL_ASIA_IN_THE_CONTEXT_OF_THE_IRANIAN_FACTOR_IN_INTERNATIONAL_POLITICS_done.pdf.

21. Rohde, "Iran Is Seeking More Influence."

22. United Nations Office on Drugs and Crime, *Afghanistan: Counter Narcotics Law Enforcement*, Update No. 6 (March 2007), http://www.unodc.org/pdf/afg/updates/cnle_update_06.pdf; Integrated Regional Information Networks, March 22, 2004; Bill Samii, "Drug Control Gets New Emphasis as Crack Gains Popularity," *Radio Free Europe/Radio Liberty*, 6 April 2006.

23. *Eurasianet*, 8 July 2006.

24. Islamic Republic News Agency, 29 August 2008.

25. Ibid.

26. Rohde, "Iran Is Seeking More Influence."

27. Waheedullah Massoud, "Iran 'Baring Its Teeth' in Afghanistan, Officials Say," *AFP*, 1 July 2007.

28. Rohde, "Iran Is Seeking More Influence"; Massoud, "Iran 'Baring Its Teeth.'"

29. Rohde, "Iran Is Seeking More Influence."

30. Muhammad Tahir, "Iranian Involvement in Afghanistan," *Journal of Turkish Weekly*, 7 February 2007.

31. Mark Mazzetti, "Arms Flow from Iran into Afghanistan, US Defense Secretary Says," *International Herald Tribune*, 4 June 2007.

32. Massoud, "Iran 'Baring Its Teeth.'"

33. Ibid.

34. Rohde, "Iran Is Seeking More Influence"; Tahir, "Iranian Involvement in Afghanistan."

35. Rubin, "US and Iranian Policy in Afghanistan," 34.

Chapter 9

The International Commitment in Afghanistan: Failure or Strategy Change? A Strategic Assessment

Hans-Georg Ehrhart and Roland Kaestner

Introduction

After the terrorist attacks of 11 September 2001, al Qaeda and the Taliban regime were driven from Afghanistan by an international "coalition of the willing," Operation Enduring Freedom, led by the United States. Germany has played a prominent role from the very beginning. The peace and reconstruction process in Afghanistan—the Bonn Process—was initiated on the Petersberg near Bonn. There the representatives of the victorious Afghan factions of the Northern Alliance, the United Nations, the United States, and other international players decided to develop Afghanistan into a democracy based on a market economy.[1] The International Security Assistance Force (ISAF) was to contribute to a safe and secure environment and support the buildup of Afghan security forces.

Four years later, in 2006, the Bonn Process was replaced by the Afghanistan Compact. This agreement, designed to be pursued until the end of 2010, sets forth a complex strategy that comprises three pillars: security, governance, and development. It provides the basis for the temporary national development plan of the Afghan government, which was adopted in the same year. Despite this comprehensive strategy, since 2005 the situation has deteriorated continuously. Developments on the ground in Afghanistan and the actions of the international community are increasingly diverging. Accordingly, a review of both the situation and the strategy is urgently required, since the vision for Afghanistan adopted at the Bucharest NATO Summit in April 2008 basically adheres to the old situation assessment and the old strategic concept.[2]

The following assessment concentrates on the current social, economic, and political conditions in Afghanistan. This is not to deny the importance of regional factors influencing the situation. Resolution of the conflict is, however, primarily dependent on internal developments in Afghanistan. Our conclusion is that the current situation and mid- and long-term trends in Afghanistan necessitate a comprehensive change of strategy.

Situation

Security

The security situation has deteriorated since 2005. The number of security events has increased from year to year, from about 3,100 in 2005 to 8,000 in 2006. According to official US information, the number of incidents rose again by about 30 percent in 2007.[3] What has increased in particular is the number of suicide attacks—which until recently had been an unknown phenomenon in Afghanistan. Whereas in 2005 only 17 suicide attacks were committed, there were 123 in 2006 and 131 in 2007. The so-called enemy elements or neo-Taliban—which may include Islamist or nationalist Pashtuns, drug dealers, local commanders, warlords, al Qaeda terrorists, foreign jihadists, religious fundamentalists, anti-centralists, and autonomous forces—are controlling or infiltrating more and more regions. According to Senlis Council estimates, these groups control 54 percent of Afghan territory and are partially present in another 38 percent.[4] According to other sources, "only" one-third of the country should be considered a high-risk zone.[5] The increasing numbers of air strikes by the ISAF and Operation Enduring Freedom (OEF), which exceed by far the corresponding number in Iraq, as well as the increasing numbers of Western soldiers killed in action, reflect the growing influence of neo-Taliban forces.[6]

The neo-Taliban is a fluid, continuously changing variable. The dynamic nature of the neo-Taliban is consistent with the tradition of Afghans pursuing their own interests in changing coalitions, with the goal of restricting the power of the government in Kabul and preserving local claims to power. Conrad Schetter points out that to Afghans the word *Taliban* no longer designates a group of individuals but a lifestyle.[7] The political attitude in the anti-government regions is characterized by anti-centralist, anti-modern, and anti-Western views and by a combination of local and militant-Islamic concepts. Apart from that, the struggle between the claim to autonomy of the local players and the claim to power of the state pervades the entire process of state development in Afghanistan. Up to now, any attempt to establish a centralist state has resulted in war.

The buildup of the Afghan security forces, the aim of which according to the Afghanistan Compact is to protect the citizens' security, is lagging far behind schedule. The strengthening of the Afghan National Army (ANA) has been relatively successful—although with a current strength of 30,000 to 33,000 operational soldiers, it presumably will not reach the 2010 target of 80,000 operational troops.[8] From the beginning, the ANA has been built up as a US auxiliary force rather than as the army of the Afghan state with the capacity to fight independently.[9] The buildup of the Afghan National Police (ANP), by contrast, has to be considered a failure. Data from the Ministry of the Interior, which is presumed to be one of the most corrupt institutions in the country and urgently in need of reform, should be handled with appropriate skepticism. The number of officially financed posts—50,000 to 70,000 men, depending on the source—presumably differs considerably from the actual number of police officers. Only about 50 percent of the officially reported ANP personnel are presumed to exist, while the salaries for the phantom police officers end up in the pockets of corrupt officials.[10] What makes matters worse is that most of the officers are illiterate, and the twenty-five nations involved in their training do not have a coordinated training concept. More and more reports suggest that the police themselves are turning into a security problem.[11] Accordingly, achieving the goal of 82,000 police officers by the end of 2010 is doubtful both in quantitative and in qualitative terms. Against this background, it is not surprising that by now both the NATO-led ISAF, which originally was to perform stabilization tasks, and the US-led OEF, which initially focused on anti-terror warfare, are involved to an increasing extent in counter-insurgency operations, with assessments of the chances of winning the war varying considerably. What is undisputed, however, is that the continued maintenance of that military commitment involves an increasingly higher price—in personnel, and in financial and ethical terms.[12]

Governance

The second reform area includes governance, rule of law, and human rights. Motivated by initial successes in the establishment of government structures (elections, parliament, constitution), the Afghanistan Compact set overly ambitious targets. Expectations regarding rapid democratization proved to be exaggerated, as was initial progress in the reform of government institutions, not least because the possibilities for "social engineering" in a strongly traditional society were misjudged.[13] Another reason for this is the state-building paradox: the very necessary aid and support provided by the international community reinforces the dependency of Afghanistan and makes it a client state.[14] Progress is judged only by bureaucratic standards,[15] and attempts to reach these governance objectives are blocked in Kabul by a patronage system that favours corruption.[16] Efforts to build subnational governance structures are hampered by a lack of commitment, the absence of coordination, and a fixation on short-term security imperatives.[17] The rapidly deteriorating reputation of President Karzai is a result of these developments, to which the international community of donors has contributed considerably with its unrealistic goals and uncoordinated approach. Afghanistan is one of the most corrupt countries in the world. The international presence has not changed that situation—the ample flow of money from donor nations has perhaps even aggravated it. In the eyes of the Afghan people, the current government is more corrupt than it was in the era of the Taliban, the mujahidin, or the communists.[18]

Development

According to the Afghanistan Compact, Afghanistan is to develop into a free market-oriented economy driven by the private sector. In a country that by many economic measures is at the bottom—where there is no working public sector and no legal security—this liberal economic approach favours only a few privileged individuals who are able to use the new system to their benefit. The living conditions of most Afghans have deteriorated. Particularly in the Pashtun regions, most of the development aid does not reach its destination, and what is constructed there is quickly destroyed again by the insurgents.[19] Additionally, other processes stimulated by the international presence, such as the "brain drain," are problematic in development-policy terms. Since, for instance, a driver employed at a non-governmental organization (NGO) earns several times the salary of an Afghan university professor, many urgently needed Afghan experts are employed in different areas and are therefore not available to work for the development of their country. Worth underlining here is the immense gap between the wealth of representatives of the international community and that of ordinary Afghan citizens; this gap, like the efforts to establish an Afghan civil society on a Western model, results in frustration.[20] Granted, the annual per capita income has increased from US$182 (in 2002–03) to US$344 in 2006–07;[21] even so, Afghans must live on less than one US dollar per day. Afghanistan remains one of the poorest and least developed countries in the world.

While there is progress to be noted in the education sector, it is marginal when compared with the rapid population growth, the high unemployment rate, and the continuing extremely high illiteracy rate. The most flourishing—and at the same time the most problematic—economic sector is the drug trade. Here, the sustained high growth rates have extremely negative implications for the functioning of government (corruption), the security of the population (violent crime), and the conflict with the neo-Taliban (funding of the war).

Development Factors

Population

Despite decades of war, the Afghan population has grown from 8.1 million in 1950 to 30 million people in 2007. The United Nations predicts that the population will reach about 60.1 million by 2030.[22] Although the population of Kabul is growing rapidly, more than 75 percent of Afghans live in the countryside, and the UN anticipates that more than 65 percent will still live in rural areas in 2030. About 45 percent of the population are children under the age of fourteen, making Afghan society one of the youngest in the world—with an upward trend.[23] Combined with unemployment and poverty, this "youth bulge" is causing considerable stress for the emergent political structures. It will also overtax the tribal structures and augurs a future full of conflict.

Resources

Afghanistan has few resources, most of which are in the hands of regional warlords and other anti-government players. Only 10 percent of the population has access to electricity, predominantly in urban centres. Public goods such as water, health, education, and administration are available to only a limited number of people. In light of the population growth, this situation is likely to worsen. According to estimates by the United Nations Office on Drugs and Crime, even the resource industry of drug production "benefits" only about 15 percent of the population, with the revenues controlled by a few powerful players.[24] Yet almost all parties involved fund their private armies using profits generated by the drug trade.

Culture

The country is characterized by considerable ethnic and linguistic diversity.[25] The Pashtuns are the largest ethnic group (roughly 42 percent), whose claim to pan-Afghan leadership is not shared by the other groups, a result of the civil war conflict with the Northern Alliance which continued until the end of the Taliban rule. Illiteracy among the adult population is more than 70 percent; among women, it is estimated to be in the range of 90 percent.[26] Given population growth and the strongly patriarchal tribal culture, the rate of women's literacy presumably will change only marginally over the next few decades. What is remarkable is that the domestic conflict in Afghanistan that broke out in 1976 (and escalated in 1979 with the invasion of Soviet forces) was sparked by the controversy with the then communist central government over the issue of mandatory school attendance for girls in the countryside.

Society

There is no modern Afghan society; at best, there are small islands of modernity in some cities. The most reliable structures are the family, the tribe, the clan, and the local community. However, these structures demand the submission of the individual to the community, which exercises a distinct social control and represents a considerable obstacle to social change. This social code is expressed in the *pashtunwali*, an informal canon of cultural rules and standards that are passed on by the family, the clan, and the tribe. The *pashtunwali* characterizes the self-concept of the Pashtuns—and, in a modified form, that of other ethnic groups—with the concepts of honour, dignity, pride, combat, and manliness. This codex provides for behavioural confidence and establishes the responsibility of the family and clan for the social security of the individual; it also shapes Afghans' behaviour toward foreigners.[27] Any attempt to replace it even partially by written law—particularly laws originating from the Western world—will not only result in considerable insecurity but will also be viewed by some elites as an attack on their power and, consequently, on their honour and dignity. This canon of values is "an uncompromising social code so profoundly at odds with Western mores that its application constantly brings one up with a jolt."[28] As long as social change is not initiated by the people themselves, the response will be a violent one. However, without social change, a modern society based on the division of labour—capable of meeting the needs of a growing number of people—is inconceivable.

Economy

Afghan society is nomadic and agrarian. As an extremely poor, landlocked country, Afghanistan depends to a great extent on foreign aid and foreign trade. About 80 percent of the people work in the agricultural sector. There is a very small industrial sector, which relies on limited quantities of gas, coal, and copper as well as on the small-scale production of textiles, furniture, cement, fertilizer, shoes, soap, and carpets. The gross domestic product (GDP) grew by more than 7 percent in 2007, but this growth has to be weighed against the background of the extremely low initial level. The official unemployment rate is 40 percent.[29] Unofficially, it is said to be approximately 70 percent in the south and up to 90 percent in the east.[30] Only two economic sectors have seen continuous growth: the drug trade and transport. The former makes up one-third of the national economy.[31] Opium production grew from 3,400 tons in 2002 to 8,200 tons in 2007, while the cultivation area in the same period increased from 74,000 to more than 200,000 hectares.[32] The other prosperous sector is dominated by the transport mafia, part of a worldwide system of organized crime that moves contraband goods from, to, and through Afghanistan.[33] Both sectors benefit from a tribal society that now has global connections.[34] This global network—the result of the emigration since the 1980s of several million Pashtuns fleeing war and poverty—spans South Asia through the Middle East to Central Asia and plays a central role in the logistic support of Pashtuns in Afghanistan.

Given the predicted growth of the population, the per capita GDP can be expected to decline from less than US$400 today—in a country already considered one of the poorest in the world. From 2002 to 2003, the number of Afghans living below the poverty line increased from 23 to 53 percent. According to information provided by the Minister of the Economy, more than 90 percent of all goods in the Afghan market are imported.[35] As the population increases, this undeveloped agrarian society will be less and less able to provide a living for the Afghan people.

Politics

In the *Failed State Index 2007*, Afghanistan ranks in the eighth-lowest position.[36] Freedom House views the country as "semi-free" and sees a downward trend in the domain of political and civil rights and liberties.[37] Afghanistan is a rents-based state that lives on nepotism and subsidies.[38] The Afghan government under President Karzai is considered incompetent, corrupt, and weak, since it has to accept people in high positions who are not primarily loyal to the government and the country. Moreover, 80 percent of the government budget is funded by the international community.[39] The donor countries justify retaining control over the relief funds in the domain of development policy by referring to extensive corruption; however, fraud, mismanagement, and shoddy work are also widespread among the international players.[40] The central state, which is promoted from outside, competes with the existing structures of a tribal society. On the one hand, the individual components of tribal society are autonomous and local in character; on the other, they are connected with the globalized world through labour migration. Thus, globalization strengthens the old local orders rather than the new state structures favoured by the international community.

Assessment

The Political Objective

In the long run, the goal stipulated in the Afghanistan Compact to establish a democratic Afghan government that rules the entire country is likely to be perceived by most Afghan social and political forces as a threat to their autonomy and traditional order—all the more so since the Karzai government is widely considered to be a puppet government appointed by Washington. Within Afghanistan, critics point to the extensive external funding of the government budget, to the presence of foreign troops, and to the government's reliance on a narrow base of "liberals" influenced by the West. The parliament, on the other hand, has become "the stronghold of dissent, Afghan style, with a kaleidoscope of nationalist, ethnic, tribal and gender-based interests that were denied space to raise questions about sovereignty."[41] The fact that the government has appointed as ministers many of those whom the Afghan population perceive as war criminals weakens it further; after all, the loyalty of those ministers has simply been bought. The objective of a central government exercising control over the rural periphery will provoke sustained resistance in Afghanistan as long as the Afghans are considered to be mere recipients of a model that is alien to them. In the long run, it is possible that other political structures will develop from the bottom up, as it were, in this tribal society. Nevertheless, the tribal structures are the most viable ones in the country today. They should be used in the political construction of Afghanistan, and the people should be granted more time for development. Given the social and economic development trends, however, this process will not proceed without conflicts.

Stability and Security

The international community has regressed from the goal of establishing security as the prerequisite for stability and development. Over the past few years, as the extension of the ISAF from Kabul across the whole country has taken place, the violent activities of the Afghan insurgency movement have also increased. The term *neo-Taliban* disguises the real causes of this increasing level of violence: the anti-Western, anti-modern, and anti-centralist attitudes of many Afghan players. Moreover, political stability and security are being undermined by the increased drug production.[42] That the disarmament of tribal militias, civil-war armies, private armies, and other players has failed indicates that—in addition to the economy of violence and the warrior culture—the tribes do not have confidence in the security institutions of the government in Kabul. Therefore, some thought should be given to whether and how security might be better ensured by regional and local actors and institutions.

Economy and Social Development

The Afghanistan Compact's goal of sustainable growth to reduce hunger, poverty, and unemployment is still a distant prospect. International assistance keeps the Karzai administration alive, but the investments made so far have not reached the majority of the population. Except for the criminal sector, economic activities tend to be declining. Successes have been achieved in education, but these improvements have no impact in the short term and are fiercely resisted by militant Islamic forces.[43] The potential for violence among the younger generation is likely to increase because of continuing high unemployment, considerable poverty, and unpromising outlook for the future. The intention to distribute massive sums of relief funds through the dysfunctional machinery of the government in Kabul is bound to feed corruption.[44] Accordingly, development aid will have to be channelled in a more intensive and coordinated way to local structures, especially those below the district level. At the same time, it should be kept in mind that not all states "are culturally capable and/or willing to accept the values of liberal market economics," especially those societies "that are essentially 'honour-based.'"[45]

Overall Assessment

Obviously, the strategic approach of the international community is failing to cope with the real situation in Afghanistan. Moreover, to a considerable extent the resistance on the ground can be attributed to this very strategy.[46] Therefore, it would seem useful to conduct a thorough analysis of the social, economic, and political conditions in Afghanistan before proceeding to correct or adjust the strategic objectives of the international community. There are many good reasons to give the Afghan people more autonomy (*Afghan face*) and more time (*Afghan pace*) in the pursuit of their development.

Options

Given the above analysis, three options for action have been identified. The first option is a quick termination of the military commitment while continuing to provide development policy support to Afghanistan on a long-term basis. In this scenario, the international community would gradually reduce its military activities to zero by 2010 and put the responsibility for the country's security policy in the hands of the Afghan government. At the same time, it would extend its commitment to the civilian objectives of the Afghanistan Compact from 2010, when the agreement is set to expire, to 2020.

The second option is to reinforce the approach pursued thus far and commit to it for the long term. This approach adheres to the mantra that the stabilization of the country in terms of security and development policy is a long-term project that requires a sustained international commitment in all three fields of action—security, governance, and development. Given the fact that the neo-Taliban have regained strength and that Afghan capabilities remain undeveloped, active military support would continue to be provided for at least another ten years—and development support for considerably longer.

The third option is a comprehensive change of strategy, which has five dimensions:

- *More modest goals:* The international community refrains from seeking to change Afghanistan into a model liberal democracy. The visionary concepts embodied in the Afghanistan Compact are replaced by more realistic and, thus, more attainable goals. It is accepted that, given Afghanistan's history and current state of development, and the limited resources and capabilities of the international donors, only pragmatic and achievable goals—not visionary ones—can be sought.
- *Afghanization of security:* Since the counter-insurgency in Afghanistan cannot be defeated by military means in the medium run, and victory will come in the long run—if at all—only at an unacceptable price, the international community will reduce its combat operations and terminate them within three to five years. The Afghan National Army and the Afghan National Police will then be solely responsible for the security of the country. At the same time, the international community will invest more in the reform of the security sector, above all in the police and in the local, regional, and national administrations managing these forces. Setting a date for the withdrawal of the majority of the NATO troops will communicate a clearly defined transition period to the sovereign government and will strengthen its responsibility for achieving viable arrangements at the local level. Since reform of the security sector is a long-term process, the international community will continue to support Afghanistan in this domain.[47]
- *Decentralized governance:* The attempt to establish central government structures, which has been pursued thus far, will be complemented by the sustained promotion of local structures. The historical-cultural fact that centralization, along with the entire pacification and reconstruction strategy, has never prevailed in Afghanistan and that local players consider it a threat is taken into account. The international community, recognizing that in tribal societies the primary loyalty of the people does not belong to the state, will reinforce decentralized governance. It is accepted that these are fluid power arrangements that serve primarily local interests whose loyalty to the central government remains relatively weak.
- *Adapted development strategy:* The goal of establishing a liberal market economy is qualified, and the development policy role of the state is promoted at all levels. Local players are strengthened, and the focus is put on local needs. Alternative production and marketing opportunities are offered in the fight against drugs. Infrastructure, education, and training are promoted, particularly in rural areas.

- *Regional integration:* The Afghanistan conflict can be resolved only in a regional context.[48] Consequently, neighbouring states—notably Pakistan and Iran—and other strategically relevant actors such as India and Russia must be involved in managing the conflict. A regional conference on security, economic cooperation, and development could be the prelude to a political process that would result in a basic agreement covering all domains, with action plans and subsequent review conferences. Core elements of this treaty would be a renunciation of force and the international guarantee of Afghanistan's permanent neutrality.

Conclusion

The first option should be rejected, because a military withdrawal of the international community at short notice would be premature and unacceptable to most NATO partners. In addition, a continuation of the development policy alone would not be sustainable. The second option should also be rejected, because long-term military involvement would impede the development of an essential aspect of Afghan sovereignty and self-reliance: Afghan ownership. At present, a significant reinforcement of the military operation is impossible due to costs and political considerations, and sustaining existing levels would be equally difficult to fund or to justify politically at home. Accordingly, a comprehensive change of strategy is required that pays heed to five imperatives: more modest goals, Afghanization of security, decentralized government structures, development oriented toward local needs, and regional integration of the Afghanistan conflict.

Notes

1. *Agreement on Provisional Arrangements in Afghanistan Pending the Re-Establishment of Permanent Government Institutions* (Bonn Agreement; Bonn, 5 December 2001), http://www.mfa.gov.af/Documents/ImportantDoc/The%20Bonn%20Agreement.pdf.
2. NATO, *ISAF's Strategic Vision. Declaration by the Heads of State and Government of the Nations Contributing to the UN-Mandated NATO-Led International Security Assistance Force (ISAF) in Afghanistan* (2008), http://www.nato.int/docu/comm/2008/0804-bucharest/index.html (accessed 29 April 2008).
3. Anthony H. Cordesman, "The Struggle for 'Pashtunistan': The Afghan-Pakistan War" (Center for Strategic and International Studies, Washington, October 2007), http://www.csis.org/media/csis/pubs/101607_pashtunistan.pdf
4. Senlis Afghanistan, *Stumbling into Chaos: Afghanistan on the Brink* (London: Senlis Afghanistan, 2007), 28.

5. Anthony H. Cordesman, "The Struggle for 'Pashtunistan': Threat Developments" (Center for Strategic and International Studies, 1 February 2008), 32, http://www.csis.org/media/csis/pubs/080201_afghanthreat.pdf.
6. Ibid., 22, 25.
7. Conrad Schetter, "Talibanistan – Der Anti-Staat," *Internationales Asienforum* 38, no. 3/4, (2007): 233-57.
8. Citha Maass, "Assessing the Afghanistan Compact," chapter 2 in this volume.
9. Antonio Giustozzi, "Auxiliary Force or National Army? Afghanistan's ANA and the Counter-Insurgency Effort," *Small Wars and Insurgencies* 18, no. 1 (March 2007): 45-67.
10. Andrew Wilder, "Cops or Robbers? The Struggle to Reform the Afghan National Police," *Afghanistan Research and Evaluation Unit Synthesis Paper Series* (July 2007), 7, www.areu.org.af/index.php?option=com_content&task=view&id=39&Itemid=.
11. Wilder, "Cops or Robbers?", International Crisis Group, "Reforming Afghanistan's Police," *Asia Report* No. 138 (30 August 2007), http://www.crisisgroup.org/home/index.cfm?id=5052&l=1; Sayed Yaqub Ibrahimi, "Afghan Police: Part of the Problem" (Institute for War and Peace Reporting, 6 June 2006), http://www.rawa.org/police-3.htm.
12. Martin Van Creveld, *On Future War* (London: Brassey's, 1991).
13. Oliver Roy, "Afghanistan: la difficile reconstruction d'un Etat," *Cahier de Chaillot* 73, Paris, December 2004.
14. Hamish Nixon, "Aiding the State? International Assistance and the Statebuilding Paradox in Afghanistan," *Afghanistan Research and Evaluation Unit Briefing Paper Series* (April 2007), www.areu.org.af/index.php?option=com_content&task=view&id=39&Itemid=73.
15. Maass, chapter 2, this volume.
16. Ute Koczy and Barbara Unmüßig, "Illusionen und Realitäten: Der steinige Weg des (entwicklungs-)politischen Aufbaus," *Zeitschrift für Afghanistankunde* 2 (April 2008): 22-55.
17. Nixon, "Aiding the State?"
18. Human Rights Watch, Open letter from Human Rights Watch to the International Afghanistan Support Conference (12 June 2008), http://hrw.org/english/docs/2008/06/10/afghan19086.htm.
19. Thomas H. Johnson, "On the Edge of the Big Muddy: The Taliban Resurgence in Afghanistan," *China and Eurasia Forum Quarterly* 5, no. 2 (2007): 122, 127.
20. Roy, "Afghanistan: la difficile reconstruction," 57-58.
21. Center for Policy and Human Development, "Afghanistan Human Development Report, Bridging Modernity and Tradition, Rule of Law and the Search for Justice" (Kabul, 2007), http://hdr.undp.org/en/reports/nationalreports/asiathepacific/afghanistan/nhdr2007.pdf.
22. United Nations Development Program, *Afghanistan Annual Report 2006* (Kabul: UNDP, 2006).

23. Central Intelligence Agency (CIA), *The World Factbook 2007* (Washington: CIA, 2007).

24. United Nations Office on Drugs and Crime (UNODC), *2008 World Drug Report* (Vienna, 2008), http://www.unodc.org/documents/wdr/WDR_2008/WDR_2008_eng_web.pdf.

25. Cordesman, "Threat Developments," 42.

26. United Nations Development Program, *Afghanistan National Human Development Report 2004 – Security with a Human Face* (Islamabad: UNDP, 2004): 301-2; ilo.org/public/english/region/asro/bangkok /skills-ap/skills/afghanistan_literacy.htm; ilo.org/public/english/region/asro/bangkok/skills-ap/skills/afghanistan_demography.htm.

27. Bernt Glatzer, "Zum Pashtunwali als ethnischem Selbstportrait," in *Subjekte und Systeme: Soziologische und anthropologische Annäherungen. Festschrift für Christian Sigraist zum 65 Geburtstag*, ed. Günter Best and Reinhart Kößler (Frankfurt: IKO-Verlag, 2000), 93-102; Thomas Barfield, Neamat Nojumi, and J. Alexander Thier, *The Clash of Two Goods: State and Non-State Dispute Resolution in Afghanistan* (New York: US Institute of Peace, 2006).

28. Charles Allen, *Soldier Sahibs 1* (New York: Carrol and Graf Publishers, 2000), 119, quoted in Johnson, "On the Edge of the Big Muddy," 121.

29 CIA, *World Factbook 2008*, https://www.cia.gov/library/publications/the-world-factbook/geos/af.html.

30. Martin Baraki, "Die Zerstörung Afghanistans," *Zeit-Fragen*, 13 August 2007, http://www.antikriegsforum-heidelberg.de/afghan/hintergrund/zerstoerung_afghanistans_baraki.html.

31. Cordesman, "Threat Developments," 55.

32. UNODC, *2008 World Drug Report*.

33. Ahmed Rashid, Taliban: Militant Islam, *Oil and Fundamentalism in Central Asia* (New Haven: Yale University Press, 2008); William Maley, ed., *Fundamentalism Reborn? Afghanistan and the Taliban* (London: Hurst, 1998).

34. Schetter, "Talibanistan – Der Anti-Staat."

35. Baraki, "Die Zerstörung Afghanistans."

36. Foreign Policy, *The Failed States Index 2007*, (n.d.), http://www.foreignpolicy.com/story/cms.php?story_id=3865&page=7.

37. Freedom House, *Freedom in the World 2008 Survey Release*, http://www.freedomhouse.org/template.cfm?page=395.

38 Florian Kühn, "Supporting the State, Depleting the State. Estranged State-Society Relations in Afghanistan," chapter 4 in this volume.

39. Matt Waldman, *Aid Effectiveness in Afghanistan*, Advocacy Series (Kabul: Agency Coordinating Body for Afghan Relief, March 2008), http://www.acbar.org.

40 Fariba Nawa, *Afghanistan, Inc., A Corpwatch Investigative Report* (Oakland, CA, n.d.), http://s3.amazonaws.com/corpwatch.org/downloads/AfghanistanINCfinalsmall.pdf.

41. Shahrbanou Tadibakhsh and Michael Schoiswohl, "Playing with Fire? The International Community's Democratization Experiment in Afghanistan," *International Peacekeeping* 15, no, 2 (2008): 252-67.
42. Roy, "Afghanistan: la difficile reconstruction."
43 Human Rights Watch, Open letter.
44. Nawa, "Afghanistan, Inc."
45. Stephen Pullinger, "European Security in 2020: Threats, Challenges and Responses," *European Security Review* 37 (2008): 12.
46. Tadibakhsh and Schoiswohl, "Playing with Fire," 263.
47. Hans-Georg Ehrhart and Albrecht Schnabel, "Post-Conflict Societies and the Military: Recommendations for Security Sector Reform," in *Security Sector Reform and Post-Conflict Peace Building,* ed. Albrecht Schnabel and Hans-Georg Ehrhart (Tokyo: United Nations University Press, 2005), 315-22.
48. Christian Wagner, "Pakistan's Afghanistan Policy in the Shadow of India," chapter 7 in this volume.

Part II

Chapter 10

No Exit: Canada and the "War without End" in Afghanistan

Kim Richard Nossal

Introduction

The debates that Canadians have had on the Afghanistan mission have always been undergirded by an assumption that it was possible—and indeed for many in the debate, desirable—to be able to specify a finite end date to the Canadian military contribution to the international coalition working to ensure Afghan security and development. The Canadian parliament has voted on the issue on three occasions—in May 2006, in April 2007, and in March 2008—deciding in each case to continue the military mission. In the 2008 vote, the House of Commons passed a compromise motion that had been negotiated by the Conservative government of Stephen Harper and the opposition Liberals. This motion extended the mission from 2009 until December 2011, a date that was widely interpreted as an end date for the Canadian military mission, and reported as such: The motion, CBC-TV reported, "also includes a firm pullout date, calling for Canadian troops to leave Afghanistan by December 2011."[1] Certainly this is how it was construed by elected politicians: as Peter MacKay, the minister of national defence, put it: "Liberals and Conservatives agree that the mission should wrap up in 2011. Liberals and Conservatives agree that we must focus our efforts on training, development and reconstruction."[2]

But on its face, a unilateral Canadian withdrawal from Afghanistan seems completely implausible. If security conditions in Afghanistan do not improve to the point that the international coalition and the govern-ment of Afghanistan are prepared to declare the mission a success, the Canadian government would have huge difficulty justifying "wrapping up" the mission by withdrawing the Canadian Armed Forces, given the likely impact on the Afghan people of a unilateral withdrawal. More-over, if the international coalition of which Canada is a part remains in Afghanistan in 2011, a unilateral withdrawal would bring with it huge political costs. Finally, given the large investment, in blood and treasure, that Canada has made in Afghanistan, it seems implausible that the government in Ottawa would be willing or able to justify walking away if the mission had not yet succeeded.

If elected politicians were willing to leave the impression that an end date to Canada's military mission had been agreed to in March 2008, two *unelected* politicians—leading members of the Senate Standing Commit-tee on National Security and Defence—greeted the March 2008 decision with skepticism that a unilateral Canadian withdrawal would ever take place in 2011. In June 2008, the chair of the committee, Liberal senator Colin Kenny, claimed publicly, "I don't think there's any chance of be-ing out of there in three years. It's a longer project and as people come to grips with that . . . they will realize it." The committee's vice-chair, Michael Meighen, a Conservative, agreed: "I don't think the troops will be out of there in 2011."[3]

To be sure, neither senator articulated precisely *why* Canada would remain in Afghanistan beyond 2011, or *how* people would "come to grips" with the fact that the Afghanistan mission was a longer-term project. But Kenny's and Meighen's skepticism and the surface implausibility of any unilateral withdrawal option suggest that the decision taken by the House of Commons on 13 March 2008 needs to be re-examined. By looking at the withdrawal debates in Canada, and the logics—and il-logics—of those debates, I conclude that the decision of March 2008 was not the decision to withdraw that was widely painted by the opposition parties—including the Liberal Party, which voted for it—and the media, but instead was a motion permitting the Canadian government to remain militarily committed to Afghanistan.

The Withdrawal Debates, 2006–2008

When Canadian governments committed armed forces to different mis-sions in Afghanistan after 2001—to the initial American-led Operation Enduring Freedom (OEF) in 2001–2002, to the NATO-led International Security Assistance Force (ISAF) in Kabul from 2003 to 2005, and then to Kandahar in 2005 to head the Provincial Reconstruction Team (PRT) in that province[4]—the deployments were always for limited periods. And on the three occasions when members of parliament (MPs) formally debated whether to extend or to terminate the Canadian contribution to the Afghanistan mission, their debates—and the wider debates within the political community—were always framed by established withdrawal dates.

In May 2006, the debate was over whether Canada should extend the mission from the original end date of February 2007 established by the Liberal government of Paul Martin in 2005. The Conservative government of Stephen Harper, which took office in February 2006, just as the Kandahar deployment was occurring, sought to extend the mission to February 2009. The government narrowly won the vote to extend the mission by 149–145.[5] In April 2007, the Liberals put an opposition motion that called on the government "to confirm that Canada's existing military deployment in Afghanistan will continue until February 2009, at which time Canadian combat operations in Southern Afghanistan will conclude." On 24 April, that motion was defeated 134–150.[6] In March 2008, the government sought to extend the mission again—to 2011, to coincide with the five-year term of the 2006 Afghanistan Compact between the government of Afghanistan and the international community, which established benchmarks for the end of 2010.[7] In that case, the House of Commons adopted a resolution by a vote of 197–77 committing Canada to the mission in Kandahar for a further two years, but with a "firm" pull-out date of December 2011.[8]

There can be little doubt that the debates among Canadians over how long the government should commit Canadian forces to Afghanistan were genuine, in the sense that there were deep fissures within the country over the appropriateness of extending the mission, first to 2009 and then to 2011. This division was reflected not only in public opinion[9] but also among the four parties in the House of Commons—the Conservative Party of Canada, the Liberal Party, the Bloc Québécois, and the New Democratic Party (NDP). And in the Liberal Party, there were marked divisions between those who wanted Canadian forces brought home sooner rather than later and those who were in favour of the mission.

To be sure, all four parties sought to position themselves on the Afghanistan issue with considerable care, since the 39th Parliament elected in January 2006 produced a minority Conservative government. In particular, between 2006 and 2008 none of the political parties in the House of Commons—government or opposition—wanted to precipitate an election, particularly not over an issue like Afghanistan. In May 2006, the Liberals were in the middle of a process of selecting a leader to replace Paul Martin, who had resigned after his Liberal government had been defeated in the January 2006 elections. And public opinion polls showed that both the Bloc and the NDP would have substantially fewer seats in an election; at the same time, however, the polls also showed that the Conservatives would not gain a majority.[10] The Bloc and the NDP opposed an extension, betting that the Liberals, who had been in government when Canadian forces were committed to the mission, would do what was necessary to avoid an election. The Liberals did not disappoint: the caucus was deeply divided on the Afghanistan mission, with many MPs agreeing with the Bloc and the NDP that there should be no extension. However, thirty Liberal MPs, including the interim leader, Bill Graham, and Michael Ignatieff, who was a candidate for the Liberal leadership, joined with the Conservatives to produce a slim 149–145 win. (The eventual winner of the Liberal leadership race, Stéphane Dion, voted against the extension.)

By early 2007, party support numbers had hardly changed at all,[11] continuing to give all of the parties a powerful reason to avoid precipitating an election. Thus when the Liberals put an opposition motion in April 2007 that essentially called on the government to terminate the mission as of February 2009, the smaller opposition parties played a careful game of aligning themselves so that the government would be sustained (even though the motion was not one of confidence): the Bloc voted with the Liberal opposition, while the NDP voted with the governing Conservatives, embracing the pretzel logic that they had to vote against any motion that would terminate the mission in February 2009 because they were in favour of bringing the troops home immediately![12]

Following the 2007 vote, and with Canadian casualties in Afghanistan mounting, Harper appointed a blue-ribbon panel, headed by John Manley, a former deputy prime minister in the Liberal government of Jean Chrétien, to advise on future options.[13] In January 2008, the Manley commission recommended that the government extend Canada's involvement beyond 2009. Harper announced plans to introduce a motion extending the mission, intimating that he would regard the vote on an extension as a matter of confidence, which meant that a defeat would trigger an election. With the polling numbers continuing to remain virtually unchanged for a second year in a row, Dion and the Liberals decided to cooperate with the Conservatives rather than continuing to use the tactic of "whipped abstentions" to ensure the government's survival.[14] The two leaders fashioned a compromise extension proposal that both parties could vote for.[15] With the survival of the Conservatives assured, the NDP and the Bloc were secure in voting against the extension.

The Logics of the March 2008 Decision

In the lengthy parliamentary debate in February and March 2008, the selected termination date for the proposed extended mandate—December 2011—essentially emerged by default as the date when it was understood that Canada would withdraw. But in fact the 2008 debate focused exclusively on the reasons why withdrawing in 2009, which was being advocated by the NDP and the Bloc, would have exceedingly negative consequences. Those speaking to the government's justifications for not withdrawing in 2009 fixed on a number of common themes.[16]

First, most of those speaking in favour of the motion cited the impact that a Canadian withdrawal would have on the people of Afghanistan in general, and on the people of the Kandahar region in particular. Many speakers invoked the spectre of the re-emergence of the Taliban, or a Taliban-like regime, and the impact on prosperity, security, and human rights in Afghanistan that such a return would bring. Many focused on the fate of women and girls in the event of a Taliban resurgence. The argument was often simply stated: as Peter MacKay, the minister of defence, put it when he moved the motion, "Afghanistan needs us."[17] Sometimes it was framed as the need to meet a Canadian "commitment" to Afghanistan and the Afghan people. For example, Michael Ignatieff (Liberal member for Etobicoke-Lakeshore), a consistent supporter of the mission, argued that Canada should have a policy that "meets the test of fidelity to the people to whom we have given our word."[18]

Second, a common connection was made between the possible return of the Taliban and the threats to Canadian security. As MacKay argued, for example,

> With an incubator and an exporter of the threat of terrorism represented in Afghanistan, Canadians undoubtedly would face increased danger because freedom, democracy and human rights and the rule of law, all things we embody and embrace as a nation, would be under threat. All of this would be an abomination to those who preach hate and practise murder if we were to walk away.[19]

Indeed, a number of contributors to the debate cited the official line of the Afghan government: "If Afghanistan is not safe, then Canada is not safe."[20]

A third argument, put most unambiguously by MacKay, was that a Canadian withdrawal would have a negative impact on Canada's allies and Canada's reputation. MacKay even added an appeal to the judgment of "history": "Do we want to tarnish Canada's reputation? Could we ever regain the confidence of allies after deserting them at a critical moment? How would history judge us, if Canada walked away from Afghanistan?" MacKay also reminded other MP's of what he called the "domino effect" of a Canadian withdrawal: "We do not want the Afghan campaign and the allied efforts to unravel. Other nations followed us into southern Afghanistan, and soon more will arrive, we hope, to fortify our efforts there. What would stop them from withdrawing if we do?"[21]

Fourth, some speakers raised the argument that to abandon the fight would be to dishonour those Canadians who had made the ultimate sacrifice to the community with their lives, because abandoning a conflict prior to winning a victory inexorably renders their deaths meaningless. For example, MacKay urged "all members to support the motion and in so doing commemorate those fallen and those who forged ahead.

Supporting the motion," he suggested, "is the best memorial we can build."[22] Others echoed these sentiments, stressing the importance of ensuring that the 78 Canadian soldiers who had died to that point on service in Afghanistan did not die in vain. For example, Greg Thompson, the minister of veterans' affairs, ended his intervention in the 2008 debate by noting: "That is what this motion is all about. We will not abandon our soldiers. We will not let their efforts or the ultimate sacrifices of their comrades be in vain. We will not walk away from them."[23] A comparable note was sounded by Jay Hill, the chief government whip, the next day: "We would want to ensure, on behalf of the sacrifice we have already made there, that the sacrifice is not in vain."[24] Indeed, Mike Wallace (Conservative member for Burlington) explicitly linked withdrawal to the idea of wasted lives and wasted effort: "If we took the New Democratic approach and left tomorrow, all the work done and the sacrifices made by our men and women on behalf of Canada in Afghanistan would be [f]or naught."[25] In a similar vein, Gerald Keddy (Conservative member for South Shore-St Margaret's), parliamentary secretary to MacKay, invoked the name of Michael Hayakaze, killed by an improved explosive device on 2 March 2008, and paid tribute to "the supreme sacrifice that Trooper Hayakaze made on behalf of the Canadian people and for the people of Afghanistan," adding, "We should not allow that sacrifice to be wasted, quite frankly. We have an obligation to stay the course for the long term."[26]

In short, an array of arguments was offered by proponents of the 2008 "compromise" for why it would be entirely inappropriate for Canada to withdraw by February 2009, and why Canada had to maintain its contribution until 2011. But there was an unspoken assumption that December 2011 would be when the mission would, as MacKay put it, "wrap up."

The Illogics of the March 2008 Decision

Although the Canadian position as of March 2008 appeared to be straightforward, the decision committing Canada to a unilateral withdrawal by 2011 involved a high degree of political legerdemain by all four political parties. In particular, all of those who constructed the March 2008 "compromise" as a Canadian military withdrawal from Afghanistan in 2011 were very careful to sidestep a thorny illogic in their position: if the objective conditions in Afghanistan do not change by 2011, all of the arguments that were advanced for not pulling out in 2009 will continue to be applicable.

First, most observers of the situation in Afghanistan appear to be agreed that the multiple objectives of the international coalition assisting the government of the Islamic Republic of Afghanistan cannot, and will not, be met any time soon. In particular, it is recognized that efforts to assist the government of President Hamid Karzai to create both security and legitimacy continue to be thwarted by a persistent insurgency whose leaders, by all accounts, enjoy sanctuary across the border in the Federally Administered Tribal Areas of Pakistan[27] and funding from bumper opium harvests in Afghanistan.[28] While both the Karzai government and the international coalition embraced five-year strategic benchmarks and timelines under the Afghanistan Compact of 31 January–1 February 2006,[29] and while reports of progress continue to be posted by NATO[30] and by the armed forces deployed to Afghanistan,[31] there appear to be few observers who seriously hold that members of the international coalition will be in a position to withdraw from Afghanistan with the mission accomplished by 2011.

On the contrary, while there are few useful comparisons to be made between the Vietnam War and the conflict in Afghanistan, the persistent inability of the international coalition forces and the Afghan security forces to prevail over those opposing the Afghanistan Compact by force has led to one paradoxical dynamic common to all guerrilla wars: As Henry Kissinger observed in 1969, "the guerrilla wins if he does not lose. The conventional army loses if it does not win."[32] It is not by coincidence that the conflict in Afghanistan is so commonly described as a "war without end."[33]

Such a long-range prognosis of the conflict is fed by contemporary assessments of the situation in Afghanistan that seem to be uniformly grim. "Afghanistan is not lost," an International Crisis Group report asserted in February 2008, "but the signs are not good."[34] A similar note was sounded by the Senlis Council in a report also released in February 2008: "The inability of domestic and international actors to counter the entrenchment of the insurgency in Afghanistan is deeply troubling, and the failure of NATO's political masters to address the realities of the security situation in Afghanistan has taken the country and the Karzai government to a precipice."[35] The Afghanistan Study Group, headed by a retired Marine general and a former ambassador, was just as blunt: "The mission to stabilize Afghanistan is faltering," the report concluded, listing "the many shortcomings in current strategies and policies" of the United States and its allies and the government of Afghanistan.[36] Similar negative notes are to be found in the assessments by the international media, non-governmental organizations, think tanks, academics, and some governments and international organizations.[37]

Three Canadian reports published in 2007 and 2008 delivered comparably negative perspectives on the ability to achieve these goals within the time frame envisaged by the Afghanistan Compact. Gordon Smith, the executive director of the Centre for Global Studies at the University of Victoria and a former Canadian ambassador to NATO and former deputy minister of foreign affairs, prepared a report for the Canadian Defence and Foreign Affairs Institute in March 2007. Smith's report suggested that the odds of achieving NATO's goal of peace and security were "daunting" but "not hopeless." However, the report concluded that "current NATO policies and programs in Afghanistan are not on course to achieve that objective, even within a period of ten years."[38]

Likewise, the *Manley Report* of January 2008 concluded that Afghanistan was a country "whose prospects still appear bleak" and where the "insurgency is far from being defeated." The report articulated what Arthur Kent has called "blistering criticisms"[39] of NATO and ISAF command structures; of corruption within the government in Kabul; and of the role of the Pakistani government in providing sanctuaries for Taliban commanders of the insurgency in Afghanistan. Nonetheless, the report recommended that Canada's commitment should be extended beyond 2009. Moreover, it is clear from the recommendations regarding "future commitments" that the panel did not doubt that there would be commitments beyond 2009.[40]

Finally, the Standing Senate Committee on National Security and Defence also reported in 2008. Its report made comparable criticisms, detailing what it called an "array of disfunctionality" (*sic*):

> Debilitating poverty, a history of violence, a weak central government, powerful warlords, endemic corruption, a feudal mindset, a paucity of education, a legacy of distrusting foreigners ... and of course, the Taliban: fuelled by religious fervour and profits from the illegal drug trade, relentless, patient, and able to recruit an endless stream of volunteers across the porous border with Pakistan.[41]

These bluntly pessimistic assessments of the situation in Afghanistan, from both global and Canadian sources, would pose a major political problem for any policy-maker who claimed to be committed to a Canadian withdrawal by December 2011. Policy-makers in Ottawa may indeed recognize that there is little prospect of imminent "progress" in Afghanistan that would allow the international community to declare success and go home by 2011; they may recognize that the global negativity about the mission in Afghanistan comes from mainstream, "blue-ribbon panel" voices and cannot be waved away as the wilful reconstructions of objective reality by "people with other agendas" (as radical critics are invariably characterized).

Most importantly, policy-makers in Ottawa may, in their heart of hearts, know that the huge tasks outlined in the Afghanistan Compact of 2006 are, quite simply, impossible to accomplish by 2011 given the short time frame, the paltry resources committed, and the objective conditions on the ground (such as the challenges of creating a Weberian state apparatus in a most un-Weberian polity, the obstacles posed by the opium economy, and the difficulties posed by the sanctuary afforded by Pakistan to insurgents). But for the government of Canada to *acknowledge* any of this, at least openly, would involve considerable costs.

First, to withdraw while at the same time acknowledging that the goals laid down by the Afghanistan Compact have not been met would be to expose the government of the day to the charge that it either was being completely illogical or was declaring the whole enterprise a failure. The illogic of withdrawing at a particular point in time that is selected without reference to the situation on the ground in Afghanistan is clear: if the job was important enough to demand a Canadian contribution in 2008, it would be entirely illogical not to see it through to completion. That logic was explicitly recognized by the *Manley Report*: "With all that needs to be done, no end date makes sense at this point."[42] Likewise, Tommy Banks, a Liberal member of the Senate Standing Committee on National Security and Defence, dismissed as "absurd" the idea of putting a time limit on the mission: "Can you imagine Winston Churchill saying we will fight until the middle of 1943 and then we'll see?"[43]

For this reason, a common theme in the Canadian debate among those not in government has been to stress the long term and the inappropriateness of setting deadlines. For example, Gordon Smith argued that "the battle for Afghanistan must be long term, requiring a sustained Canadian commitment in development assistance for a minimum of ten years."[44] Likewise, speaking at a news conference in Kandahar on 25 October 2007, the Chief of the Defence Staff, General Rick Hillier, admitted that Afghan military capacity cannot be built "overnight," and that "it's going to take ten years or so just to work through and build an army . . . and let them meet their security demands here."[45] Paul Tellier, a member of the Independent Panel, put it succinctly: "Dites-moi quand l'armée et la police afghanes pourront assurer la sécurité du pays et je vous dirai quand le Canada pourra retirer ses troupes."[46]

More importantly, however, to engage in a unilateral withdrawal before the mission was completed would be to signal very publicly that the mission was a failure, and that therefore those other members of the international community who remained behind were engaged in a failed mission. A unilateral Canadian withdrawal would stick an unambiguous finger in the eye of all those participating in the Afghanistan Compact process: fifty-one participating governments, including all five permanent members of the United Nations Security Council and all Canada's friends and allies; thirteen observer governments; and ten participating organizations including the United Nations, the World Bank, the International Monetary Fund, the European Union, NATO, the Organization of Islamic Conference, two development banks, and the Aga Khan Foundation. And it is highly unlikely that the implicit criticism entailed in a unilateral Canadian withdrawal would be met impassively by this wide array of global actors. Bluntly put, one just does not declare to the international community that it is engaged in completely useless activity without there being a huge and costly backlash.

Third, some of the contributors to the Afghanistan mission would regard a unilateral Canadian withdrawal as a major threat to their interests. As MacKay recognized so clearly in the 2008 debate, there would undoubtedly be a "domino effect": a Canadian withdrawal would invariably galvanize public opinion in other countries contributing to the mission, and perhaps lead others to question their commitment to the mission. Because of the possibility that a Canadian withdrawal would precipitate a bandwagon effect, other contributors to the mission—particularly those with forces in the more volatile areas of Afghanistan—would most assuredly move to punish Canada either to convince Canadians to reconsider their withdrawal or to discourage others from following suit.

Finally, any government seeking to actually implement the March 2008 withdrawal decision would not be able to easily sidestep the "sunk cost effect"[47] of the significant number of fatalities suffered by the Canadian Armed Forces in Afghanistan. As the Manley panel noted, "Canadian interests and values, and Canadian lives, are now invested in Afghanistan. The sacrifices made there, by Canadians and their families, must be respected."[48] To note, as Paul Robinson did,[49] that this is to be "mired" in the "sunken cost fallacy" is not, however, to gainsay its persuasive power. The connection between the mission, the fallen, and those who remain behind is inevitably tight—however much one may complain, as Robert Thibault (Liberal member for West Nova) did that "supporting the troops and supporting the decisions of government are two completely different things."[50] On the contrary, it has been common in the Canadian debates for supporters of the mission to paint those who sought an immediate withdrawal as failing to "support our troops"[51]—to the point where it was *de rigueur* for those opposing the extension and arguing for an earlier withdrawal to pronounce that they nonetheless supported the troops.

It is for this reason that a unilateral withdrawal before the job is done, particularly if the armed forces of other states remain in Afghanistan, will likely expose any government seeking to implement the 2008 decision to considerable domestic criticism. Not only will there be the obvious criticism that the lives of all those members of the Canadian Armed Forces were given "for naught," but there will be the additional problem that members of the CAF would be none too happy to be forced by their political masters to "cut and run" while their colleagues from other NATO countries remained behind. However, this would not simply be an armed forces issue: it could be argued that one of the consequences of the refurbishing of the Canadian military since 2003 is that Canadians in general are more likely to be concerned about the armed forces, and thus it is possible that concerns over the implications of a pullout would be felt more widely.

Reconstructing the Logics of the March 2008 Decision

If it is seen as a decision to withdraw by December 2011, the March 2008 motion of the House of Commons is puzzling, because of the very high political and diplomatic costs to Canada of a unilateral Canadian military withdrawal from Afghanistan. But if the motion is seen as a way for the Harper government to remove an issue from the parliamentary agenda in the short term while retaining maximum freedom of action in the medium term, the motion agreed to by the Conservative government becomes more understandable.

First, when the motion is read *literally*, it is clear that there is no military withdrawal from Afghanistan promised or anticipated, in 2011 or later. The key parts of the motion read,

> It is the opinion of the House:

> that Canada should continue a military presence in Kandahar beyond February 2009, to July 2011 . . .

> that . . . this extension of Canada's military presence in Afghanistan is approved by this House expressly on the condition that:

> . . . (c) the government of Canada notify NATO that Canada will end its presence in Kandahar as of July 2011, and, as of that date, the redeployment of Canadian Forces troops out of Kandahar and their replacement by Afghan forces start as soon as possible so that it will have been completed by December 2011.[52]

In other words, while it was commonly interpreted as the Conservative government's committing itself to ending Canada's military engagement in Afghanistan over the course of 2011, this is in fact *not* what was agreed to. The commitment was to redeploy CAF units out of Kandahar, not out of Afghanistan.

Second, even the commitment to redeploy troops out of Kandahar in 2011 must be seen as essentially fluid and flexible. Given the contingent nature of war-fighting, the condition laid down in the March 2008 motion readily could (and probably would) be revisited should conditions change. Thus, for example, while the motion requires the government in Ottawa to negotiate a change of its mandate in Afghanistan with NATO, it is highly unlikely that the Canadian government would unilaterally leave the Kandahar region if Afghan forces were not prepared to take over, or if other coalition partners could not be found to replace the Canadians.

Third, it is noteworthy that Prime Minister Stephen Harper did not contribute to, or participate in, the March 2008 parliamentary debate—other than to vote in the divisions to a standing ovation by his caucus.[53] Although no reason was formally offered for Harper's non-participation in a long debate to which 128 MPs (55 Conservatives, 40 Liberals, 11 Bloc members, 20 NDP members, and 1 independent) contributed over a period of five days, it would be unusual if his decision not to contribute to the debate were not politically calculated. While numerous reasons could be adduced for his absence from the debate, one possibility is that the Prime Minister wanted to put some distance between himself and the ambiguities of the March 2008 motion—in order to keep options open for the future.

Conclusion

In sum, it can be argued that, despite the March 2008 motion, the Canadian government's position had not much changed since March 2006, when Harper was being pressed to hold a Commons debate on the recently deployed troops to Kandahar. At that time, Harper summarily dismissed the need for a debate in the House on the grounds that the result would be a "foregone conclusion," since both the Conservatives and the Liberals supported the mission. Moreover, he expressed concern that a debate in parliament could send the wrong message. Noting that "Canadians don't cut and run at the first sign of trouble," Harper said that he had no intention of questioning that mission. "To do so would not only be not in the best interests of Canada's international reputation . . . it would be a betrayal of the men and women—the brave men and women we have in the field—who are in danger."[54]

But the parliamentary debate in March 2008 over the future of the Canadian contribution to the Afghanistan mission did encourage Canadians to believe that it would be possible to withdraw unilaterally from the military role to which the Liberal government of Paul Martin had agreed in 2005. By allowing—if not encouraging—a highly ambiguous interpretation of the motion passed on 13 March to prevail, MPs also encouraged Canadians to believe that Canadian troops will no longer be engaged in the conflict in Afghanistan after 2011. I have argued in this chapter that the motion passed by the House of Commons on 13 March does not commit the government of the day in 2011 to withdraw the Canadian Armed Forces from Afghanistan. On the contrary, there is no unilateral exit from Afghanistan: if in 2011 the international coalition of which Canada is a part is still engaged in the NATO-led mission,[55] both diplomatic and political realities will conspire to ensure that whichever party forms the government in 2010–2011 will continue to contribute to the "war without end" in Afghanistan.

Notes

1. CBC News, "House Votes in Favour of Extending Afghan Mission," 13 March 2008. For comparable coverage, see Steven Chase, "Afghan Mission Extended until 2011," *Globe and Mail*, 14 March 2008, A4; Allan Woods, "Conservatives, Most Liberals, Back Afghanistan Extension," *Toronto Star*, 14 March 2008, A1; Alec Castonguay, "La mission en Afghanistan est prolongée jusqu'en 2011," *Le Devoir*, 14 March 2008, A7.
2. Canada, Parliament, House of Commons, *Debates*, edited *Hansard* online, no. 053, 25 February 2008, 12h20.
3. Steven Chase, "Senators Forecast Military Deployment Past 2011," *Globe and Mail*, 12 June 2008, A4.
4. For a history of the Canadian mission in Afghanistan to 2007, see Janice Gross Stein and Eugene Lang, *The Unexpected War: Canada in Kandahar* (Toronto: Viking Canada, 2007); Independent Panel on Canada's Future Role in Afghanistan, *Report,* John Manley, chair (Ottawa, 2008), http://dsp-psd.pwgsc.gc.ca/collection_2008/dfait-maeci/FR5-20-1-2008E.pdf (hereafter *Manley Report*).
5. House of Commons, *Debates*, 39th Parliament, 1st Session, 17 May 2006, 1501.
6. Ibid., 24 April 2007, 8647.
7. Afghanistan Compact, 31 January–1 February 2006, http://www.nato.int/isaf/docu/epub/pdf/Afghanistan_compact.pdf.
8. House of Commons, *Debates*, 39th Parliament, 2nd Session, 13 March 2008, 18h05.
9. In a Decima poll in April 2006, 45 percent of Canadians polled approved of the mission and 46 percent were opposed. In February 2007, an Angus Reid poll showed that 46 percent wanted Canadian troops brought home; by April 2007, that number jumped to 52 percent. As of May 2008, 54 percent of Canadians opposed an extension of the mission. See the April 2006 poll at www.angus-reid.com/polls/view/11588/canadians_divided_over_Afghanistan_mission; the February and April 2007 polls at www.angusreid-strategies.com/uploads/pages/pdfs/2007.04.25 Afghanistan Press Release.pdf; and the May 2008 poll at www.angus-reid.com/uppdf/ 2008.05.12_Afghanistan.pdf.
10. See all poll results for the party standings from February 2006 to April 2008 listed at http://www.nodice.ca/elections/canada/polls.php.
11. By early 2007, the Conservatives were stuck at the high 30 percent range of the vote, the Liberals at high 20 percent/low 30 percent, the NDP at 12–15 percent, and the Bloc at 8–10 percent nationally (i.e., 30–40 percent in Quebec): see http://www.nodice.ca/elections/canada/polls.php.
12. "MPs Defeat Motion to Pull Troops from Afghanistan by 2009," *CBC News*, 24 April 2007.

13. The other members of the Independent Panel on Canada's Future Role in Afghanistan were Derek Burney, chair of the board of CanWest Global Communications, a former diplomat, chief of staff to Prime Minister Brian Mulroney, negotiator of the Canada-US Free Trade Agreement, former chief executive officer of Bell Canada International and CAE Inc., and a member of Stephen Harper's transition team; Jake Epp, chair of the board of Ontario Power Generation, and a minister in Mulroney's cabinet; Paul Tellier, a former Clerk of the Privy Council and former president and CEO of Bombardier and Canadian National Railways; and Pamela Wallin, former TV journalist with CTV and CBC and former Canadian consul-general in New York.

14. In October 2007, the eagerness of the Liberal opposition to avoid an election had led Dion to authorize the use of "whipped abstentions"—where the party whip insists that an MP abstains on a crucial vote to ensure that the government is not defeated.

15. In the end, several Liberal MPs defied their whip: Bonnie Brown (Oakville), Mario Silva (Davenport), and Joe Volpe (Eglinton-Lawrence) all absented themselves from the vote; Bill Matthews (Random-Burin-St George's) openly voted against the motion.

16. House of Commons, *Debates*, 39th Parliament, 2nd Session, edited *Hansard* online, nos. 053-066 passim. The debate began on 25 February 2008 and was continued on 26 February and then again on 10, 11, and 13 March. On 10 March, there was additional time for debate on Afghanistan since the Liberals moved an opposition motion under Business of Supply ("That the House take note of the ongoing national discussion about Canada's role in Afghanistan").

17. House of Commons, *Debates*, 39th Parliament, 2nd Session, 25 February 2008, 12h20; the same point was made by Jay Hill, the government whip (26 February 2008, 11h20) and Bev Oda, minister of international cooperation (26 February 2008, 16h15).

18. House of Commons, *Debates*, 13 March 2008, 11h10; also see 26 February 2008, 10h35.

19. Ibid., 25 February 2008, 12h25.

20. Dave MacKenzie, parliamentary secretary to the minister for public safety, citing Sima Samar of the Afghanistan Independent Human Rights Commission, House of Commons, *Debates*, 11 March 2008, 20h00. Hamid Karzai, speaking to a joint session of the Canadian parliament in 2006, noted that Canadians had sacrificed their lives "so that we in Afghanistan may have security, and they have sacrificed [their lives] to ensure the continued safety of their fellow Canadians from terrorism." Afghanistan, Office of the President, Press release, 22 September 2006, http://www.president.gov.af/.

21. House of Commons, *Debates*, 25 February 2008, 12h45.

22. Ibid.

23. Ibid., 25 February 2008, 19h20.

24. Ibid., 26 February 2008, 11h35.

25. Ibid., 10 March 2008, 21h30.

26. Ibid., 10 March 2008, 23h45. Other Conservative MPs who mentioned the importance of remaining true to the memory of the fallen included Blaine Calkins (Wetaskiwin), James Lunney (Nanaimo-Alberni), and Joy Smith (Kildonan-St Paul).

27. Barnett R. Rubin and Abubakar Siddique, "Resolving the Pakistan-Afghanistan Stalemate," *Special Report 176*, United States Institute of Peace, October 2006.

28. United Nations, Office on Drugs and Crime, *Afghanistan Opium Survey 2007* (Vienna, August 2007); for a good discussion of the paradoxes of the opium economy in Afghanistan, see Vanda Felbab-Brown, "Afghanistan: When Counternarcotics Undermines Counterterrorism," *Washington Quarterly* 28, 4 (Autumn 2005): 55–72.

29. Afghanistan Compact, Annex I, Benchmarks and Timelines, http://www.nato.int/isaf/docu/epub/pdf/Afghanistan_compact.pdf; also http://president.gov.af/english/np/security.mspx.

30. See, for example, the figures reported by NATO at http://www.nato.int/issues/Afghanistan/factsheets/reconst_develop.html.

31. For example, US Department of Defense, American Armed Forces Press Service News Articles, "Afghanistan News," http://www.defenseclink.mil/news/articles.aspx?SectionID=13; United Kingdom, Ministry of Defence, "Defence Factsheet: Operations in Afghanistan: Background Briefing 2," 20 February 2008, http://www.mod.uk/DefenceInternet/FactSheets/OperationsFactsheets/; Australia, Department of Defence, "Operation SLIPPER" (2009), http://www.defence.gov.au/opslipper/default.htm; Netherlands, Ministerie van Defensie, http://wwwmindef.nl/missies/Afghanistan/uruzgan/index.aspx.

32. Henry Kissinger, "The Viet Nam Negotiations," *Foreign Affairs* 47, no. 2 (January 1969): 214.

33. For example, A.C. Thompson, "War without End," *The Nation*, 2 December 2001; Dilip Hiro, *War without End: The Rise of Islamist Terrorism and the Global Response* (London: Routledge, 2002); David Rhode, "Concern Rises in Pakistan of a War without End," *New York Times*, 1 November 2004; Severin Carrell, "On the Frontline: War without End—Afghanistan," *Independent on Sunday*, 18 September 2005; Robert Fisk, "War without End," *The Independent*, 30 December 2005; "War without End: Not Winning, but Not Losing Either," *The Economist*, 25 October 2007; *Afghanistan: War without End*, History Channel, 2 November 2007. Perhaps not coincidentally, the "war without end" trope was often applied to the war waged by the mujahidin against Soviet forces after the Soviet Union's invasion of Afghanistan in December 1979: "A War without End," *Time*, 10 January 1983. "Afghanistan: War without End?" was the title of a feature on the MacNeil/Lehrer NewsHour on PBS, 27 December 1985. It is also commonly used in the context of the war in Iraq and the "global war on terror": see, for example, "Bush's Illusions and a War without End," editorial, *International Herald Tribune*, 27 May 2007.

34. International Crisis Group, "Afghanistan: The Need for International Resolve," Asia Report No. 145, 6 February 2008.

35. Senlis Afghanistan, *Afghanistan: Decision Point 2008* (London: Senlis Council, 2008), 4, http://www.senliscouncil.net/documents/decision_point_08.

36. Center for the Study of the Presidency, *Afghanistan Study Group Report: Revitalizing Our Efforts, Rethinking Our Strategies*, 2nd ed., General James L. Jones, USMC (Ret.) and Ambassador Thomas R. Pickering, co-chairs (Washington: Center for the Study of the Presidency, 2008), 8, 17, http://www.thepresidency.org/pubs/Afghan_Study_Group_final.pdf.

37. Googling "situation in Afghanistan" reveals the depth and extent of global gloominess about the prospects for Afghanistan.

38. Gordon Smith, *Canada in Afghanistan: Is It Working?* (Calgary: Canadian Defence and Foreign Affairs Institute, 2007), 4.

39. Arthur Kent, "Ottawa Misses Manley's Best Points," *Policy Options* (March 2008): 50-53.

40. *Manley Report*, esp. 10-18; recommendations, 37-38.

41. Canada, Parliament, Senate, Standing Senate Committee on National Security and Defence, 39th Parliament, 2nd Session, *How Are We Doing in Afghanistan? Canadians Need to Know* (Ottawa, June 2008), 2, http://www.parl.gc.ca/39/2/parlbus/commbus/senate/com-e/defe-e/rep-e/rep09jun08-e.pdf.

42. *Manley Report*, 4.

43. Chase, "Senators Forecast Military Deployment Past 2011."

44. See Smith, *Canada in Afghanistan*, 24.

45. "Afghans Years Away from Taking Over Own Security: Hillier," *CBC News*, 25 October 2007; for reaction, see "Hillier Says He's on 'Same Sheet of Paper' as PM," *CTV.ca News*, 26 October 2007.

46. Alec Castonguay, "Mission Impossible?" *L'Actualité*, 15 March 2008, 44.

47. See Hal R. Arkes and Catherine Blumer, "The Psychology of Sunk Cost," *Organizational Behavior and Human Decision Processes* 35, no. 1 (February 1985): 124. The "sunk cost effect" is the "greater tendency to continue an endeavor once an investment in money, effort, or time has been made. The prior investment, which is motivating the present decision to continue, does so despite the fact that it objectively should not influence the decision." It is also known as the "Concorde fallacy"—after the supersonic airliner that both the British and French governments continued to invest in despite vast overruns in costs.

48. *Manley Report*, 32.

49. Paul Robinson, "No End in Sight," *Ottawa Citizen*, 23 January 2008.

50. House of Commons, *Debates*, 39th Parliament, 2nd Session, 13 March 2008, 12h45.

51. For example, Greg Thompson, minister of veterans' affairs, asserted that the NDP "do not believe in the mission, they do not support our veterans, and they do not support our men and women in uniform. That is the sorry

state of the NDP… The NDP record is deplorable. Those members should be ashamed of themselves." House of Commons, *Debates*, 39th Parliament, 2nd Session, 25 February 2008, 19h30.

52. House of Commons, *Debates*, 25 February 2008, 12h00.
53. CBC News, "House Votes in Favour of Extending Afghan Mission," 13 March 2008.
54. Mike Blanchfield, "Harper Refuses to 'Cut and Run,'" *Calgary Herald*, 8 March 2006, A1.
55. It must be stressed that the analysis in this chapter would not apply if there were to be a multilateral decision by the international coalition, or even by NATO, to bring the Afghanistan mission to an end by 2011.

Chapter 11

Afghanistan and the Limits of "Unlimited Solidarity": A Farewell to *Schicksalsgemeinschaft*

Davɪᴅ G. Haɢʟᴜɴᴅ

Introduction

An editorial cartoon in the *Globe and Mail* nicely depicted the juncture at which Canada's military commitment to Afghanistan found itself at the start of 2008. The Harper government was sending clear signals that failure of (some) NATO allies to do more of the fighting in that troubled Central Asian land would assuredly result in Canada's doing less, come next year. The cartoon revealed a burly, but not bright, soldier relaxing over a glass of wine and pondering a crossword puzzle, seeking a four-letter word for "render assistance." This soldier wore a NATO patch on his shoulder, but Canadian readers would not have needed too much imagination to envision this towheaded non-combatant sporting the German flag instead of the NATO patch (in which case, the puzzle would have to demand a five-letter word, *Hilfe*).[1]

It is hard to remember that a scant half-dozen years have passed since Germany's foreign minister, Joschka Fischer, journeyed to the United States in the wake of the terrorist attacks on New York and Washington to pledge "unlimited solidarity" between Germany and its American ally in the struggle against terrorism—a struggle whose first powerful manifestation took form a month later, when fighting began to rid Afghanistan of the Taliban, and presumably to bring to that failed state a new prospect for order.[2] Even harder is it to recall those more distant years of superpower struggle known as the Cold War, when Germany was at one and the same time the "central front" as well as the ultimate geostrategic prize of the contest between the United States and the Soviet Union—a contest that, as the Germans could be counted upon to insist, bound all of us together existentially in a "community of fate" (*Schicksal-sgemeinschaft*). Alexandre Dumas himself could not have expressed better than German elites the injunction that, in the transatlantic community, it really was supposed to be "one for all, and all for one."

For sure, much water has flowed under the geostrategic bridge since the ending of the Cold War and the demise of the Soviet Union, and Josef Joffe does well to remind us of how much the earlier sentiment of "existential" solidarity had been dependent upon an assessment of shared security interests in a moment of self-evident threat.[3] Still, the Fischer pledge (ratified by then-Chancellor Gerhard Schröder)[4] was made a good decade after the Cold War ceased to be, so one might have expected this commitment to solidarity to be reflective less of bygone strategic realities and more of a set of shared Western "values." That value set would shortly be put to a hard test as a result of the crisis in the alliance triggered by the Iraq war,[5] which led many, and not just in Europe or in Germany, to ponder the wisdom of what used to be styled the GWOT (global war on terror).

Moreover, the allies seem to have had little difficulty, singly and collectively, in differentiating between an Iraqi "theatre" (said by many of them to be a snare and a diversion) and an Afghani one, held by most sentient observers of global security to constitute today, as it did a half-dozen years ago, the key to resolving the primordial security challenge represented by the nexus between "failed states" and terrorist networks.[6] No NATO government, least of all those most adamant about staying as far away from the south of the country as they possibly can, denies the ethical and political merits of "reconstructing" Afghanistan, though a growing "peace movement" among the German left appears to have convinced itself that even "peacekeeping" in that war-ravaged land is an illegitimate, because a militaristic, undertaking, one with which the German military should have no truck. The peace movement in Germany and other NATO countries aside, Afghanistan continues to be adjudged by governments to be the "good" front in the struggle against terrorism, however that struggle might be construed.

And though it would be inaccurate and unfair for anyone, in Canada and elsewhere, to single out the Germans from among all the other "usual suspects" thought to be only too happy to absent themselves from the receiving end of enemy IEDs and bullets, there is an unmistakable undercurrent of discontent with Berlin getting expressed, usually *sotto voce*, in Canadian media. So while Peter Worthington may put matters too strongly (and indelicately) in complaining that Germany has "chickened out of the heavy peacemaking process, and won't let its troops near the danger zone,"[7] his critique, even if not his manner of stating it, nonetheless has echoes elsewhere, with even the international press beginning to notice this Canadian disquiet.[8] Germany, it is felt, is letting down the side, and Canada in particular. Nor is it just the failure to deploy combat troops alongside Canadians that rankles. Other lapses of solidarity are cited, and as one former high-ranking civil servant with long-standing foreign policy experience notes disapprovingly, "the media tell us that useful tactical information gleaned from Germany's *Luftwaffe* photo reconnaissance flights has been denied to Canadians in the south of Afghanistan on the basis that the Germans insist they were there only for peacekeeping purposes and as a result were prohibited from conveying tactical information to war-fighting allies."[9]

Notwithstanding these less-than-flattering references to Germany's ersatz (or at least, Pickwickian) sense of solidarity and the implication that it has become high time for Berlin to demonstrate its alliance bona fides, the Harper government actually looks elsewhere than to the German capital for support: as this is being written, attention is focusing more and more upon Paris.[10] Canada, it appears, has simply written the Germans off as being likely to come to its aid—though it does so ruefully. NATO, by contrast, gets no such pass, especially the non-German members who constitute the remainder of the suspects' list (namely France, Spain, and Italy). As the *Manley Report* has made clear, should NATO not provide an additional thousand combat troops in the south, along with medium-lift helicopters and other equipment needed by the Canadian Forces, then Canada would be well advised to end its combat role within a year.[11]

Thus to many in Canada, including Prime Minister Stephen Harper, much is at stake should the allies not do their duty by the alliance, or at least by Canada—not only the virtual guarantee of an impending end to the Canadian combat role in Afghanistan, but something even more perilous. In words betraying his own and the country's growing exacerbation with the gimcrack qualities of the alliance's "community of fate," the prime minister has signalled the ultimate danger facing NATO: "Canada has done what it said it would do and more. We now say we need help . . . [and] if NATO can't come through with that help, then I think, frankly, NATO's own reputation and future will be in jeopardy."[12]

Two striking ironies have surfaced during the current Afghan debate. The first concerns the remarkable role-reversal experienced by Ottawa—all of a sudden a NATO capital that finds itself lecturing other allied capitals on the need to make a more credible commitment to the common effort. For so much of NATO's history, this used to be a criticism launched at Canada itself, and in the following section I address some of the conceptual and theoretical background of that history, with a view to illuminating what it is about the alliance that makes the temptation to shirk instead of share the burden so hard to resist.

The second irony inheres in the manner in which the current dispute calls into question one of the cherished myths of certain Canadian atlanticists, namely, those who have managed to convince themselves that there existed a "special relationship" forged within alliance circles between the Canadians and the Germans, conceived in their minds to be the alliance's gold-dust twins. This I address in the penultimate section of the paper.

The Bearable Lightness of the Democratic Alliance

More than a decade ago, Richard Gwyn pondered the curious diminution (and likely future disappearance) of the "nation that dares not speak its name"—English Canada. He did so within an overall critique of Canadian nationalism, which he somewhat enigmatically deemed to be a burden characterized by "unbearable lightness."[13] With apologies to Gwyn, we might remark of the "bearable lightness" of the burden carried (or not) by the members of the transatlantic alliance, the epitome of the so-called democratic alliance. It is fitting that the theoretician who has done more than anyone else to conceptualize the democratic alliance should be a German scholar, Thomas Risse, of the Free University of Berlin.[14] It is fitting because to contextualize the alliance's current Afghan dilemma we can find no better starting place than Risse's book *Cooperation among Democracies*, especially because of what his theory of the democratic alliance has to tell us, however inadvertently, about the generic issue of "burden-sharing" within NATO.

As noted in the introduction, it is unusual that Canada should be wagging the burden-sharing finger at recalcitrant allies, for it used to be an alliance truism that Canada itself was among the most prominent burden *shedders* in the transatlantic community. As with all platitudes, this one expressed enough truth to appear credible, but not enough to be totally reliable. It is true that during many years of NATO's Cold War existence, Ottawa's per capita spending on defence could and did leave it open to the charge, if not of "free riding," then certainly of what Joel Sokolsky neatly characterized as "easy riding."[15] But it is no less true that at times during the Cold War (for instance, throughout most of the 1950s), Canada was more than pulling its "weight" among Western militaries.[16] Moreover, even after the decision had been taken (in 1992) to end the long-standing deployment of Canadian Forces in Germany, it simply did not follow that Canada "left" Europe or otherwise turned its back on European security, as some commentators in Europe mistakenly appear to believe.[17] Canada simply shifted the area of its European operations farther east, to the Balkans, where by the end of the 1990s Canadian troops were actually engaging in combat operations—something its German-deployed units had never had to do during the period 1952 to 1994.[18]

"Burden sharing" has been a constant bone of contention within the alliance, and some member-states understandably tend to get upset when too much attention is lavished upon the level of their commitments. Lost in the near constant wrangling about buck-passing and burden shedding is the conceptual and theoretical source of the problem. Ironically, the quality of the "democratic alliance" that contributes to its durability is also the very quality that guarantees that just as there is likely to be "no end of alliance,"[19] there is also likely to be no end of bickering. It is not only, as some analysts want to believe, a function of "rational actors" confronting the perhaps insoluble dilemmas associated with the provision of collective goods;[20] rather, the problem inheres in the alliance's very value structure. In other words, the problem is also "cultural" in nature, given that the values upon which the democratic alliance rests present to some member-states powerful disincentives to increasing their level of commitment.

Risse's book appeared in the early post-Cold War years, when it looked as if NATO itself might be at mortal risk because of the disappearance of the Soviet Union. He sought, above all, to show that democratic alliances such as NATO did not really need existential threats to stay in business (though most people would argue they did require them to come into existence in the first place); such alliances are qualitatively different from, and therefore more durable than, traditional collective-defence arrangements. Because they comprise cognate liberal democracies, they have developed a pattern of dispute resolution within their alliance structures that resembles the way in which each member-state resolves political conflict domestically: to wit, they are mechanisms for "externalizing" and extending domestic "zones of peace."

Two implications flow from this observation, but generally only the first of these gets much attention. This is the inference that *because* of their respective dispute-resolution and interest-articulation mechanisms, allies who are liberal democracies not only have no need or desire to exit the alliance, but they also possess the uncanny ability to inject "voice" into collective decision-making and even—for the smaller allies—manage to influence the manner in which the alliance leader conceives of its *own* "national" interest. This upside of democratic alliances accounts for the remarkable pattern of NATO's growth: no one wants to leave it, so that notwithstanding the conviction of some international relations theorists in the early post-Cold War decade that NATO's demise was at hand,[21] the alliance has merrily continued along the expansionary path it first trod during the Cold War, when it grew from an initial dozen to an eventual sixteen countries, prior to attaining, after the Cold War, its current (for how long?) membership level of twenty-six. Illustratively, it has known only one period in its nearly six-decade existence when it actually shrank (though in terms of territory not membership), namely, in 1962 when Algeria won its independence from France.[22]

But every upside has its downside, even and especially within the comforting confines of the democratic alliance. Precisely *because* of the level of trust that member-states have in each others' essentially irenic disposition (at least toward other members of the group), not a single member of the alliance, no matter how small or powerless it might be, worries much about being "punished" if it does not pull its weight. Therefore, while it is fair to say that democratic alliances tend to be longer lived than, and even normatively superior to, other sorts of alliances, they do possess the distributive downside of encouraging some allies to "under-commit" to the common good.

Those who are quick to imagine that NATO is in danger of expiring should it not "succeed" (however success be measured) in Afghanistan should ponder one important fact: no one has ever sought to quit NATO—not even France when it pulled out of the alliance's integrated military structure in 1966. Indeed, though it is well known that the alliance has a provision for accommodating new members (Article 10 of the Washington treaty of 1949), hardly anyone is aware that there also exists a statutory means of exiting NATO (Article 13 of the same treaty).[23] We remember Article 10 because it has been so frequently invoked, while Article 13 might as well not even exist, which is another way of stating the obvious: for all the grumbling associated with it, no member state shows the slightest inclination to decamp from the alliance—not even those who demonstrate the greatest dexterity today at minimizing the burden they are expected to carry.

Burden shedding, or easy riding, is an inherent, one might say almost *structural*, feature of the democratic alliance. At the very least, it is a behavioural orientation that frequently gets put on display, in no small measure because members of the democratic alliance live in such minimal fear of being "abandoned," and this notwithstanding that abandonment is said by some international relations theorists to be an aspect of the "security dilemma" inevitably associated with alliances.[24] The democratic alliance looks to have eradicated that generic aspect of the alliance security dilemma: underperforming allies will certainly not avail themselves of any "notice of denunciation." They do not fear much in the way of vigorous retribution; at most, they face a bit of shaming. And they cannot be bounced from the club.

For these reasons it might even be said of alliance membership that it constitutes the contemporary geostrategic epitomization of what the fire insurance industry in the nineteenth century called "moral hazard." In its original usage, moral hazard applied both to character and to circumstance, with greater stress being laid on the former than on the latter; but as evolved under the tutelage of economists during the second half of the twentieth century, moral hazard grew to be associated almost entirely with circumstance (i.e., incentive structures) and hardly at all with the character of the "insured."[25] This is why the earlier usage has greater applicability to the democratic alliance than the later one, given the importance of liberal-democratic norms and values (i.e., "character") to the workings of such an alliance.

And this gets us to the important issue of public opinion as a constraint upon the provision of collective goods appertaining to security and defence. Burden shedding is not just a function of the incentives provided by the "insurance" afforded by NATO (primarily the American security guarantee); it is also reflective of the character (call it "strategic culture") of the alliance membership. In this respect, the moral hazard associated with alliance membership owes at least as much to culture as it does to circumstance, and few would doubt that Germany's strategic culture today gravitates more to "Venus" than to "Mars." To be sure, amid the current grumbling about German unwillingness or inability, or both, to assist Canada and other allies fighting in southern Afghanistan, one sometimes comes across reminders such as that expressed so wryly by Geoffrey Wheatcroft, that "some of us cannot see it as an occasion for pure regret if the Germans have changed character so drastically."[26]

Thus when Peter Schmidt, of the Berlin-based Stiftung Wissenschaft und Politik, recently remarked that "partners in an alliance have to also understand the domestic debates in a partner country like Germany,"[27] he was merely restating one of the facts of life in the democratic alliance: all leaders of democratic states find themselves in the same boat in having to appeal to their electoral base, and because each knows the feeling, at some time or other, of being held hostage to public whim, each is inclined toward a sympathetic assessment of a colleague's plight, albeit even if only reluctantly.[28] Nor is the tendency to want to shed the burden of combat a particularly German affliction; Canada as well has on occasion (though not, at the moment, in Afghanistan) displayed a similar allergy toward deployment of expeditionary forces within the context of collective commitments, and has done so for reasons not totally dissimilar to Germany's.[29]

The End of a "Beautiful Relationship"?

What the Afghan experience demonstrates is that "unlimited solidarity" has some obvious limits. It also reveals that there is nothing particularly blessed about the bilateral ties between Canada and Germany, which far from constitute a geostrategic marriage made in *Himmel*. In fact, this bilateral relationship turns out to be quite a "normal" one, insofar as relationships within the Western world go. It would not even be necessary to draw anyone's attention to the fundamental normality of Canada-Germany relations were it not for the cult of "specialness" that has been allowed to grow up around this tandem, for reasons related to both sides' political interest in romanticizing the relationship. Germans, understandably, find it easier to deal with a North American country that is smaller than their own than to deal with one that is the world's ranking power. And since it will probably take another half-century before Canada becomes as large as Germany, we might expect to see a prolonging of the impulse to accord to Canada some benefit of doubt that only begrudgingly gets extended to the United States, with whom it has not only become easier for Germans to disagree but seems to be almost obligatory for them to do so.[30]

As Canada emerges, in the German construction, as the better proportioned of the two North American allies, it also appears to be "nicer" because it is more normatively attuned to German preferences; indeed, Canada is frequently stylized as almost "German" due to its ostensible commitment to a "multilateralism" validated first and foremost through the United Nations.[31] Thus, it has not been difficult for Germans to conceptualize a natural community of interests with Canada in the area of international security, one whose primary expression has been "peacekeeping."[32] To a certain extent this image was accurate, at least into the 1990s, even if it was possible to overstate the commitment of both countries to UN operations as well as to understate the centrality that both accorded to NATO.

From the Canadian perspective, Germany during the Cold War was being increasingly imagined as a large part of the solution to a series of perceived foreign policy and even economic challenges. Regarding the latter, during the Trudeau era when Canada was questing after a "third option" that was not only supposed to minimize its economic dependence upon the United States but also to provide tangible commercial advantages, Germany was considered to be the gateway to, and backbone of, the tempting European market. As well, for many years the metaphorical (some say metaphysical) conceptualizing surrounding Germany's place in Canada's future featured the notion of "counterweight," by which Germany and Europe were supposed to provide great psychological and political succour to a Canada confronting a peculiar geopolitical predicament—that of being, in Herman Kahn's memorable words, "a regional power without a region."[33]

So Germany was being counted upon to help resolve the sempiternal Canadian identity crisis, no less! However, even during the height of the Cold War the romanticized relationship had been encountering problems as it came up against real-world challenges, and Germans from time to time were known to query (quietly if they could, noisily if they had to) whether Canada was as "committed" to the defence of the central front as the logic of *Schicksalsgemeinshaft* required it to be.[34] Nor was the period following the Cold War free of bilateral strain—not that the Canadian public dwelt upon, or even much noticed, some particular episodes when it could be said that Germany was objectively letting Canada down (e.g., when it sided with Spain during the "Turbot War" of 1995, or when it went along with France in early 2003 to "coax" Airbus into cancelling a decision to award a lucrative contract to Pratt & Whitney Canada to build 180 engines for the European military transport, A400M).[35] This is simply to acknowledge the obvious: that when Germany has to choose Canada or "Europe," it plumps for the latter. Less obvious, but no less important, is that when it has to choose which Canada it prefers, the Canada of "peacekeeping" or the Canada of "peacemaking," it opts for the former.

Conclusions

So what does it mean for the transatlantic alliance if the erstwhile gold-dust twins turn out to be sprinkled with pyrite flakes instead? Not very much, and for two reasons: First, and alarums to the contrary notwithstanding, Germany's failure to assist Canada in combatting the Taliban in southern Afghanistan will almost certainly not constitute a body blow to alliance credibility; much less will it result in the impending death of the alliance. NATO may not be like the proverbial cat in possessing nine lives, but it certainly has shown a remarkable ability to survive a number of apparently lethal crises over its six-decade existence.

Consider, by way of illustration, what so looked to be ailing it over the decades of its existence: (i) the years 1949–1958 featured an awkward period of adjustment for two European colonial powers (Britain and France) forced to come to grips with a new "imperial" order in Europe, one that needed a severe crisis over Suez to be brought fully into focus; (ii) NATO's second decade (1959–1968) was consumed in near-constant skirmishing between Charles de Gaulle and whoever happened to be the American president; (iii) from 1969 to 1978 the alliance wrestled with the contradictions of "regional détente" at a moment when some allied leaders were suspicious that Germany might just trade alliance solidarity for the lure of unification; (iv) NATO's fourth decade (1979–1988) saw member-states playing a mug's game of trying to perfect the imperfect-ible, "extended deterrence," resulting in bruising battles over so-called Euro missile deployments; (v) 1989 to 1998 was expected to be the *coup de grâce* by many NATO watchers, convinced as they had become that life without an enemy meant no life at all; and (vi) the latest decade (1999–2008) has provided the stage for the grand and ongoing melodrama billed as NATO's "transformation"—that is, its ability (or lack thereof) to adapt to a radically different set of security challenges from those it had known in the past.

For sure, only a fool would want to claim that NATO's travails in Afghanistan are good for it; the point is that hardship is nothing new to a transatlantic democratic alliance from which no one—neither the alliance leader nor any of the followers—has shown any desire to depart. It is difficult, in face of the various interest-based calculations of the membership, to identify what actually *could* render NATO defunct. One thing, however, does seem obvious in light of the current impasse: NATO will remain an operational entity about which it has to be said that the whole is much less than the sum of its parts. By this is meant that NATO, militarily, will be characterized in future more as the means of generating coalitions than as a full-blown alliance marching in lockstep to "victory" (whatever that might be said to be). The metaphor of the "tool box" may not be a popular one, but it is a realistic one for guiding our thinking about NATO's future as a military organization.[36]

Finally, there is the question of the European Security and Defence Policy and how, if at all, the German failure to assist Canada in Kandahar might play out with respect to Canadian involvement in any future security operations mounted under the aegis of Europe. It might be tempting to conclude that because of that failure, "payback time" is around the corner for those in Europe who would count upon Canadian support in some hypothetical European Union operation. But there will be no such payback. Things really do not work that way, for many reasons, not least of them being that should Canadian policy-makers in future ponder the likelihood (not very high, but at least conceivable) of Canada's getting involved militarily in an operation on which NATO has taken a "pass," they will always have the reminder that when Canada needed support from European allies in the south of Afghanistan, it was able to count on the British, the Dutch, the Danes, and the Romanians, Europeans all—and who can say, perhaps even the French?

Notes

1.   *Globe and Mail*, 24 January 2008, A20.
2.   Jim Garamone, "Germany Offers America 'Unlimited Solidarity,'" American Forces Press Service News Articles, 19 September 2001.
3.   Josef Joffe, *Überpower: The Imperial Temptation of America* (New York: W.W. Norton, 2006).
4.   Markus Kaim, "Friendship under Strain or Fundamental Alienation? Germany-US Relations after the Iraq War," *International Journal* 49 (Winter 2003–2004): 130.
5.   On that crisis, see Elizabeth Pond, *Friendly Fire: The Near-Death of the Transatlantic Alliance* (Pittsburgh and Washington: European Union Studies Association/Brookings Institution Press, 2004).
6.   Writes one observer of the reaction to the campaign to unseat the Taliban in the autumn of 2001: "The regime change was broadly welcomed by the 'international community,' despite the very obvious precedent that had

been set." Niall Ferguson, *Colossus: The Price of America's Empire* (New York: Penguin Press, 2004), 152.

7. Peter Worthington, "Seriously, Folks," *Toronto Sun*, 14 September 2007.

8. Marcus Gee, "Where Are Our Allies? Where Is Germany?" *Globe and Mail*, 14 September 2007; Judy Dempsey, "Merkel's Election Fear Drives Afghan Refusal," *International Herald Tribune*, 6 February 2008, 3. Dempsey states that "several NATO allies—including Canada, which has 1,730 [*sic*] military personnel in Afghanistan, most of them in the south—have questioned Germany's sense of solidarity with the alliance."

9. Robert R. Fowler, "Alice in Afghanistan: Canada Has Gone to War with Complete Confusion of Purpose," *Literary Review of Canada* 16 (January–February 2008): 5.

10. Campbell Clark, "France Hints It Will Offer Canada Troop Support," *Globe and Mail*, 8 February 2008, A10.

11. See the report of the five-member commission established in October 2007 to advise the government on Canada's Afghan deployment post-February 2009, *Independent Panel on Canada's Future Role in Afghanistan* (Ottawa: Minister of Public Works and Government Services, 2008). NATO members with troops deployed mainly in parts of Afghanistan that have the strongest Taliban and al Qaeda presence include the United States (15,000), the United Kingdom (7,750), Canada (2,500), the Netherlands (1,650), Denmark (780), and Romania (535).

12. Campbell Clark, "Harper Backs Manley and Vows to Press NATO," *Globe and Mail*, 29 January 2008, A1, A4. This has been a constant refrain of Canadians for nearly half a decade. In early December 2003, the minister of national defence, John McCallum, gave a talk at London's Chatham House in which he warned that if NATO could not emerge successful in its newly discovered vocation of bringing peace and stability to Afghanistan, its credibility in handling security challenges elsewhere would be severely damaged, with all that this implied for the alliance's very future. See Janice Gross Stein and Eugene Lang, *The Unexpected War: Canada in Kandahar* (Toronto: Viking Canada, 2007), 115-16.

13. Richard J. Gwyn, *Nationalism without Walls: The Unbearable Lightness of Being Canadian* (Toronto: McClelland and Stewart, 1995), 114-15.

14. Thomas Risse-Kappen, *Cooperation among Democracies. The European Influence on U.S. Foreign Policy* (Princeton: Princeton University Press, 1995).

15. Joel J. Sokolsky, "Realism Canadian Style: National Security Policy and the Chrétien Legacy," *Policy Matters* 5 (June 2004): 11.

16. Although in later years the image of Canada as the alliance's "odd man out" became a staple of discourse, in NATO's early years Canada was actively engaged in the defence of western Europe, and by 1953 it was allocating more than 8 percent of its gross domestic product to defence spending. At that time, Canada's defence/GDP ratio stood fourth highest in NATO, and its defence budget of nearly $2 billion accounted for 45 percent of all

federal spending (compared with today, when its defence outlays are equal to 1.2 percent of GDP, and its defence budget is about 6 percent of total federal spending). See David J. Bercuson, "Canada, NATO, and Rearmament, 1950–1954: Why Canada Made a Difference (but Not for Very Long)," in *Making a Difference? Canada's Foreign Policy in a Changing World Order*, ed. John English and Norman Hillmer (Toronto: Lester Publishing, 1992), 104-5.

17. See, for instance, Julian Lindley-French, "Reconnecting Canada to the World (via Europe)," *International Journal* 60 (Summer 2005): 651-65.

18. For a good summary of the Canadian Forces experience in Germany, written shortly before the commitment was terminated, see Roy Rempel, "Canada's Troop Deployments in Germany: Twilight of a Forty-Year Presence?" in *Homeward Bound? Allied Forces in the New Germany*, ed. David G. Haglund and Olaf Mager (Boulder, CO: Westview, 1992), 213-47.

19. Geir Lundestad, ed., *No End to Alliance: The United States and Western Europe—Past, Present, and Future* (New York: St. Martin's, 1998).

20. See, for instance, Todd Sandler and Keith Hartley, *The Political Economy of NATO: Past, Present and into the 21st Century* (Cambridge: Cambridge University Press, 1999).

21. In particular, Kenneth N. Waltz, "The Emerging Structure of International Politics," *International Security* 18 (Fall 1993): 44-79.

22. It is often forgotten that Algeria, unlike France's two other North African holdings (Tunisia and Morocco), was considered to be within the alliance's original "area." See Irwin M. Wall, *France, the United States, and the Algerian War* (Berkeley: University of California Press, 2001), 12.

23. Article 10 states that the members of the alliance "may, by unanimous agreement, invite any other European state in a position to further the principles of this Treaty and to contribute to the security of the North Atlantic area to accede to this Treaty." According to the provisions of Article 13, once the treaty had been in force for twenty years, namely, as of 1969, "any Party may cease to be a Party one year after its notice of denunciation has been given to the Government of the United States of America." North Atlantic Treaty Organization, *NATO Handbook* (Brussels: NATO Office of Information and Press, 1995), 233-34.

24. On the abandonment problem in alliances, see Glenn H. Snyder, "The Security Dilemma in Alliance Politics," *World Politics* 36 (July 1984): 461-95.

25. Tom Baker, "On the Genealogy of Moral Hazard," *Texas Law Review* 75 (December 1996): 237-92.

26. Geoffrey Wheatcroft, "War's Vanishing World in Europe," *International Herald Tribune*, 9–10 February 2008, 8. This article was a review of a new book by James J. Sheehan, *Where Have All the Soldiers Gone? The Transformation of Modern Europe* (New York: Houghton Mifflin, 2008).

27. Quoted in Helene Cooper, "Rice Urges Europeans to Step Up Afghan Role," *International Herald Tribune*, 7 February 2008, 3.

28. William J. Dixon, "Democracy and the Peaceful Settlement of International Conflict," *American Political Science Review* 88 (March 1994): 14-32.

29. See David G. Haglund and Stéphane Roussel, "Is the Democratic Alliance a Ticket to (Free) Ride? Canada's 'Imperial Commitments' from the Interwar Period to the Present," *Journal of Transatlantic Studies* 5 (Spring 2007): 1-24.

30. Though France is often held in the United States to be the cynosure of "anti-Americanism" within the transatlantic community, some analysts argue that it is Germany that serves as the more profound, and disturbing, critic of America, and does so on "cultural" grounds. See, for this assessment, Russell A. Berman, *Anti-Americanism in Europe: A Cultural Problem* (Stanford: Hoover Institution Press, 2004).

31. Jens Fey, *Multilateralismus als Strategie: Die Sicherheitspolitik Kanadas nach dem Ende des Ost-West-Konflikts* (Köln: SH-Verlag, 2000).

32. See, for instance, Hans-Georg Ehrhart and David G. Haglund, eds., *The "New Peacekeeping" and European Security: German and Canadian Interests and Issues* (Baden-Baden: Nomos Verlagsgesellschaft, 1995).

33. Quoted in Peter C. Dobell, *Canada's Search for New Roles: Foreign Policy in the Trudeau Era* (London: Oxford University Press/Royal Institute of International Affairs, 1972), 4.

34. For a critical assessment of the Canadian-German relationship, see Roy Rempel, *Counterweights: The Failure of Canada's German and European Policy, 1955–1995* (Montreal and Kingston: McGill-Queen's University Press, 1996).

35. See Donald Barry, "The Canada-European Union Turbot War: Internal Politics and Transatlantic Bargaining," *International Journal* 53 (Spring 1998): 253-84; and CBC News, "Pratt & Whitney Loses Big Deal to European Lobbying," *cbc.ca*, 7 May 2003.

36. On this point, see Sten Rynning, *NATO Renewed: The Power and Purpose of Transatlantic Cooperation* (New York: Palgrave Macmillan, 2005).

Chapter 12

Canada in Afghanistan: Strategic Perspectives

M.D. (Mike) Capstick

"The powerful exact what they can, and the
weak grant what they must."[1]

Introduction

There are few places in the world where Thucydides' cynical expression of political realism applies more than in Afghanistan. Invaded by outsiders, seized by religious extremists, forgotten for long stretches of time by the international community, and victimized by criminals and warlords, the people of Afghanistan have suffered "what they must" for far too long.

Since the overthrow of the Taliban regime, the world has turned its attention to Afghanistan. This is not to say that the attention has always been positive, focused, or concerted. Even in Canada, despite the size of our investment, our almost continual military commitment and, most importantly, the blood of our soldiers and a diplomat, public attention toward Afghanistan has been inconsistent at best. The report of a high-level panel[2] and an extensive parliamentary debate[3] notwithstanding, media coverage of the Canadian contribution continues to focus on combat operations in Kandahar, the details of military equipment, and suicide bombers. There has been very little analysis of our "whole of government" or 3D (defence, diplomacy, and development) approach. This approach is based on the idea that no single element of national power is sufficient, on its own, to deal with all of the complexities of failed and failing states, and therefore a coordinated and concentrated whole of government effort is necessary to secure the strategic effects desired by the international community, by Canada and, most importantly, by the people affected by state failure.

To illustrate how this concept should work, this paper will discuss how the Canadian military is supporting the Afghanistan Compact and Afghanistan's National Development Strategy. Although this paper concentrates on the contribution of the Canadian Forces, it also recognizes the subordinate, supporting role that the military plays in those areas that are within the competence of Canada's Department of Foreign Affairs and International Trade (DFAIT), the Canadian International Development Agency (CIDA), and the other federal departments and agencies involved in the Afghan mission.

What Canada is really trying to do is to help the weak of Afghanistan develop the strength that they need to deny the strong the ability to "exact what they can." This paper will, in short, describe the Canadian Forces' focus on this vital objective, one that is clearly informed by the long-standing Canadian values of "peace, order and good government."

Afghanistan's Future

Three decades of insurgency, invasion, resistance, civil war and, ultimately, the American-led attack on the Taliban have left Afghanistan shattered. Despite this legacy of violence, the progress between 2001 and 2005 was impressive. The Bonn Agreement was, in essence, a political roadmap that has allowed Afghans to take control of their own future.[4] Even with the pressure of an ongoing insurgency, Afghanistan has promulgated a constitution, held two very successful elections, opened the parliament, and restored a sense of normalcy in most of the country. Yet major problems have persisted: insurgency, opium, criminality and, most importantly, grinding and endemic poverty. Determined to overcome these obstacles, the Government of Afghanistan in partnership with the international community is taking the next steps as mapped out in two crucial documents, the Afghanistan Compact and the Afghanistan National Development Strategy (ANDS),[5] both presented and approved at the London Conference in 2006.

The result of extensive consultation and a concerted effort by both the international community and, most importantly, all elements of the Afghan government, the Compact and the ANDS received an extraordinary degree of consensus at the London Conference as well as rare endorsement by a unanimous resolution of the UN Security Council. Together, these strategies map the future of Afghanistan and, if properly implemented, will establish the conditions necessary for Afghans to achieve their vision of a peaceful, just, democratic, stable, and prosperous Islamic state.

Both the Compact and the ANDS are built around three "pillars": security, governance, and development. Security includes the international military contribution, defeat of the insurgency, reform of the Afghan National Army (ANA) and the Afghan National Police (ANP), and the disbandment of illegal armed groups. The second pillar encompasses governance, rule of law, and human rights. It entails reform of the machinery of government, revitalization of the civil service, justice reform, the fight against corruption and the poppy economy, and reform of the institutions of the state to make them work for the people. The third pillar, economic and social development, is the real heart of the matter. It is under this pillar that the bulk of the reconstruction effort falls. Development is, in essence, the central objective of the ANDS.

Canadian Forces' Support for the Three Pillars

Canada and the Afghanistan Compact

The three-pillared structure of the Afghanistan Compact suggests that there is a neat division of labour among the three lead Canadian government departments and the agencies in Afghanistan with respect to their engagement. This is true in broad terms: the Department of National Defence and the Canadian Forces leads on security issues, Foreign Affairs and International Trade leads on governance, rule of law, and human rights, and CIDA leads on the economic and social development front. Other Canadian departments and organizations also contribute. For example, the Royal Canadian Mounted Police (RCMP) has officers serving in the Kandahar Provincial Reconstruction Team and in the United Nations Assistance Mission Afghanistan (UNAMA) headquarters, as does Corrections Canada.

Despite this apparent clarity, the reality is rather more complex on the ground, and no Canadian government agency can operate strictly in one pillar or another. Although it is not necessarily obvious, the Canadian Forces plays a role in each of the three pillars as part of the cohesive whole of government approach that Canada is trying to apply as a means of achieving the best effects. In turn, Foreign Affairs and CIDA both have significant influence on, and are active in, the security sector. For example, the ambassador and the head of aid played key roles in the Disarmament, Demobilization, and Reintegration (DDR) Program, a function of the security pillar. Thus, each committed department and agency has a vital role to play in supporting all three pillars of the Afghanistan National Development Strategy. This discussion, however, will focus primarily on the role of the Canadian Forces in sustaining each of the pillars.

The Canadian Forces has been engaged in Afghanistan since the deployment of a combat unit to Kandahar in late 2001 as part of the American-led coalition Operation Enduring Freedom (OEF). Although the number of troops has varied, the Canadian Forces has made major contributions to both the OEF and the International Security Assistance Force (ISAF), the mutually supporting multinational forces in the country.[6] From March to November 2006, Canada assumed lead-nation status in Regional Command South. This region covers some of the most unstable provinces in the country, including Kandahar, Uruzugan, Helmand, Nimroz, and Kunduz. The commitment included the lead of the Multi-National Brigade Headquarters, which exercises command over the Canadian, British, American, Dutch, Romanian, and Australian units in the region.

The Canadian commitment of around 2,500 troops currently includes an infantry battle group in Kandahar Province and personnel with the Kandahar Provincial Reconstruction Team and the Observer Mentor Liaison Teams embedded with Afghan national army and police units in the province. This commitment was initially part of Operation Enduring Freedom and, as a result, became conflated in some quarters with the more unpopular aspects of US foreign policy. The Canadian mission (and Regional Command South) came under the command of the ISAF at the end of July 2006, and the Canadian-led command structure was instrumental in establishing the conditions for the successful transition from US to NATO command.

In addition to the troops in Regional Command South and in Kandahar, the Canadian Forces has a strong presence in Kabul. Canadian officers serve in both the ISAF and the Combined Security Assistance Command – Afghanistan (CSTC-A) headquarters, and a fifteen-soldier training team works with ANA units to prepare them for deployment to the provinces. In addition, a small military-civilian team of planners (Strategic Advisory Team – Afghanistan) has worked directly with Afghan government agencies to assist in the development of the strategic plans necessary to achieve the objectives of the Afghanistan Compact.

The Security Pillar

It is clear that security is the non-negotiable prerequisite for the success of the Afghanistan Compact. In the absence of security, economic and social development is almost impossible. In addition, the insurgency presents a direct threat to the development of good governance structures and practices. As a result, the security pillar will continue to be the main focus of the Canadian Forces' effort in Afghanistan for some time to come. Despite this emphasis, the Canadian Forces' Campaign Plan for Afghanistan has three lines of operation that mirror the ANDS pillars.[7]

The battle group in Kandahar is organized and equipped to assist the provincial governor and the Afghan national army and police in their efforts to establish the legitimate government's "monopoly on the use of lethal force" in the province. The Provincial Reconstruction Team with its military members, police and corrections officers, diplomats, and CIDA development specialists is also heavily engaged in the security pillar. The PRT reinforces the authority of the Afghan government in and around Kandahar and helps local authorities stabilize and rebuild the region. Its tasks are to monitor security, to promote the policies and priorities of the national government with local authorities, and to facilitate reform in the security sector.[8] An analysis of this mandate reveals that the PRT concept illustrates the reciprocity among security, governance, and development goals.

With the exception of the Strategic Advisory Team in Kabul, almost every other Canadian Forces member in the Kabul area has been engaged with the security pillar. Canadian staff officers and troops at the ISAF and various coalition headquarters are fully integrated into those organizations. The Afghan National Army training team and the Observer Mentor Liaison Team are also fully committed in this pillar as their work is hands-on tactical training of Afghan soldiers at the small unit level.

The Governance, Rule of Law, and Human Rights Pillar

In this ANDS pillar, the most obvious examples of Canadian Forces' support are found in the Provincial Reconstruction Team and in the Strategic Advisory Team – Afghanistan. The PRT is, by its mandate, intended to "reinforce the authority of the Afghan government."[9] Although its focus has been on security because of the prevailing situation in Kandahar Province, it has provided significant support to the provincial governor, the Afghan National Army, the Afghan National Police and, by virtue of its development work, the line ministries of the central government. This level of support will continue to grow as the intent is to co-locate part of the PRT headquarters in the governor's office.

The Strategic Advisory Team (active until late 2008) had a direct role in the governance pillar as its planning teams supported of a number of Afghan ministries including the Ministry of Rural Rehabilitation and Development (MRRD)—the main Afghan government agent for reconstruction outside of Kabul. The team assisted in the development of the MRRD strategic plan, which includes the establishment of a comprehensive governance structure for development that will extend from the village to the national level. In all cases, the Strategic Advisory Team formed working partnerships with international organizations such as the World Bank and the United Nations Development Program. Those bodies brought expertise in governance to the table, while the team provided the skills necessary to integrate their input and to assist Afghan managers in the formulation of a coherent strategy. This work was a clear demonstration of the potential of military staff to transfer skills to the civil sector in a post-conflict society that has had little time to develop viable public institutions and a culture of good governance.

The Economic and Social Development Pillar

Within the security envelope provided by the battle group in Kandahar Province, the PRT is focused on development and reconstruction. This includes support to alternative livelihood programs, rural rehabilitation, and any number of public infrastructure projects. At the same time, the ISAF in general and the PRT in particular have renewed their emphasis on good governance. For example, the PRT provides direct support to the newly established Provincial Development Councils and to their district- and village-level equivalents. The PRT unit is by far the best example of the whole of government concept at the tactical level as it includes a senior diplomat, CIDA experts (augmented by staff from both the British Department for Foreign International Development and USAID), and RCMP officers. It is the CIDA component, not the military, that plans and coordinates development activities, while the Canadian Forces provides the basic security envelope and the essential support framework.

In addition to the Kandahar focus in the economic development pillar, the Strategic Advisory Team in Kabul was directly involved with a planning team supporting the Afghan-led ANDS Working Group. Similar to the effort in support of the Ministry of Rural Rehabilitation and Development, in this initiative the ANDS Working Group and the international experts provided the substantive and technical content while the Strategic Advisory Team applied military strategic-planning methodology to ensure coherence, synchronization, and sequencing in the same way that it would for a military campaign.

The Future of the Canadian Commitment

It is evident that Canada's whole of government approach has matured greatly in the past two years and that the recent striking of a cabinet committee, supported by a task force located in the Privy Council Office, promises to strengthen the cohesion of the Canadian effort. With the passage in early 2008 of a parliamentary motion extending Canada's military contribution until 2011, a special parliamentary committee on Afghanistan will be able to exercise oversight of the mission and ensure ministerial accountability.

These positive steps must now be supported by the development of a comprehensive *public* strategy that defines Canadian objectives in

Afghanistan (the "ends"), the organizations, methods, priorities, and benchmarks to accomplish these goals (the "ways"), and the resources, both human and financial (the "means"). This strategy must accord with the Afghanistan Compact and provide authoritative guidance for Canada's "whole of government" effort. It would permit parliamentarians to monitor progress and, at the same time, would fully inform Canadians as to their national objectives in Afghanistan and how the government intends to achieve them. Taken together, the new cabinet committee, the Afghanistan Task Force in the Privy Council Office, the special parliamentary committee, and the articulation of a public Afghan strategy can only improve national strategic coherence.

Canada and its international partners realize that the principal objective of the Afghan effort must be the establishment of an effective government in Kabul that has the confidence of the people. To accomplish this, every single Canadian effort in the security, governance, and development pillars of the Afghanistan Compact must be designed to strengthen the legitimacy of the Afghan government.

Much of CIDA's support of national programs has been successful in this regard. For example, support from CIDA and other overseas development agencies for Afghanistan's National Solidarity Program has not only resulted in the establishment of grassroots community development councils but has also been one of the major reasons that the Ministry of Rural Rehabilitation and Development is one of the most credible arms of the Afghan government. Making more ministries and the administration of Kandahar Province just as effective should be Canada's objective.

There is so much need in Afghanistan that each development partner must set priorities and leverage its strengths. The single greatest need, cited in report after report, is human security—the kind of security that can be provided only by a clean and effective government supported by a professional public administration system, effective conflict resolution and judicial systems, and security forces that perform their "duty with honour." Canada should focus its traditional strengths in these areas at both the national and subnational levels.

Public administration and governance reform efforts in Kabul have been undisciplined and fragmented since the fall of the Taliban regime. Despite the expenditure of large amounts of money and the presence of hundreds of international technical assistants, there is still no comprehensive strategy to reform the entire system and its processes. Canada should exercise leadership in this area by working closely with the United Nations and the World Bank to develop the necessary strategy and to focus international efforts. The actual shape of this effort needs further analysis but could range from providing senior officials to manage the program to building on the work of the Strategic Advisory Team with governance professionals.

There is also a desperate need to extend good governance to Kandahar Province. The entire subnational governance structure in Afghanistan is problematic—corruption, weak capacity, and arbitrary decision-making are all common. Clearly, projects intended to correct this situation in Kandahar should be a Canadian priority. These projects must address reform of the public administration system, the police and security forces, the penal system, and the control of public finances. At the same time, Canadian efforts must also focus on assisting the Afghan government in its efforts to deliver basic services to the population.

In simplest terms, most Afghans want the same things that Canadians wanted in 1867—peace, order, and good government. Canada's development aid efforts must focus on helping them to achieve these goals.

Conclusion

The importance of this mission to the people of Afghanistan cannot be overstated. This chapter took as its text one of the best-known quotes from Thucydides' Melian Dialogue—"the powerful exact what they can, and the weak grant what they must"—because it summarizes the plight of the Afghan people. This expression of political realism has characterized Afghan history, politics, and society for far too long. Overcoming the predators is crucial to the future of Afghanistan and its people. This will take time—a long time. It is simply impossible to repair the damage wrought by three decades of conflict in a matter of a few years. It is easy to see the physical damage to the country's infrastructure and institutions, and this is repairable with money and time. On the other hand, it is far more difficult to see the damage that constant conflict has done to the social fabric of the country—and the shortcomings of human security, good governance, and human capacity are far more difficult to fix than are bridges, roads, and schools.

The international community has failed, because of a lack of strategic vision and, in some cases, an excess of strategic hubris, to establish the conditions required for human security and good governance. Canada can help rectify this situation by exercising leadership internationally and in Kabul. The first steps have been taken in Ottawa. The formulation of a public Afghan strategy and a development focus that reinforces the legitimacy of the Afghan government in both Kabul and in Kandahar would, over time, correct most of the strategic errors of the past few years.

Afghanistan and Afghans are often complex and contradictory. Proud, hard-working, resilient, the Afghan people have learned to survive the worst. The Soviet invasion, a vicious civil war, the Taliban, US bombing, and now a persistent insurgency have combined to destroy the state's institutions and the society's traditional mechanisms of conflict resolution. The international community has, thus far, not been successful in its efforts to assist the Afghans in developing an effective governance system. Afghans' biggest fear is that the international community will, in its frustration with slow progress, confusing politics, and weak governance, "blame the victim" and simply abandon them again.

Others have made the national-interest argument against this course of action. Perhaps strangely for a former soldier, I would rather emphasize the human aspects of this mission. Afghanistan is at or near the bottom of every single ranking of UN Human Development indicators. Canada, a country at or near the top of the same rankings, made a strong commitment when it signed the Afghanistan Compact in 2006. Canada reinforced that commitment when the UN Security Council endorsed it and has further strengthened it with the human sacrifice that we are all too well aware of.

Opponents of the mission often recite the litany of failures as proof that stabilizing Afghanistan and alleviating its grinding poverty is "mission impossible," and that abandoning the country is the only option. This is simply wrong-headed and would consign Afghans to more decades of predation and violence. At the same time, it would be folly to adopt a simplistic stay-the-course approach, which would result only in the repetition of the strategic failures that have had such an adverse impact on the Afghan mission.

The only moral response is to absorb the lessons of the past few years and exercise the kind of political leadership needed to make the necessary changes to the Afghan strategy. Canada's political leaders have forged a parliamentary consensus that extends the military commitment in Kandahar until 2011. There should be no doubt, however, that the Afghan state-building enterprise will take decades. Success will require both strong political will and strong political leadership. Canada and Canadians have reason to be proud of their traditional leadership role on any number of international issues—the formation of NATO and the United Nations, the land-mine treaty, the International Criminal Court, and peacekeeping all come to mind. It is time for Canada's leaders to move beyond the politics of their domestic debate and to grasp the challenge of international leadership presented by the Afghan mission.

Notes

1. Thucydides, *The Peloponnesian War,* ed. Benjamin Jowett (Oxford: Clarendon Press, 1900), 5:89.
2. Independent Panel on Canada's Future Role in Afghanistan, *Final Report* (Ottawa: Ministry of Public Works and Government Services, 2008), http://dsp-psd.communication.gc.ca/collection_2008/dfait-maeci/FR5-20-1-2008E.pdf. This report, chaired by former Liberal deputy prime minister John Manley, recommended the extension of the Canadian military mission

in Kandahar until 2011, with some conditions. It served as the basis of the subsequent parliamentary debate.

3. For the CBC report of the 13 March 2008 vote in the House of Commons, see CBC News, "Revised Conservative Motion on Afghanistan," *cbc.ca*, 14 March 2008, http://www.cbc.ca/news/background/afghanistan/revised-motion-afghanistan.html. The full text of the motion is posted.

4. "Agreement on Provisional Arrangements in Afghanistan Pending the Re-establishment of Permanent Government Institutions" (Bonn Agreement; Bonn, 5 December 2001), http://www.un.org/News/dh/latest/afghan/afghan-agree.htm.

5. Both are available at http://www.ands.gov.af/main.asp.

6. Canada, National Defence and the Canadian Forces, "Canadian Forces Operations in Afghanistan" (Backgrounder, 25 November 2005), http://www.forces.gc.ca.

7. Brigadier General David Fraser, Canadian Armed Forces, Comd RC (S), interview with author, 11 February 2006.

8. Canada, National Defence, "Canadian Forces Operations."

9. Ibid.

Chapter 13

The Construction of a War

CHRISTOPH REUTER

Introduction

Kabul, late autumn 2007, on patrol with British soldiers in a slum. Heavily armed but not nervous, fifteen soldiers move through the narrow alleys carrying signal jammers against remotely detonated mines (which the German patrols do not have) and stable sleeves with tourniquet-pressure bands for gunshot wounds on arms and legs (which the Germans also do not have). Before moving out, commander Doug Fisher repeats the phrase heard time and again in Afghanistan: "Stay *in the bubble*, between the first and last soldiers!"

The "bubble" means security. Being in the bubble also describes the NATO troops living in the gigantic bases in Afghanistan under the International Security Assistance Force (ISAF) mandate. The bases span several square kilometres, artificial cities where thousands of soldiers live. The soldiers rotate every few months, and many of them do not leave the bases at all during their tours of duty. When new soldiers arrive, the officers project an ideal world in snazzy Power Point presentations: the mission is to win Afghan "hearts and minds," to build streets, schools and hospitals, and to fight the Taliban. Since the Taliban no longer oppose the superior Western troops in open battles as they did in 2006, in the officers' ideal world the enemy is on the road to defeat.

The reality is quite different, but in their "bubble" the troops hardly notice. Afghanistan is about as opaque as Germany during the Thirty Years' War—ethnically and religiously torn apart, paralyzed by the power of countless warlords big and small, many of whom appear to cooperate with Western troops while using their own militias to support their violent rule at home. Moreover, various Taliban wings operate on this perplexing playing field. Although they present a unified front to the outside, they are internally divided in pursuit of different goals. Those wings supported by the Pakistani secret service, the Inter-Services Intelligence (ISI), seek to destroy and overthrow President Karzai, while others want local power and control.

Which War Are We Fighting?

The problem with the bubble is not only that there is minimal interest in looking outside of it, but also that the bubble itself is taken for reality. Stubborn to the point of denying reality, Washington clings to the myth that the Taliban must be militarily defeated in order to save Afghanistan—even though the government's own investigative commission evaluated this approach as a failure. In January 2008 the Afghanistan Study Group, co-led by an ex-ambassador and a high-ranking ex-general, in cooperation with two additional Washington think tanks, presented its findings. "You can win every battle, but fail to win the war," Senator John Kerry summarized their conclusions. "We are there to lose [the war]."[1]

Many military leaders, not just the Americans, still believe the war can be won. But they usually fail to drag their memories back six years: the Taliban are not only still around, they are back in strength after literally disappearing at the end of 2001. This is one of the forgotten truths of this war, which says quite a bit about how successful the war strategy has been so far. Security has not improved in the course of the US military action in southern and eastern Afghanistan (NATO has been active in these areas only since 2006), but worsened. In the summer of 2002, foreigners could move unmolested anywhere in Afghanistan. This author, working as a journalist, travelled for weeks in the currently contested Pashtun provinces of Oruzgan, Helmand, and Kandahar—something unthinkable today.

In the hot summer of 2002, our team drove through a confused land: full of mistrust, full of hope. Outside of Kabul, power still meant the power of the tribe. After the Taliban's fall, old feuds were taken up again, the Akhundzadas and Popolzais (Hamid Karzai's tribe) facing the Itzhakzais and others with new strength. There were tensions but no common enemy. Yet the United States was interested in one thing only: hunting the Taliban, the terrorists, and Osama bin Laden. Everything else came second. Those not for the Americans were against them. Dependent on local rulers and translators, the US military increasingly let themselves be used in tribal feuds. They bombed the opponents, denounced as "al Qaeda," of their Afghan "friends." They failed, though, to understand what the Taliban had done so forcefully: establish order. Not democratic order—it was misogynistic and murderous for non-Pashtun minoritites, but it was order nonetheless. It ensured that money, land, and daughters could not be indiscriminately stolen as they had been during the civil war, and that traders could drive unmolested through the country without encountering highway robbers every few kilometres.

Yet there was no room for former Taliban leaders under the new Afghan leadership that had been hand-picked by Washington. New resistance slowly grew against the US occupiers, whose brutal responses to opposition won them new enemies. This spiral of resistance and retaliation allowed a new Taliban movement to become powerful in southern and eastern Afghanistan, where most of the Pashtuns, the largest single group, comprising 40 percent of the population, live.

Since 2001, the United States has constructed a conflict that mirrors its own ideology of "Enduring Freedom"—freedom versus terrorism, forever—a construct that does not apply to realities on the ground. Afghans do not know what to do with this approach. From the perspective of the farmers and traders who no longer wanted to be subject to the whims of the countless militias, the parameters of the numerous single conflicts were power, affluence, and even a certain legal security. By stipulating new roles and bringing in their overwhelming military strength, the US armed forces have caused the Afghan factions to align themselves accordingly, like iron filings under a magnet.

How to Create Mortal Enemies

The United States created terrorists and mortal enemies from the outset of the campaign. Afghan warlords eagerly supplied the Americans with targets using false information, harnessing the militarily superior US forces for their own purposes. From December 2001 onward, "bombing on demand" hit the wrong targets by the dozen: a tribal delegation in the east, massacred on the way to a Loya Jirga; less surprisingly, Taliban opponents; opponents of the ruling warlord in Khost, Khan Zadran, who had immediately entered into an alliance with the Americans; and numerous villages in the central province of Oruzgan, where at least forty-eight people died in the bombings of July 2002—including members of a wedding party.

The Pentagon lied to the public about these operations, which it passed off as aircraft-crew self-defence. In reality, US ground troops, led by the then chief of the Kandahar governor's secret services, simultaneously marched into extremely remote villages (a twelve- to eighteen-hour drive from Kandahar). The chief had a feud with the leading clan of the Dehrawud precinct, who were of the Popolzai tribe—Karzai's tribe. In a bitterly ironic turn of events, the Afghan president's strongest supporters died in a bombing by his protective guardians.[2]

In the northeastern province of Kunar, once richly wooded, the United States offered to find and fight terrorists. The Taliban molded two mafia groups competing in the cedarwood-smuggling business into the desired combination: "good" Afghans and "bad" Afghans, friends of freedom and friends of the Taliban. One group had gone over to the US troops early on and denounced its competitors. The second group was duly attacked, upon which it mounted the counterattack that proved that it was, indeed, the Taliban.

Hence, as foreigners interpret "their" Afghanistan according to their own interests and imaginings, most Afghans live in a world where perceptions are refracted by radical mullahs, by rumours and conspiracy theories. In a country where more than half of the population cannot read or write, and where electricity is scarce, the village elder's crank-powered radio is often the only source of information other than rumours. Thus, how is farmer Habibullah to know whether the heavily armed strangers in his village do not actually want to occupy Afghanistan forever and wage war against Islam?

Once this new conflict configuration was established, since 2003–2004 the fight has become self-perpetuating. Attacks on US troops created new US enemies who were all subsumed under the heading "Taliban." Whether one speaks with American foot soldiers in the field or with officers in Afghanistan, one often encounters a sweeping generalization: not only are the Taliban and al Qaeda one and the same, but they are also delusional terrorists who cannot be dealt with through negotiation. The only way to handle these terrorists, they say, is "kinetically," as shooting is more nicely termed.

SPD Defence Minister Peter Struck's now-famous dictum that Germany's freedom would be defended at the Hindu Kush followed the same line; it just did not go quite so far. Rhetoric that alternates between the domestic political exploitation of lack of knowledge and the fear of terrorism has led to the assumption that the alliance between the old al Qaeda under Osama bin Laden and the former Taliban regime, which dissolved during the war in 2001, still exists. This assumption dictates that supporters of these groups who are still on the ground must be fought and halted in order to foil their next attacks on Europe and elsewhere.

The fear of terrorist attacks is—in the long shadow of 11 September 2001—a powerful lever in political decision-making, from implementing more stringent punishments to dismantling data protection to extending tours of duty for Afghanistan. The "terrorist threat from Afghanistan" thesis is tempting for us in the West to believe. Yet it is no longer supported by reality, as the actors have changed enormously under the pressure of the events of the last seven years. The old al Qaeda, with its hierarchical structure, has crumbled under the pressure of US searches. The assassinations committed or attempted by al Qaeda followers in Europe have been the work of migrants, converts, or immigrant Arabs—not those under the direct command of Afghanistan or Pakistan. The perpetrators seldom have any contact with the old al Qaeda leadership. The

"Western attack" on Afghanistan is one of the reasons assassins give for their actions, yet none of them come from there. Instead, violence-prone jihadists have been travelling to Afghanistan (even from Germany) for some time.

Furthermore, the old al Qaeda doctrine of the "distant enemy" who must be attacked (as in 2001) has in many conflict zones (Pakistan, Iraq, Lebanon, Afghanistan)[3] yielded to the simpler fight against the near enemy. It is no longer about war against the rest of the world but about control of one's own home turf. Al Qaeda's decline in Iraq should be noticed in light of this shift, as its claim to omnipotence collides with its former sympathizers' power structures. In Afghanistan the jihadist "travelling cadres" comprise a small minority in comparison to the local Taliban who fight in their home districts for their own interests.

Division into Good and Bad

A further problem has resulted from the division into evil (Taliban) and good (Hamid Karzai's government): even the supposed good guys do not behave in ways that make the country more democratic, more legally secure, more drug-free, and less a breeding ground for Taliban ideology and power.

After many years of delay, the knowledge is leaking out that Hamid Karzai's government, installed under massive American pressure at the Petersberg conference near Bonn at the end of 2001 and confirmed in free but by no means fair elections, is in many areas more a part of the problem than the solution. Universal corruption, the involvement of governors and members of Karzai's family in the heroin trade, the persistent dominance of the Tajik Northern Alliance, and Karzai's pacts with warlords have all discredited the government among wide sections of the population. The government is unable to give the people what they most urgently demand: legal security. In the eyes of large segments of the population, Karzai is a puppet of the United States, one who rests his power on corrupt governors, on old and new military leaders, all of whom are no less involved in the opium trade than were the Taliban. The drug police devote themselves far less to fighting the drug trade than to proportionately distributing its profits. The justice system is a travesty, the police notorious. When in late 2007 a Western diplomat in Kabul asked about the new police checkpoints along the main route from Kabul to the south, an Afghan countered with a sad smile, "You mean the new toll stations?"[4]

Although Karzai fiercely denies that his own family or members of his government are involved in the drug trade, internal reports from the American Drug Enforcement Agency (DEA) leave little doubt that they are. And the suspects themselves make little effort to disguise their activities. For example, General Daoud, responsible for the war on drugs within the Ministry of the Interior, succeeded in having his home district specially exempted from all measures to eradicate poppy fields.[5]

Even if he wanted to, Karzai no longer has the power to select his allies. Thus, he is instead trying to compete with the Taliban in fanaticism: he reinstalled the Taliban's notorious ministry for "promoting virtue and combatting vice." Even the laws passed by the parliament read like a repetition of the Taliban era. First, Indian soap operas were banned in April 2008 for their alleged blasphemies. Then, official government clerics fiercely protested against the immensely popular pop-star talent contest "Afghan Star," while independent mullahs have no problem with it and even the Taliban have been silent regarding the program. At the end of April, a parliamentary group moved that T-shirts, loud music, billiards, video games, open contact between non-married men and women, and even the release of tamed doves all be summarily forbidden. "We have the same ideas as the Taliban," said parliamentarian Quazi Naseer Ahmad. "We want sharia law in our country. Women must ask permission from their husbands before they leave the home, and they must not wear clothes that are against Islam."[6]

Karzai said nothing in protest when Afghan journalist Sayed Perez Kambaksh was sentenced to death for alleged blasphemy in a secret trial with no defence lawyer. Kambaksh had downloaded a text critical of the Qur'an from the Internet and distributed it. This was enough for a death sentence. Parliament even confirmed the decision at an initial hearing—until at a later date it declared itself not the competent authority.

Thin Line for the Soldiers

All foreign troops walk a fine line in the current situation. They must act as a military power in order to keep the omnipresent local commandos in check. The relative calm in the north, where the German troops are deployed, was never self-evident. German units tactically disarmed former warlords, contributed massively to deposing corrupt police chiefs in Kunduz, and created a halfway-functioning order in the area. At least, these conclusions were the results of an investigation into how troops have been accepted in the north. Researchers from the somewhat awkwardly named "Special Research Sector 700" at the Free University of Berlin questioned more than two thousand households in two northern provinces. More than 80 percent replied that security had improved in the last two years—thanks to the foreign troops, but also thanks to their own government.[7] "We were positively surprised," said Berlin ethnologist and project coordinator Jan Köhler. "In the eastern provinces, for example, the mood worsened massively in the same time period."[8]

After heavy fighting, particularly in 2006, the country has since become calmer. Yet, we cannot conclude that because the Taliban are avoiding open battles, they are getting weaker. They have shifted tactics, now conducting attacks like that on the Serena Hotel in Kabul at the beginning of 2008 as well as making silent infiltrations, constantly advancing nearer to Kabul. They control the villages rather than the cities, the nights rather than the days. In Wardak, a province south of Kabul, government troops venture out only in heavily armed convoys. The Taliban have established their own jurisdiction in the province's countryside and regulate disputes over land, water, and theft. The well-off flee Jalalabad, not wanting to pay "jihad tax" to the Taliban. In Kabul, Afghans working for foreign troops or organizations plan their own emigration. The Taliban have infiltrated the government security apparatus to such a degree that they are able to carry out attacks such as that near Hamid Karzai at the military parade on 27 April 2008.

As the public mood changes, the soldiers are seen as occupiers; resistance arises, and the spiral of fighting and retaliation begins. Thus, for example, the Canadian contingent in Kandahar at the beginning of 2006 was caught in the middle of a war where fighting was not a question of choice but of self-protection. By the end of May 2008, eighty-three Canadians had died in this mission, and at home pressure on the Canadian government was growing with no victory in sight. In February 2008, Canada gave the other NATO states an ultimatum: if at least 1,000 additional soldiers were not sent to Kandahar, then Canada would withdraw its 2,500-soldier contingent in February 2009. Discontent is also fermenting among the Dutch, who have nearly 2,000 soldiers stationed in neighbouring Oruzgan.

The military courses of action chosen by its allies do not suit the US government at all. The Dutch have in effect arrived at a ceasefire agreement with the Taliban. Their ex-commander, General van Loon, openly conceded in an interview with *Stern Online* in October 2007 that "it makes no sense to fight when Afghan government institutions simply do not exist on the ground."[9] British military and secret service officers in the opium province of Helmand have long negotiated with Taliban members (who were occasionally costumed as village elders). They chose these paths not out of sympathy but because war alone just creates new enemies. The Taliban believe that they do not need to win fights at all; they need only to survive until the foreign troops withdraw when governments can no longer withstand the pressure at home.

Therein also lies the German units' problem. The federal government has continually kept the population in the dark about the nature of this mission—out of fear of the electorate, since a majority of Germans already disapprove of the mission and every death adds to their number. Yet the power of the German armed forces rests on the Afghans' assumption that German soldiers, weapons, helicopters, and Fenneck-armoured reconnaissance vehicles can be sent in when required—not offensively, but in case of need. This assumption was undercut when, in the aftermath of the suicide attack in May 2007, Defence Minister Franz Josef Jung wanted to forbid all patrols and barricade the soldiers in the camp. The armed forces have been walking a fine line in Afghanistan for seven years: deploying not too much but also not too little military strength.

Still, the German mission has, overall, allowed the north to develop into one of the most successful areas of the country. Of course, the north never was "Taliban country," and discontent never enjoyed the same solid foundations as in the south. Yet this success is also due to the type of mission the Germans are conducting. The same holds for the former Norwegian and other contingents in the north.

The Divided Country

While the north and west have remained comparatively calm, the Pashtun south and east continue to be trapped in a spiral of violence. Too often, US troops have killed civilians. Time and again, they have bombed the wrong targets and with astonishing regularity covered it up afterward. The distinction between the UN-mandated ISAF mission and the purely American hunt for the Taliban under the banner of "Enduring Freedom" has long been blurred. Afghans simply cannot tell under which mission mandate a troop of US soldiers enters their village. Regardless of the approach used by the new ISAF contingent in the south, it is too late to make a new and friendly start. The enmity has cemented. The Canadian contingent in particular painfully experienced this reality as it entered Kandahar, which lies in the main fighting zone.

Here one often hears the same argument about statistical inequality from politicians, military men, and journalists alike: "blood" is the currency "that must be paid." The Germans in the north, some point out, have avoided paying the same blood tax as the Americans, the British, and the Canadians in the south. This inequality is unfair, they continue, and should be corrected by transferring German troops to the south. But if others have more casualties, does that inevitably make their actions more meaningful? As elegant as the statistical inequality argument sounds, its premise is quite flawed. To emphasize only the numerical difference in the casualty count, the "fair" division of the burden, is to posit that, overall, the operations are meaningful and that all participants are pursuing the same goals. Both assertions are faulty.

The US Operation Enduring Freedom, which aims with immense brutality only at eliminating all enemies, has not contributed to Afghanistan's security and pacification but has escalated the level of violence and insecurity. The situation in the south and east continually worsened from 2002 until the summer of 2008 with more attacks, more battles, and a progressive loss of control by the central government. Moreover, the practice of taking the number of Taliban killed as a measure of success fails to account for the effects of such "successes." Not only do many civilians fall victim to the bombings, but the killings and house raids incite hatred among the affected populations. It is naive to think that one must simply eliminate the bad guys: shoot the Taliban, and there will be calm. Each dead Taliban member creates new Taliban supporters and fighters. Southern and eastern Afghanistan have become the final destinations for jihadist pilgrims, primarily from Pakistan. Their preference is to go wherever Americans are being fought, and they are prepared to be killed there.

Hundreds of thousands of Afghans share the opinion that Afghanistan has long been a divided country in which the north and west prosper while the south and east stagnate. In past years they have confirmed this assessment with their actions, fleeing to the calmer regions where an entire network of interconnected activities is improving living standards. Schools and roads are being built, providing work. Microcredit banks make it possible to establish businesses, whose existence is facilitated by the massively improved road network. Kunduz, for example, is flourishing. This city, which houses the second-largest German contingent after Mazar-i-Sharif, looks like a single construction site, producing streets as well as kitschy villas. Much of it is being built with drug money, says Afghan journalist Yacub Ibrahimi, "but still [the money] is invested in construction here. In the Taliban era no one built here!" The bazaar sells everything from Chinese DVD players to Pakistani bananas. The number of children attending school in Kunduz city and province has jumped from about 15,000 in 2001, when the "schools" were often in open tents, to about 210,000 in 2008. The number of permanent schools has grown from six to approximately 150.

Outlook

In the international community, this north-west/south-east gap is often lamented. Yet why not make use of the circumstances? Even where the Taliban are powerful, as in Zabul and Ghazni provinces, the people have a highly ambivalent opinion of the movement. The people value (or at least did at the start) the legal security of the Taliban's "mobile courts," whose rulings cannot be evaded by bribery. They equally value the protection the movement offers from encroachments by the corrupt police and army, whose leadership is recruited from the former Northern Alliance, the enemy in the old Taliban era. Yet the more powerful the Taliban become in a region, the more corrupt and overbearing the Taliban leaders also become. Their courts lose their aura of incorruptibility, and their active hindrance of infrastructure-building weakens their popularity. Indeed, the Taliban face increasing resistance because of their failure to improve infrastructure (roads, wells, schools, hospitals). Not only do the Taliban refuse to undertake these projects but they prevent others from doing so. They even dismantle water pumps, announcing that a well built by a non-believer produces only contaminated, "infidel water."[10]

However, the attitude of Afghans toward US and NATO troops is equally ambivalent. Those who cooperate with the Taliban—and many Taliban commanders inconsiderately operate very near villages—fear brutal retaliation by the superior Western forces. And those who cooperate with foreign troops fear falling victim to the Taliban's revenge when the militias pull out (as has happened many times). Military operations may eliminate individual Taliban members, but in large areas of Afghanistan the foreign troops have not maintained a long-term presence.

It would be helpful to Afghanistan if the nations waging war did not view the country as a playing field to be used in the pursuit of external priorities, from the US fixation with the "war on terror" to NATO's preoccupation with survival. As a German officer in conversation with British colleagues in the garden cafeteria at ISAF headquarters in Kabul agreed, "ISAF must not fail! For NATO's sake!" Should such a debacle come to pass, NATO as a functioning alliance would be through, he continued, "and then the Americans would go it alone, do whatever they want!" For Afghanistan, such a consensus means that, in the end, loyalty to the Atlantic alliance outweighs mission success, and that the US tendency to shoot first and build wells later will continue. But what about the preservation of NATO should interest Afghans? Every foreign power involved in Afghanistan has its own agenda. The US government will not allow itself to fail there, because it has already failed in Iraq. Tehran, in turn, has no interest in a calm Afghanistan as long as the United States continues to threaten Iran with an attack. Pakistan's sinister secret service would like to continue using Afghanistan as a safe haven so that it can send Islamist militants into play in the endless war with India.

As long as Afghanistan remains simply the playing field for external conflicts and interests, the stated goal—stabilizing Afghanistan—will be reached only at immense cost, and even then only partially. Sometimes nothing will happen, and sometimes well-intended actions will prove to be counterproductive. The sole possible route to some sort of success is to win over the population, which will take a generation, because people must learn to read and write before they can oppose the mullahs' monopoly on religious interpretation. Quick military victory is therefore an illusion. To the extent that it is useful to offer a domestic model of success based on the (still comparatively) calm northern and western regions where there is more work, drinking water, schools, and electricity compared with the Taliban areas, a reduction of military activities would offer long-term, decisive advantages. After all, the Taliban have nothing to offer beyond fighting. The fewer fights there are and the more regions that prosper and present an alternative to stagnation and poverty, the more clearly Afghans will perceive this one-sidedness. In the end, Afghan citizens will have to decide for themselves what kind of world they want to live in.

Notes

1. See Center for the Study of the Presidency, *Afghanistan Study Group Report: Revitalizing Our Efforts, Rethinking Our Strategies*, 2nd ed. Co-chairs General James L. Jones and Ambassador Thomas R. Pickering (Washington: Center for the Study of the Presidency, 2008), http://www.thepresidency.org/pubs/Afghan_Study_Group_final.pdf.
2. "Tod auf Bestellung," *Stern* 33 (8 August 2002).
3. Whether we refer to the numerous radical Sunni "emirates" that have been proclaimed in Iraq since 2005, the casualty-heavy battles for control in the northern Lebanese refugee camp Nahral-Barin, or the fight for the "Red Mosque" in Islamabad, in all cases the fighters, who felt as if they belonged to al Qaeda or at least agreed with it ideologically, wanted simply to bring their location or region under control. These attempts, as might be expected, failed against overwhelming military force and thus removed much of the horror and fear of the terrorist threat, since it was no longer about a small group of terrorists striking any chosen location at any given time but about hundreds of fighters facing a superior opponent in conventional warfare and being defeated.
4. Interview with a Western ambassador in Kabul.
5. Interview with an American DEA officer in Kabul, March 2008.
6. *Christian Science Monitor*, 21 April 2008.
7. See Jan Köhler and Christoph Zürcher, *Internationale Akteure in Afghanistan* (February 2008), http://www.sfb-governance.de/media/news_links_data/SFB_700_Handout_Afghanistan.pdf.
8. Interview with the author.
9   "Wir müssen uns starker engagieren," *Stern.de*, 11 October 2007, http://www.stern.de/politik/ausland/599754.html (accessed 20 June 2008).
10. Interview with an ex-mullah in Andar Region, Ghazni Province.

Chapter 14

Security Sector Reform in Afghanistan: The Canadian Approach

DAVID M. LAW

Introduction

The involvement in Afghanistan has been of seminal importance for Canada in several respects. The Afghan campaign has been Canada's first foray into a war-fighting environment since the Korean War. It signals the country's coming out as a nation that is ready to engage in heavy conflict if necessary after decades of proudly wearing a peacekeeping mantle. This process has been accompanied by an effort on the part of Canada to return to the ranks of leading military nations after a sustained period of governmental neglect of national defence capabilities. It has also been tragically marked by the proportionally highest casualty rate of any national actor in the post-2001 phase of conflict in Afghanistan, save Afghanistan itself.

If Canada's involvement in Afghanistan was sparked by a need to show military solidarity with a traumatized post-9/11 America, it has also brought in its wake conceptual and organizational changes in the way the country goes about its activities on behalf of development and reconstruction abroad. Afghanistan has initiated a long overdue debate about the nature and needs of effective development assistance, and about the overall relationship between development, security, and justice. At the same time, 9/11 has had a significant impact on the country's understanding of governance, obliging politicians and bureaucrats in Ottawa to rethink the way the various federal departments of government engage in war zones and troubled states, and what this means for their interface in Ottawa. These trends have evolved in parallel with

Canada's efforts at home to protect its population, infrastructure, and land mass from terrorist attack and deny use of its territory for actions against its allies.

A number of conceptual innovations have accompanied these processes: the 3D approach, the "whole of government" approach and, in particular, Security Sector Reform (SSR)—the focus of this chapter. We will look at these conceptual developments in the second section. But first, we examine the factors that have driven and shaped change in Canadian thinking about security, development, and governance in third-world countries, including the strategic shift that occurred with 9/11. The third section addresses the main features of Canada's SSR role in Afghanistan: what Canada has been doing in this theatre, how it has been pursuing its activities there, how its approach compares with that of other countries, and how Canada's efforts have been conditioned by those of the international community in Afghanistan. The final section puts forward some recommendations for Canadian policy-makers that may also be relevant for other countries facing similar circumstances.

Drivers of Change

In the Canadian context, several factors have conspired to reshape the way that the country approaches security and sees its relationship with development, justice, and governance. This is a process that began in the early 1990s but has received several new impulses since.

With the end of the Cold War, Canada, like many other countries, began to reconceptualize its approach to security. This process meant that Canada put a new emphasis on the security of populations and the role of public security forces in this regard, and downplayed the bloc-to-bloc, state-focused security concerns and military issues that had dominated during the East-West conflict. At the same time, security perspectives, which had previously been segregated into external and internal components, began to collapse into a seamless continuum.

A second factor was the enhanced globalization of the security environment post-Cold War. Where previously the East-West standoff had tended to marginalize third-world conflict, in the changed strategic circumstances it rapidly became clear that a strategic problem virtually anywhere on the globe could have serious repercussions for a country's security. Canada, as a country traditionally open to trade and immigration, would increasingly find itself trying to cope with the impact of international information systems, global transport links, and ethnic and religious communities dispersed across countries and continents. Security globalization engendered a growing concern about the ability of fragile and conflicted states to control their security forces and their borders, and to ensure that they would not become vehicles for the proliferation of weapons of mass destruction.

A third factor shaping changes in Canada's world development view was the country's experience with the failed states of the 1990s, in particular Haiti and Somalia where Canadian troops were stationed in the largely failed international interventions of the early part of the decade. These deployments spotlighted the necessity of a secure environment to effectively convey resources for development. This led to the emergence of what has come to be called the security-development nexus: the notion that development is not possible without security, and that security can be neither provided nor sustained without development. Canada has been an enthusiastic participant in the consultations undertaken by donors in the OECD Development Assistance Committee (OECD DAC) from roughly 1995 onward, with the aim of enhancing the effectiveness of donor assistance.

A fourth factor also emerged at mid-decade when Canada, together with its NATO allies, began thinking seriously about the prospects of the organization enlarging to include democratizing states of the former Warsaw Treaty Organization. As this process gathered strength, it became clear that it was not enough for the military of these countries to be efficient, effective, and professional; they also had to be democratically controlled and overseen if they were going to be capable of making a positive contribution to alliance security, let alone not act as spoilers of democratization. At the same time, it was understood that NATO had to be similarly concerned with candidates' other security forces—the police, paramilitary agencies, intelligence services and so on, which had traditionally represented a security threat to the populations in communist countries.[1] It was this realization that encouraged Canada to work with other member states of the Organization for Security and Co-operation in Europe (OSCE), under European Union leadership, to elaborate the OSCE Code of Conduct on Political-Military Relations, which came into effect in 1995.[2]

The fifth driver of change came with the complex peace support operations in which Canada was involved as of the second half of the 1990s in the former Yugoslavia. The deployment in Bosnia-Herzegovina sent a number of very important messages. One message was that the traditional Canadian paradigm of peacekeeping, observing the peace between formerly belligerent parties, was a thing of the past. Another was that fundamental reform of a post-conflict country's security sector was essential if a return to large-scale violence was to be prevented. Bosnia-Herzegovina, a new state emerging out of the ashes of the Yugoslav wars, was a particularly daunting challenge in view of the ethnic cleansing that had occurred during the war, the fragmentation along ethnic lines of the political structures prevailing in the country postwar, and the reflection of this in the organization of its security sector. An additional message emanating from the Bosnian experience was the need for viable systems to coordinate the policies and activities of the kaleidoscope of actors that tend to be active in post-conflict settings—in addition to national and regional governments, foreign donors, intergovernmental organizations, private military and security companies, and an army of non-governmental organizations, both local and international. These were not entirely new phenomena for Canada to have to deal with, but this was probably the first time that these factors had all come together so dramatically.

The sixth factor shaping Canada's approach was the shift in strategic thinking provoked by the events of 11 September 2001, and the vulnerabilities in the US security posture that these attacks exposed. As the US National Security Council admitted, a superpower's strategic self-understanding was taken down for the price of a tank.[3] Canada lost over thirty civilians in the 9/11 attacks but it was, of course, less concerned by the strategic implications than was the United States. On the other hand, Canada quickly understood that its vital trading relationship with America—and the long, at that time relatively unprotected, border over which goods, services, and people had to pass if Canada was to remain economically viable—called for a series of measures to reinforce security at the border and internally. The subtext was as follows: Canada's security forces needed to be retooled to deal with new strategic challenges, in particular those emanating from the confluence of such phenomena as failed states, weapons of mass destruction, and strategic terrorism; they needed more resources than they had had at their disposal through much of the previous half century; and they needed to be able to work together as synergistically as possible.

Thus, Canada took measures to reinforce control of its border with the United States, including the arming of its previously unarmed custom officials. The immigration regime was reviewed to reduce the threat of foreign terrorists securing access to the country. There was a noticeable rapprochement with the United States on security issues under the Liberal government, one that was reinforced by its traditionally more pro-US Conservative successors when they formed a minority government in 2006 after thirteen years in opposition. Resources for defence were massively increased, rising by more than a quarter in 2007–08 compared with pre-9/11 levels and placing Canada as the sixth-highest military spender in NATO, well surpassing Canada's performance during the post-Korean phase of the Cold War.[4] Relations among key ministries were reorganized. A new Department of Public Safety was created, a kind of Canadian version of the Department of Homeland Security. Overall, security issues were re-mainstreamed in public and campus life,[5] after spending the better part of four decades out in the cold.[6]

Finally, the Canadian approach has also been shaped by the emergence in this decade of SSR as a policy framework for a growing number of its national development partners as well as for key international organizations (IGOs) of which Canada is a member and with which it cooperates, such as the OECD Development Assistance Committee, the European Union, and the United Nations. For example, Canada was involved in the OECD DAC consultations that led to the elaboration of its guidelines in *Security System Reform and Governance* in 2005 and its *Handbook on Security Sector Reform: Supporting Security and Justice* in 2007.[7] Canada also played a key role in efforts underway at the United Nations as of 2005 to mainstream SSR in post-conflict settings.[8] And, of course, as Canada has participated in these activities, its own thinking on SSR has evolved.

These drivers of change are summarized in Table 1. As we shall see, the Canadian deployments to Afghanistan have tended to bring these factors together and, in several respects, to accentuate them.

TABLE 1
Drivers of Change in the Canadian Approach to Security and Development

1. Reconceptualization of link between external and internal security
2. Security globalization
3. Security-development nexus
4. NATO enlargement
5. Third-generation peacekeeping
6. Strategic terrorism
7. Changes in partners' approaches

Source: Author's compilation.

Conceptual Frameworks

Since the end of the Cold War, Canada has adopted four overarching frameworks for conceptualizing and orienting its activities on behalf of development and, in particular, on behalf of troubled states: human security, the 3D approach, the whole of government approach, and security sector reform. While these concepts have entered the policy discourse at different intervals, they are not mutually exclusive; they tend to enjoy simultaneously a certain currency, and they all figure to varying degrees as mobilizing constructs for Canada's involvement in Afghanistan.

Human Security

Human security (HS) was mainstreamed in Canadian foreign policy practice after 1993, when the Liberal party returned to government looking for a concept to order its actions abroad in the post-Cold War era. Under the leadership of a dynamic foreign minister, Lloyd Axworthy, the government adopted a human security agenda as a way of underscoring that the purpose of its efforts abroad was to support populations in their strivings to live in security and under improving material and social conditions. In the Canadian vision, human security was not a substitute for state security; rather, state security was a precondition for the state's meeting its responsibility to help populations live in freedom from both want and fear. As a manifestation of the attractiveness of this idea, a Human Security Network was established in 1999 with a dozen like-minded states from around the world.[9] The HS star began to fade after the departure of Lloyd Axworthy from government in 2000, but the Department of Foreign Affairs continues to fund projects under this heading. The weak point of human security has revolved around the question of how to operationalize the concept with robust programs in the field.[10]

The 3D Approach

The 3D approach of defence, diplomacy, and development was adopted by the Liberal minority government in 2004 and mainstreamed in Canadian policy practice in 2005 with the publication of the country's new national security policy.[11] This document sought to integrate external and public security issues, traditionally handled as separate and largely unconnected domains. Likewise, it called for the main Canadian departments that had traditionally been active in crisis settings—the Canadian International Development Agency (CIDA), the Department of Foreign Affairs and Foreign Trade (DFAIT), and the Department of National Defence—to work closely together in the field, the implication being that traditionally this had not always been the case.

The concept of 3D has its limitations, however. To quote from a speech delivered in 2007 by David Mulroney (the Canadian deputy minister currently responsible for coordinating government policy on Afghanistan), defence, diplomacy, and development are not parts that "equal the whole"; there needs to be "an overall policy construct that sits above 3D" to motivate, validate, and connect everything that Canada does.[12] These departments need, moreover, to be approached not as distinct domains but as entirely interrelated ones, "as are (their) objectives and expertise."

Beyond this, while 3D rests on an expanded vision of security, the actors given centre stage by this approach are not capable of dealing with all the issues that need to be addressed in the field. Which of the 3D departments, for example, is to deal with policing, a crucial issue determining the success or failure of the international community's commitments to fragile and post-conflict states (the latest being Afghanistan)? Who is to deal with prisons? Who, with debt reduction? Who, with gender? And who would deal with all those other issues that are essential to putting a troubled or conflicted country back on its feet? Clearly, 3D falls short as a vehicle for mobilizing all the actors that matter in the Canadian development and security context—for example, the Department of

Finance, the Department of Public Safety, the Royal Canadian Mounted Police (RCMP), and the Correctional Service of Canada.

The 3D approach has also been criticized in the Canadian context as a vehicle that attempts to camouflage the fact that funding for Afghanistan has been heavily weighted in favour of the military. A 2006 report by a Canadian NGO claimed that defence expenditure has outpaced development funding by a factor of ten to one, while noting that the exact figures are difficult to come by. The numbers have prompted Canada's former minister of foreign affairs, Lloyd Axworthy, to assert that 3D has become one big D—for defence.[13]

The Whole of Government Approach

The whole of government approach, sometimes also referred to as the joined-up government approach, was introduced in the Canadian discourse by the Conservative government as an alternative of sorts to the 3D approach. The concept is, however, rather different in nature. The whole of government approach revolves around the issue of what mechanisms can be devised to ensure that the various governmental actors involved in a particular issue area work together synergistically. This is a challenge for governments around the world, and certainly not just in security and development but also in areas as diverse as health care, gender, and climate change. But the core problem is the same. The purposes for which a particular ministry has been established— sometimes very early on in the Westphalian epoch—can be outlived in part or whole by changing realities. When this happens, what do governments do in response? In the post-9/11 environment, does one create a new ministry, say, a ministry for security, writ large? Does one establish a new framework for traditional actors to consult about new realities while preserving their individual prerogatives and structures? Or does one end up somewhere in between?

Canada, like the United States, has embraced all three approaches to varying degrees. It has created a new ministry (Public Safety), it has created new structures for interdepartmental consultation, and it has recently established a coordinating mechanism for Afghanistan in the prime minister's office in an effort to ensure coherence and effectiveness on the part of the various governmental actors involved. But as we shall see, the whole of government concept is still much more an ambition than a norm: whole of government can easily descend into Hell of Government, with energies and resources being dissipated under the impact of "coordinationitis" and "cooperationism."[14] Much more thinking is needed on how to enhance the efficiency of mechanisms and methodologies for coordination and cooperation in environments at home and abroad where multiple governmental actors are active.

Security Sector Reform

SSR, as with the other concepts under review here, is relatively new. The term was coined a decade ago by the British minister of development, Claire Short, and it figured in the Canadian *International Policy Statement* of 2005. This concept too has emerged in response to the need to take a broader view of development and security, and of the interrelationships among different policy communities.

The OECD Development Assistance Committee uses the term *security system reform* to highlight the notion that security needs to be approached from a broad perspective, and the term *security and justice system reform* to stress that justice is not to be considered as being subordinate to security, nor is justice to be subordinated to security considerations—to be "securitized," as the discourse would have it. The more widely used term is *security sector reform*, which both the European Union and the United Nations have adopted when developing their SSR programs in response to the groundbreaking work of the OECD Development Assistance Committee, as have many donors in developing their national SSR agendas. We shall use SSR to denote both approaches as their core propositions are virtually identical.

SSR has many manifestations and variants, but its key propositions can be reduced to three. One is the need to take a holistic approach toward the understanding of the actors and factors involved in security, justice, development, and governance. Another is that security must be delivered professionally, efficiently, and at a reasonable cost, one that is commensurate with a country's resources. The third proposition is that the security forces as well as the ministries that manage and direct them need to be subject to democratic control and oversight. This is essential if these security forces are to be accountable, transparent, representative, and responsive—and in consequence to enjoy the confidence of the population, whose security should be their foremost concern. For an interpretation of the key norms pertinent to SSR, see Table 2.

SSR is versatile. It offers a framework for thinking about which actors play central or supporting roles in a country's security. It proposes a methodological dimension, for it insists on the need to take a comprehensive approach to the challenges of security, justice, development, and governance, and for security resources to be used for the public good. It says, for example, that police reform should not proceed without the implications for justice and correctional institutions also being addressed or that it can be deleterious for the population's security to build the capacity of security forces without ensuring that they are subject to democratic oversight and control. At the same time, it acts as a connector of a plethora of traditionally disparate policy strands: those of the security and development communities; the external actors supporting SSR and

TABLE 2
Decalogue of Key SSR Norms

1. The security forces are capable of delivering security professionally, at a reasonable cost, and in a way that helps to ensure that justice for all individuals and groups in society is served.
2. The security sector is representative of the population as a whole. It is inclusive, adequately reflecting a country's various communities and fairly providing opportunities to both genders.
3. The security forces operate transparently. Information about their activities is accessible to the public, save where legitimate national security concerns justify keeping information classified.
4. A country's security objectives and policies are set out in a national security strategy and in supporting documents that define the respective tasks and responsibilities of the various components of the security sector.
5. The executive and civil management authorities in charge of the security forces are capable of giving the security forces proper direction and management.
6. The security forces are overseen by and accountable to civilian, democratically constituted authorities. In particular, the legislature is empowered and able to oversee the policies and activities of the security forces as well as the executive and civil management authorities in charge of their activities.
7. The security sector is subject to a robust judicial and legal framework.
8. Civil society and non-governmental actors with a role in monitoring the governance of the security sector are active and can operate independently.
9. Domestic security sector actors are capable of interfacing smoothly with one another.
10. Domestic security sector actors are well integrated into regional and international security frameworks.

Source: This material first appeared in David. M. Law, "Taking Stock, Moving Forward," in *Intergovernmental Organisations and Security Sector Reform*, ed. David M. Law (Berlin: Litverlag, 2007), 248.

the implementing national governments; programs focusing on different actors or dimensions of security and development (for example, police and military, security forces' performance and oversight issues); regional, national, and local initiatives, and so on.[15]

Thus, SSR goes substantially further than either the 3D or whole of government approaches. It takes a much broader approach to the question of which actors—external or domestic—should be involved in questions of security and development than does the 3D approach. It goes much further than does the notion of whole of government; for example, SSR says that it is important not only for government departments to be joined up but for a wide gamut of other actors as well, and that how different actors interface with one another is a decisive factor in their overall effectiveness. Unlike the 3D and whole of government approaches, SSR lays out key objectives for government action.

While the Canadian take on SSR has been largely inspired by the OECD Development Assistance Committee, Ottawa has tended to emphasize certain aspects that, while not at odds with OECD orthodoxy, set different accents. For example, DFAIT twins SSR with rule of law in the description it provides on its website, explaining that a security sector cannot be functional unless rule of law prevails.[16]

The four conceptual frameworks described above are often perceived as contrasting or even opposing elements. If we look at the core ideas behind them, however, we see that they are largely complementary. Figure 1 attempts to capture this.

FIGURE 1
Human Security, 3D, Whole of Government, and SSR

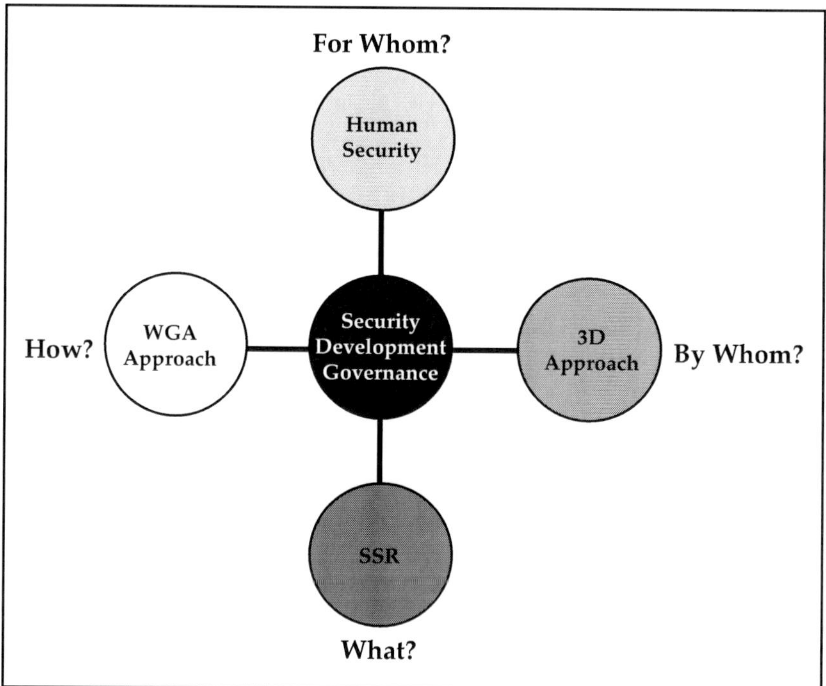

Source: Created by author.

Canada in Afghanistan

The Context

Afghanistan, as is now widely acknowledged, represents an extremely challenging environment for outside efforts to help bring stability and development to the country. The country is dirt poor, ranked 174 on the list of 178 nations in the United Nations Human Development Index.[17] The median age in this country of 33 million souls is 17.6 years. Literacy is low, pegged at 43.1 percent for males and only 12.6 percent for females. The last figure available for unemployment, from 2005, is 40 percent. The country has no history of central government control over its territory and borders. It is ethnically diverse: its largest group, the Pashtuns, making up some 42 percent of the population, are the second-largest group in bordering Pakistan. Officially approved political parties number over eighty.[18]

Afghanistan has known internal strife and conflict for over three decades now, provoked and/or exacerbated by a series of external interventions and involvements across its largely porous borders—notably the Soviet invasion of 1979 and their ten-year presence before a humiliating withdrawal that helped spark systemic change in the USSR, and now Taliban elements from Pakistan supporting home-grown Taliban as well as al Qaeda militants from around the Muslim world. The largely subdued violence of 2001–2005 has since reappeared with a vengeance, as the overall situation in Afghanistan's region has deteriorated. It is against this background that countries like Canada and Germany have found themselves struggling to make a significant improvement to the circumstances in which the Afghan people live and to help rebuild their state, a process that has involved nurturing a culture of governance that is largely new in the Afghan experience.[19]

Canada's Objectives

Canada's objectives in Afghanistan have varied little since the initial engagements in 2001–2002 and the three changes of government that have taken place throughout this period. Canada has essentially four objectives:

- to prevent Afghanistan from again becoming a sanctuary for strategic terrorism;
- to support the UN peace enforcement mission for Afghanistan in accordance with Chapter VII of the UN Charter;
- to act in solidarity with Canada's allies in NATO, which represent twenty-six of the thirty-nine countries in the ISAF coalition; and

- to foster stability and development in Afghanistan, in keeping with Canada's general commitment to promoting human security in fragile states.[20]

A fifth objective, that of strengthening Canada's relationship with the United States, has also been apparent during this period, particularly under the Conservative government in power after January 2006.[21]

Since 2001, Canadian governments have made five major decisions on Afghanistan. All decisions have been dominated by the security situation in the country, and by the need to secure a safe environment for reconstruction and governance capacity-building initiatives to proceed. The first decision was made in October 2001 under a Liberal majority government when Canada deployed a special forces unit and 750 troops to Afghanistan to support the US campaign there. At the same time, naval and air surveillance units were deployed to the Arabian Sea. The second decision came in February 2003 when 1,700 ground troops were deployed to Kabul as part of the NATO-led International Security Assistance Force (ISAF). In March 2005, the third step—this time under a Liberal minority government—was taken when it was announced that the troops in Kabul would be redeployed to Kandahar in February 2006. After the Conservative Party came to power in January 2006, two more situation-shaping decisions were made. In May 2006, parliament approved a two-year extension of the Canadian deployment. In January 2008, parliament approved another extension—this time to 2011—on the condition that an ally would provide an additional 1,000 soldiers to support Canada's role in Kandahar. This followed the recommendations of a study commissioned by the government in October 2007 on Canada's future role in Afghanistan which, while critical, was supportive of the continuation of the mission.[22]

Table 3 tracks the evolution of the Canadian presence in Afghanistan as a function of the government in power in Ottawa, the command to which the deployment has been subordinated, the number of Canadian personnel deployed, and the lethality of the deployment environment.

Public Opinion

Opposition to Canada's involvement covers a broad swathe of concerns: the prospect of defeat, Canadian policy being subordinated to US interests, burden-sharing, "Canada first" inclinations, and the need for Canada's involvement to be first and foremost about development and peacekeeping, not about war-fighting. These arguments are, however, not necessarily representative. The Canadian public has, until recently, tended to be more or less evenly divided in its attitudes toward Canada's role in Afghanistan—even into 2006 when Canadians began to suffer

TABLE 3
Overview of Canadian Military Involvement in Afghanistan

Government	Period	Command	Forces Deployed	Theatre of Deployment	Lethality of Environment
Liberal majority	As of October 2001	Canadian Operation Apollo; Canadian Naval Task Group under US Command (OEF)	(at peak) 6 warships, 1,500 Navy, long-range transport aircraft, two surveillance and maritime patrol aircraft	Persian Gulf/ Arabian Sea	Relatively benign (0 casualties)
Liberal majority	January– August 2002	US Command (OEF)	850	Kandahar	Still benign but less so (4 casualties)
Liberal majority and Liberal minority as of June 2004	August 2002– August 2005	Operation Athena; NATO Command (ISAF)	1,700	Kabul	Relatively benign (3 casualties)
Liberal minority	August 2005– January 2006	US Command; Canada assumes command of K-PRT	1,000	Kabul to Kandahar	Relatively benign (1 casualty)
Conservative minority as of January 2006	February 2006– August 2008	Operation Archer (OEF) and ISAF Operation Medusa; NATO command (ISAF)	2,000; increased to 2,500 between 2006 and 2007	Kandahar	Increasingly malign (85 casualties)

Note: Casualties current as of 25 August 2008. For the most up-to-date list of Canadian casualties, see CBC News, "In the Line of Duty: Canada's Casualties," *cbc.ca*, http://www.cbc.ca/news/background/afghanistan/casualties/list.html.

Source: Duane Bratt, "Mr Harper Goes to War: Canada, Afghanistan and the Return of High Politics in Canadian Foreign Policy" (2007), www.cpsa-acsp.ca/papers-2007/Bratt. pdf, Independent Panel on Canada's Future Role in Afghanistan, *Final Report* (Ottawa: Minister of Public Works and Government Services, 2008), http://dsp-psd.tpsgc.gc.ca/collection_2008/dfait-maeci/FR5-20-1-2008E.pdf.

dramatically higher casualties. While Canada has been in Afghanistan since late 2001, eighty-five of its total of ninety-three casualties as of August 2008 have occurred in the last two years, essentially corresponding to its second deployment to Kandahar. Not surprisingly, the last couple of years have seen a corresponding drop in support for the Canadian mission (see Table 4).

TABLE 4
Opinion Polls on Afghanistan

Regarding Canada's military involvement in Afghanistan, do you... (%)

	2002		2004		2006 Mar		2006 Jun		2006 Oct		2006 Nov	
Strongly approve	38		26		21		25		23		19	
		75		61		49		56		48		50
Somewhat approve	37		35		28		31		25		31	
Somewhat disapprove	11		15		16		15		18		18	
		33		35		48		40		50		48
Strongly disapprove	12		20		32		25		32		30	

Do you think in the end the Canadian mission in Afghanistan is likely to be successful or not successful? (%)

Successful	34
Not successful	58
Don't know / No answer	7

Source: "CBC-Environics Public Issues Poll," *cbc.ca*, November 2006, http://www.cbc.ca/news/background/afghanistan/afghanistan-survey2006.html.

Skepticism as to whether the Canadian mission would be successful was already quite pronounced in 2006, with almost 60 percent of Canadians polled doubting that the engagement would be successful. More recent polls show dwindling support. In a July 2008 poll conducted by Angus Reid Strategies, only 36 percent of Canadians agreed with the decision to extend Canada's military mission in Afghanistan through 2011. This represents a sharp drop from 41 percent in a similar poll done in May 2008.[23]

Actors

Canada's involvement in Afghanistan has been played out through the actions and interactions of a bewilderingly complicated landscape of actors.[24]

Canadian Government Departments in Ottawa. As mentioned above, these include Defence, Foreign Affairs, CIDA, Public Safety, Justice and Finance, as well as other actors such as the Canadian parliament and its recently established Special Committee on Afghanistan, and coordinating mechanisms in Ottawa both on the political and the working level. Their interactions can be outlined as follows:

- All the main departments of government involved in Afghanistan have an Afghanistan Task Force. These, until recently, were coordinated through the Department of Foreign Affairs; in response to the *Manley Report*, the coordination function has been relocated to the Privy Council, which supports a newly created Cabinet Committee on Afghanistan.[25]
- START, the Stabilization and Reconstruction Task Force, is an across-departmental structure located in the Department of Foreign Affairs. START is a major funder of Canadian activities in Afghanistan that are not clearly developmental (financed through CIDA) or military (financed through the Department of Defence) in nature. START primarily supports activities in the area of rule of law: police reform, judicial reform, and prisons reform.[26]
- The SSR Working Group is another whole of government mechanism embedded in the DFAIT, which since March 2006 has brought together functionaries from across government to ensure coherence in SSR policy, coordinate SSR deployments, and ensure that those deployed on SSR missions have the requisite training.

Intergovernmental Organizations. Canadian government departments deliver many of their policies and programs for Afghanistan through intergovernmental organizations, including NATO, the United Nations, the World Bank, the International Monetary Fund, the G7, and the Organization for Security and Co-operation in Europe. Programs are delivered at the headquarters of these organizations and in some instances through in-country offices and structures, for example, NATO's International Security Assistance Force, the United Nations Assistance Mission for Afghanistan (UNAMA), and the World Bank's Afghanistan Reconstruction Trust Fund.[27]

In-Country Multilateral Coordination Mechanisms. These mechanisms include

- the Joint Coordination and Monitoring Board set up in 2006 to oversee the implementation of the Afghanistan Compact, the road map for the country's further efforts in the areas of security, development, and governance, with seven representatives from the Afghan government and twenty-one from the international community, including Canada;[28]
- the Law and Order Trust Fund for Afghanistan, created to finance priority policing activities;[29]
- the Policy Action Group, established by President Karzai in 2006 to manage four working groups addressing such issues as intelligence, security, strategic communication, and reconstruction and development. Representation includes the Afghan president (the chair), the Afghan ministers of Defence, Internal Communications, and Education, representatives of UNAMA, ISAF, and Operation Enduring Freedom (OEF), as well as the ambassadors of the United Kingdom, the Netherlands, and Canada;
- US-led structures of which Canada is a part, such as the Combined Security Transition Command – Afghanistan (CSTC-A) that works with the Afghan government and the international community to help the Afghanistan National Security Forces to carry out organizational reforms.[30]

Canadian Representation in Afghanistan. Canada is represented by its ambassador, the highest-ranking Canadian official in the country; by the Joint Task Force – Afghanistan (JTF-AFG), now under NATO command in the ISAF and stationed in Kandahar; as well as by a number of special bodies with multidepartmental representation subordinated to them, such as the following:

- the Kandahar Province Reconstruction Team, one of twenty-five PRTs operating in Afghanistan. The Kandahar PRT has roughly 350 personnel from various departments of government, protected by a dedicated Canadian Forces infantry company. Their task is to deliver reconstruction and development aid in Kandahar province, supported by a variety of international donors and contractors including representatives of the United States Agency for International Aid (USAID) and Afghan central ministries;[31]
- the Canadian Operational Mentor Liaison Team (OMLT or informally, "omelette"), which works with the Afghan Nation Army (ANA) and the Afghan National Police (APA) to build capacity to a level where

these national institutions can assume responsibility for security in Kandahar province;[32]

- the Strategic Advisory Team – Afghanistan (SAT-A), which from 2005 to late 2008 worked to support capacity-building for Afghan central ministries. While SAT-A was a military unit, it worked closely with the Canadian ambassador, the CIDA representative in Kabul, and a senior representative of the Afghan government;[33] and
- the Canadian Afghan National Training Centre Detachment in Kabul, which provides some fifteen trainers for Afghan army personnel.[34]

Clearly, a major challenge to Canada has been to ensure certain coherence in the objectives, programs, and actions of this army of actors. We will return to the subject in the concluding section.

SSR and SSR-Related Program Activities

Canada's combat mission in Afghanistan has been the precondition for a range of SSR and SSR-related activities. The overarching framework for these activities is laid out in the Afghanistan Compact and in the more detailed Afghanistan National Development Strategy (ANDS), which set out a five-year program of cooperation between the Government of Afghanistan and the international community in three areas: security; governance, rule of law, and human rights; and economic and social development (with counter-narcotics as a cross-cutting fourth program area).[35] The activities of the main Canadian governmental departments engaged in Afghanistan have dovetailed closely with the first of these program areas.

Thus, the Department of National Defence and the Canadian Forces have led on cantonment of heavy weapons, demining, and training of the Afghan National Army. CIDA has led on infrastructure repair, rural development, education, and local governance. Public Safety has led on police training, through the RCMP, and on prisons regime improvement, through the Correctional Service of Canada.[36] The Department of Finance has been involved in many of these activities through World Bank, International Monetary Fund, and G7 funding mechanisms as well as in other initiatives such as providing advice to the Government of Afghanistan on trade and investment, private sector development, economic governance, DDR (disarmament, demobilization, and reintegration programs), and anti-narcotics actions.

The jewel in the crown in Afghanistan as concerns SSR has, however, been the work of the Provincial Reconstruction Teams. PRTs are civil-military partnerships designed to facilitate the development of a secure environment and reconstruction in the Afghan regions. Only the military elements of PRTs are integrated in the ISAF chain of command. As described on the NATO website, the primary purposes of PRTs are

- to help the Government of Afghanistan extend its authority through the country;
- to facilitate the development of a secure environment in the Afghan regions, including the establishment of relationships with local authorities; and
- to support, as appropriate, security sector reform activities and, within means and capabilities, to facilitate the reconstruction effort.[37]

Canada took over the Kandahar PRT from the United States in 2005–2006 when it redeployed its troops from Kabul to Kandahar. This PRT is top-heavy in military personnel owing to the security situation, but staff also include representatives of Foreign Affairs, CIDA, the RCMP, Canadian municipal police, and the Correctional Service of Canada, as well as a few representatives of various US agencies.[38]

Currently, there are twenty-six PRTS headed up by thirteen NATO member countries. Figure 2 shows their locations, and Table 5 summarizes the different national approaches. Those that are led by the United States tend to downplay governance and emphasize security; most other PRTs focus on both development and governance issues. Some other PRTs, such as the one in Faryab led by Norway, focus on DDR and ANP training and mentoring. While similar to other PRTs in

TABLE 5
National Approaches to PRTs

Country/PRTs	*US (12)*	*UK (1)*	*Germany (2)*	*CDN (1)*
Personnel per PRT	75	100	450	335
Composition	Mainly military	Civil-military	Civil-military	Civil-military
Role	Focus mainly on infrastructure repair: small scale, quick impact programs to win "hearts and minds"	Focus on both security forces efficiency and governance of security sector (identified as such as SSR)	Focus on both security forces efficiency and governance of security sector	Focus on both security forces efficiency and governance of security sector
Environment	Eastern – malign	Southern – malign	Northern – benign	Southern – malign

Source: Author's compilation.

FIGURE 2
International Security Assistance Force

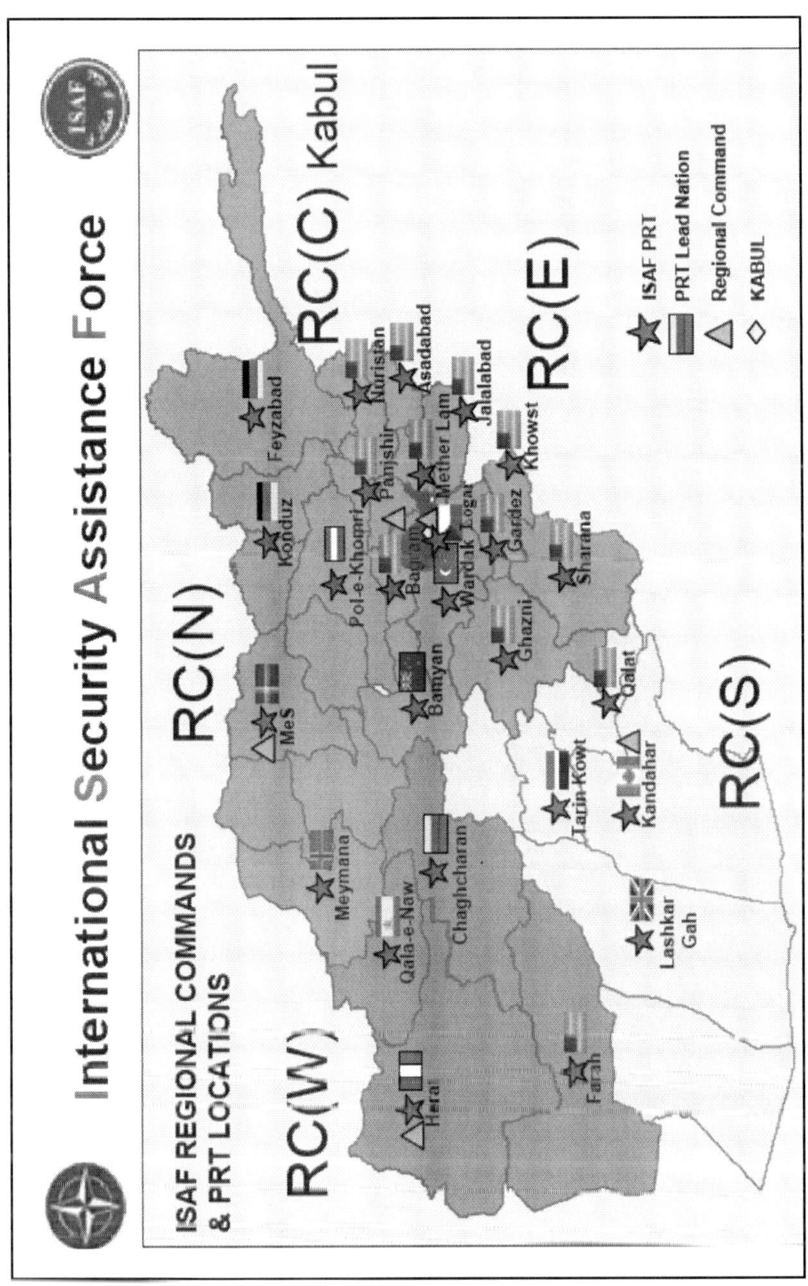

Source: For the map and more information on the PRTs, see www.nato.int/multi/map-afghanistan-htm.

that it has military and civilian pillars, the Norwegian model is distinct because it does not engage directly in development work in its province but channels development funds through the Norwegian Embassy in Kabul, working in cooperation with two civilian employees from the embassy stationed at the PRT. In this way, the Norwegian PRT model is more centralized than others.[39]

Budgets

Canada gives more money to Afghanistan than to any other country.[40] Other countries identified as priorities for Canadian policy such as Haiti and Sudan lag well behind. According to the Canadian Broadcasting Corporation, the military costs for the mission in Afghanistan reached $2.6 billion in March 2007, or nearly $1.3 million per day of the mission.[41] As in the case of US spending for Iraq, assessments of the costs of military action vary widely. For example, one Canadian research organization puts the cost to date at three times as much.[42]

Canada is a leading donor to Afghanistan for civilian activity, with over $1 billion pledged to 2011.[43] Generally, estimates of the relationship of military to civilian costs run about ten to one. This proportion was criticized by the *Manley Report*, as was the fact that much of Canadian spending goes through multilateral aid agencies (35 percent) and the central government (50 percent), leaving little for "locally managed quick action projects that bring immediate improvement to everyday life for Afghans" or for "signature projects readily identified as supported by Canada."[44]

There has also been criticism of the high proportion of contract budgets that stay with Canadian contractors as opposed to local Afghan actors, as well as the fact that the Afghan government has apparently been incapable of accounting for money put at its disposal. A recent article in the *Globe and Mail* claimed that the Afghan government had not been able to substantiate roughly one-third of the $15 billion entrusted to it since 2001.[45]

Policy Reorientation

In follow-up to the *Manley Report* of January 2008, Ottawa has published a report entitled *Canada's Engagement in Afghanistan: Setting a Course to 2011* (hereafter, *Engagement in Afghanistan*).[46] The report offers a candid assessment of the situation in Afghanistan. As concerns security, it notes that the situation deteriorated through 2007 and into 2008. As concerns governance, it decries persistent shortcomings owing to the weak capacity of Afghan government institutions and waning public trust because of continuing widespread corruption. As concerns development, the report acknowledges that while the economy has been expanding at a remarkable rate, it will take many years of "sustained growth to reach reasonable levels." *Engagement in Afghanistan* lays out a number of initiatives that have been taken in response to the *Manley Report* recommendations and others that go beyond it. These initiatives are summarized below.

First, *Engagement in Afghanistan* revamps Canada's governance approach to Afghanistan at home. As mentioned above and as recommended in the *Manley Report*, a cabinet committee on Afghanistan has been created, and interdepartmental coordination of Canadian policy has been moved to the Privy Council from Foreign Affairs, with a dedicated full-time staff headed by deputy ministers from Foreign Affairs, Defence, Public Safety, and CIDA.

Second, Ottawa has committed itself to making quarterly reports to parliament and its newly created Special Committee on Afghanistan, and to ensuring a better flow of information on policy to the Canadian media and public. Ottawa has also promised to develop a system of benchmarks for measuring progress on the security, governance, and development fronts in Afghanistan and Canadian efforts in these areas.

Third, the Canadian approach within Afghanistan has been recalibrated in the direction of "Kandaharization" and "civilianization" of the Canadian involvement. The process of concentrating energies on Kandahar, initiated by the Liberal Party in 2005, is to be reinforced. More resources will be allocated to the province, with the amount it is to receive rising from 17 percent to 50 percent of all Canadian aid to Afghanistan. Canada is attempting to showcase three "signature" development projects in the province. Training of Afghan police and military is to be pursued, the objective being that these forces will able to sustain a secure environment and rule of law by 2011, the date when the Afghanistan Compact governing cooperation between the Afghan government and the international community is due to conclude, and when the Canadian presence will presumably wind down. A senior-level civilian representative is to be appointed to the PRT in Kandahar, the number of civilians involved is set to increase significantly, and Canadian actors are to be given more discretion in the making of policy to address local conditions. Canada is committed to pursue its efforts to advance Afghanistan's capacity for democratic governance and effective government decision-making, as well as to help bring about national political reconciliation.

Fourth, Canada has put its NATO allies on notice that it expects them to field an additional 1,000 combat troops if Canada is to maintain its own presence. This appeal is in part conditioned by the high number of Canadian casualties, but also by the growing criticism levelled by the Afghan government toward coalition governments regarding civilian casualties owing to mistargeting from high-level bombing operations. Everything points to the fact that insufficient soldiers on the ground necessitates greater use of air-power which, while having greatly improved in accuracy in recent years, still remains a blunt instrument, often incapable of discriminating between Taliban and civilian targets.[47]

Fifth, *Engagement in Afghanistan* calls for a changed leadership paradigm for international efforts in Afghanistan, coming out strongly for the United Nations to assume a much more important coordinating role in Afghanistan and enthusiastically supporting the appointment of the Norwegian Kai Eide as the UN Secretary General's Special Representative in the country.

While much of what is proposed appears to be very sound, the *Engagement in Afghanistan* report raises more questions than it answers. The reorganization in Ottawa makes sense in theoretical terms, but it remains to be seen whether the now centrally located task force will have the necessary clout to make coherent policy and to implement it effectively. There still remains a considerable degree of stove-piping in the Canadian departmental system (and in that of most other countries), despite 3D and whole of government efforts. The situation in and around Afghanistan, and in particular in such southern provinces as Kandahar, will have to contend with formidable political challenges in 2008–2009: in particular, the instability and uncertainty engendered by elections in Pakistan, Afghanistan, the United States, and Canada itself. The call for additional support from NATO allies comes none too soon. But just how the allies will respond, in view of reservations in public opinion and the material constraints they face when it comes to putting soldiers in the field, remains to be seen. Still, allied countries deployed in more secure parts of the country and under restrictions to be active elsewhere are now under notice from Ottawa that this must change. Finally, there is definitely a need for enhanced coordination of the various initiatives underway in Afghanistan. On the other hand, a UN umbrella under existing international circumstances may not be the ideal framework for organizing the leadership of such a complex endeavour as Afghanistan.

Assessment

The Canadian approach to SSR in Afghanistan is now seven years old. What kind of balance sheet can now be established? Basically, the Canadians have attempted to take a comprehensive and integrated approach in their efforts and to encourage other governments—donor countries as well as the Government of Afghanistan—to do likewise. A balance has been sought between governance initiatives and those seeking to enhance the ability of the Afghan national security forces to assume responsibility for security delivery on the behalf of their population. These positive elements form an integral part of the current Canadian government's new approach to Afghanistan and should be accentuated as they are implemented. This being said, there is much that the Canadian government needs to do in order to fully operationalize its approach to SSR, both in Afghanistan and more generally.

First, Canada should develop its own concept of SSR. This is not to suggest that Canada should try to reinvent the wheel in this regard. However, the country has a long tradition of involvement abroad that has been articulated and implemented through a variety of departmental policy portals with different operational cultures, objectives, procedures, and the like. These now need to be brought together in an overarching Canadian concept that is elaborated by the various Canadian government departments involved in SSR. More likely than not, such a concept will end up closely resembling the OECD Development Assistance Committee concept described above. But Canadians need to take ownership of their own national approach and use this process to support efforts to encourage national actors to work together as part of a common endeavour.

Second, to this end, Canada should redouble its efforts to build the capacity of government representatives working both in Ottawa and abroad to operate in an SSR mode. Canada has been one of the first member countries of the Organisation for Economic Co-operation and Development to engage in the capacity-building consultations on SSR offered by the OECD Development Assistance Committee. The Canadian experience in Afghanistan underscores the importance of having staff capable of supporting and spearheading, as the situation may demand, the rebuilding and creation of ministries, security forces, and systems for managing government departments and their personnel and finances, not to mention the all-important structures for overseeing and controlling the security forces and their masters.

Third, Canada needs to think about how to create incentives for its staff to coordinate and cooperate more effectively at home and in the field. The stance taken by ministers, including the prime minister, is crucial in this regard. Beyond this, there is much that can be done to encourage symmetries among different departments at the staff level. Involving staff in the elaboration of interdepartmental memoranda of understanding MOUs would be a step in the right direction. Another would be the insertion of incentives in staff-promotion packages that would reward efforts to enhance coordination and cooperation. Canada might also use its world-class International Development Research Centre to explore new avenues for improving effective coordination and cooperation among the multiple actors who typically find themselves working shoulder to shoulder in such environments as Afghanistan.

Fourth, in view of the challenges discussed above, it may be worthwhile to think about creating dedicated international departments in those ministries that are called upon to provide capacity for programs, together with a policy framework for coordinating and integrating their efforts. As part of this process, Canada might review whether START, the centralized funding mechanism located in Foreign Affairs, might not be more effective as a central fund of government subordinated to a central policy framework along the lines of the Afghanistan Task Force located in the Privy Council Office. Similarly, there should be a review of whether SSR and SSR-related funds now dispensed through CIDA and the Department of National Defence should be reallocated to such a repositioned START. Centralization of funding is a device to which other governments, such as the United Kingdom and the Netherlands, have resorted with success. A related step in this area will be to rethink the way that international service is rewarded in the career paths of civil servants. The current system sometimes fails to take into account experience won in the field relative to experience gained in the corridors of powers in Ottawa.

Fifth, Canada should redouble its efforts to encourage its allies to step up to the plate. Already, the appeal for more troops has resulted in the French government deciding to deploy another seven hundred troops to Afghanistan. Canada has earned the credibility to demand more of its allies.

At the same time, Canada needs to pursue its efforts to be able to field military forces that can create a secure environment, carry out reconstruction efforts with and for local populations, and work together with other actors—military and others—in the field. If the experience of Western countries in Afghanistan since 2001 has shown nothing else, it has underscored the importance of being able to bring sufficient military forces to bear to create an environment in which development can proceed. It has also shown that the norm for third parties is to have to deal with environments that are both post-conflict and conflictual in nature, and often the borderlines between the two are ill-defined and subject to rapid change.

Conclusions

Canada has been an important player in Afghanistan, punching above its weight, certainly if one considers the development resources it has brought to the table and the military responsibilities it has assumed in the conflict in view of its traditional peacekeeping role. But Canada is only one actor in an army of other countries and their peace-support forces, as well as NGOS, IGOs, private military and security companies, and local and international media, not to mention the Government of Afghanistan itself. The fortunes of Afghanistan do not depend on the Canadian effort alone, just as Canada's successes and failures are in large part conditioned by those of other actors.

Much has been written about the trials and tribulations of the international community in Afghanistan, and there is no need to revisit these debates in detail.[48] But in conclusion it may be useful to highlight the main shortcomings of the external actors' efforts.

A first observation is that while the international community's involvement has not been tainted with the brush of illegitimacy as it has in Iraq, this bonus has been losing relevance as the number of civilian casualties from aerial bombings has soared. There is a straight line between insufficient firepower to create a secure environment and overreliance on airpower to defeat the Taliban and al Qaeda.

Second, the approach of the international community in Afghanistan has suffered from the beginning from the lack of a coherent strategy. Any effort in this direction was skewered from the outset by two things: the preponderance of the US-led GWOT (Global War on Terror) agenda in determining the policies of the international community, and the unintegrated approach to Afghan security that was institutionalized by the decisions taken at the Bonn donors conference in 2002. The strategic malaise goes, however, well beyond this. It has included an abject failure to think creatively about how to give the Pashtuns—Afghanistan's largest ethnic group—a stake in the country's stabilization and development. If the Sunnis of Iraq can be brought back into the fold, why cannot the Pashtuns of Afghanistan? A related strategic issue concerns how the international community has approached other players in Afghanistan's region—obviously, Pakistan, but also others such as Iran, India, and the Central Asian republics.

A third major fault line has concerned the ability of the many actors involved in Afghanistan to work together. Examples of this dysfunction are legend. To take just a few, there are the efforts of the international community to promote rule of law in Afghanistan. It is clear that programs in the related areas of policing, courts, and corrections are uncoordinated. It is clear that approaches to these policy areas differ from province to province and from district to district as a function of which external donor is in the lead. These donors tend to propagate the norms and objectives that they are most familiar with from national practice. There are, as yet, no common international reference points for reform efforts. What happens at district and provincial levels tends to be disconnected from what happens at the national level, and in turn there is little interface between programs concerning policing and those that address the military, notwithstanding the interdependence of these two subsectors of the security sector in providing for the public's security in Afghanistan.[49]

Last but not least, there is the issue of resources. Afghanistan is Iraq's poor sister in this regard, with the latter profiting from substantially greater resource inputs from abroad and, more recently, also from internally generated resources such as oil. The comparison of Iraq and Afghanistan in Figure 3 drives this message home.

FIGURE 3
Battlespace Comparison

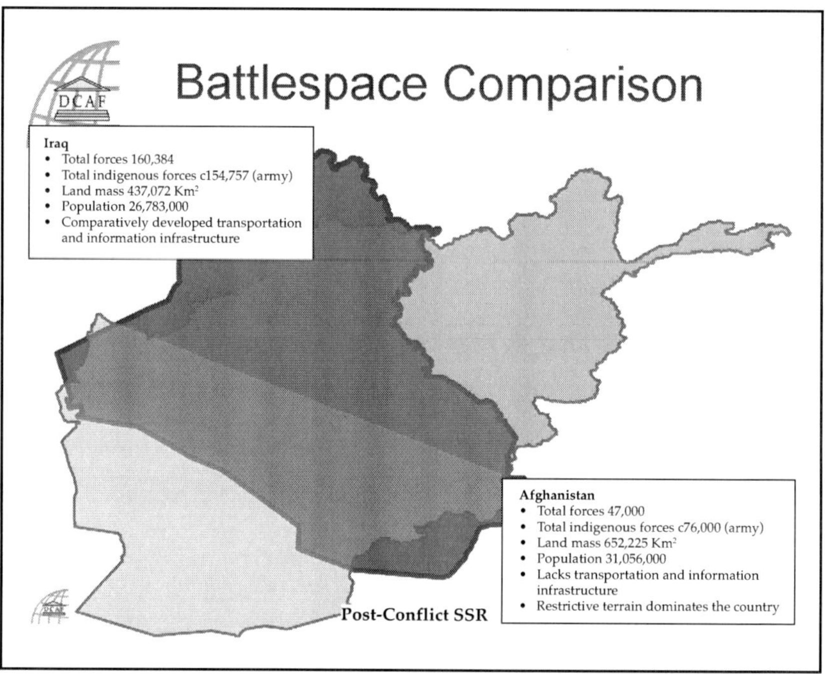

Source: Adapted from a similar version presented by Brigadier General Richard E. Nugee, Chief Joint Fires and Influence Branch, Headquarters Allied Rapid Reaction Corps (Brussels, 1 April 2007).

Afghanistan has proven to be a major testing ground for a number of opposing approaches championed by different stakeholders in the Canadian context. One has revolved around the best use of the Canadian Forces, in particular, the issue of whether they should uphold their traditional post-Korean War role as peacekeepers or whether they need to be capable of participating in combat operations, as they have been required to do in Afghanistan. This deployment has also seen Canada struggling with a choice between its more traditional stance as an ally that fell into line and one that is now prepared, when pressed, to set conditions for other allies to fulfil. A third area of challenge has involved the government's public information policy, whereby the choice has lain between the continuation of long-standing efforts to control the public debate by attempting to seal issues off from public scrutiny, to a more recent attempt to engage parliament and the public through regular reporting on developments and the accompanying implicit invitation for them to exercise greater oversight.

Alongside such general public policy issues, debates that are more specific to the SSR agenda have raged as well. In particular, there is the question of the proper mix between long-term development programs such as those sponsored by CIDA, and shorter-term, quick-fix projects advocated by the Department of Defence and the Canadian Forces. The response for the time being appears to be that both are needed and that, if the latter are particularly required, they should be embedded in a long-term development perspective. Also dear to the SSR agenda has been the question of intergovernmental coordination and cooperation, where much progress has been made, even if much more needs to be done. Finally, in recent years, Canada has moved toward a comprehensive, integrated approach to security and development, justice and governance. The movement has been slow, incomplete, and imperfect, but it has definitively taken place. This is a promising trajectory that warrants continuing support on the part of both the Canadian public and Canada's partners.

Notes

This chapter was prepared with the help of my research assistant, Gabriel Real de Azúa, who did much of the research and advised me on successive drafts. His contribution is greatly appreciated.

1. Saša Janković, "The Status of Serbia's Intelligence Reform and Its Challenges," in *Security Sector Reform in South East Europe – From a Necessary Remedy to a Global Concept*, ed. Anja H. Ebnöther, Ernst M. Felberbauer, and Mladen Staničić (National Defence Academy and Bureau for Security Policy, 2007), 150-56, http://www.bmlv.gv.at/pdf_pool/publikationen/10_wg13_global-concept_200_jankovic.pdf.

2. David M. Law, "Rethinking the Code of Conduct in the Light of Security Sector Reform," in *Consolidating the OSCE*, PSIO Occasional Paper 4, ed. Daniel Warner (Geneva: Program for the Study of International Organizations, HEI, and Federal Department of Foreign Affairs, 2006), 83-105, http://graduateinstitute.ch/webdav/site/iheid/shared/iheid/514/OP4_2006_EDITED_FINAL.pdf

3. National Security Council, "The National Security Strategy of the United States of America" (September 2002), http://www.whitehouse.gov/nsc/nss.pdf.

4. Steven Staples and Bill Robinson, "More Than the Cold War: Canada's Military Spending 2007–08," *Foreign Policy Series* 2, no. 3 (Canadian Centre for Policy Alternatives, October 2007), http://www.policyalternatives.ca/documents/National_Office_Pubs/2007/More_Than_the_Cold_War.pdf.

5. The author was involved in the efforts of the Department of National Defence to reintroduce lecturers from the military into university campuses in 2001–02. The response of students, many of whom were first- or second-generation

Canadians whose families had come from fragile, conflict, or post-conflict countries, was particularly enthusiastic.

6. Despite efforts to re-establish a credible security role for Canada at home and abroad, the process is still in its infancy and will likely take several years. For example, an article entitled "Between the Lines of the Manley Report" by *Globe and Mail* journalist Jeffrey Simpson (Toronto, 29 January 2008) claimed that the most soldiers that Canada—a G8 member and 33 million people strong—was able to field at any one time was 1,000.

7. Organisation for Economic Co-operation and Development (OECD), *Security System Reform and Governance*, DAC Guidelines and Reference Series (Paris: OECD Publishing, 2005), http://www.oecd.org/dataoecd/8/39/31785288.pdf; OECD, *The OECD DAC Handbook on Security System Reform (SSR): Supporting Security and Justice* (Paris: OECD, 2005), http://www.oecd.org/dataoecd/43/25/38406485.pdf.

8. See, for example, Geneva Centre for the Control of Armed Forces, "The UN Approach to SSR in Post-Conflict Peacebuilding" (Factsheet, n.d.), www.dcaf.ch/un_ssr_pcpb/_index.cfm?navsub1=31&nav1=3.

9. Human Security Network, "The Vision of the Human Security Network" (20 May 1999), http://www.humansecuritynetwork.org/menu-e.php.

10. It has been argued that human security was sidelined after 9/11 as Canada moved toward the US approach in the War on Terror, which prioritized national security considerations as opposed to concerns about the security of individuals and their communities. See Stefan Gänzle, "The Impact of 9/11 on Human Security in Canada's Foreign Policy" (draft paper presented at a Canadian Political Sciences Association conference in Saskatoon, 1 June 2007), http://www.cpsa-acsp.ca/papers-2007/Ganzle.pdf. For an examination of the relationship between human security and SSR, see David. M. Law, "Human Security and Security Sector Reform: Contrasts and Commonalities," *Sicherheit und Frieden* 1 (2005).

11. Department of National Defence, "Canada's International Policy Statement. A Role of Pride and Influence in the World: Defence" (Cat. No. D2-168/2005, Department of National Defence, Ottawa, 2005), http://merln.ndu.edu/whitepapers/Canada_Defence_2005.pdf.

12. The quotes are taken from a speech by David Mulroney entitled "Canada in Afghanistan: From Collaboration to Integration," delivered 2 May 2007 when he was Canadian associate deputy minister of Foreign Affairs and interdepartmental coordinator for Afghanistan. He has since become a deputy minister in the Privy Council Office, roughly the prime minister's dedicated civil service, with similar responsibilities.

13. Taylor Owen and Patrick Travers, "3D Vision," *The Walrus*, 8 August 2008, http://www.walrusmagazine.ca/articles/2007.07.Afghanistan-and-Canada/.

14. David M. Law, "Cooperation among SSR-Relevant IGOs," in *Intergovernmental Organisations and Security Sector Reform*, ed. David M. Law (Berlin:

Litverlag, 2007), 43-62; and David M. Law, "Taking Stock, Moving Forward," in *Intergovernmental Organisations and Security Sector Reform*, 239-52.

15. As a developing concept, SSR has a number of dimensions that need further conceptual work, ideally supported by empirical experience from the field. For example, the borders between what qualifies as SSR and what does not remain weakly defined. Is a *train and equip* program for the military SSR if it does not have a dimension designed to ensure that those who are trained and equipped are subject to effective democratic control? Or is this consideration moot if other actors are involved in governance issues that are designed to promote democratic governance? Likewise, the costs and benefits of SSR have not yet been subject to a rigorous comparative analysis. Furthermore, methodologies for assessing security sector performance or the effectiveness of SSR programs are yet in their infancy, and so on.

16. See "Security System Reform and Rule of Law" at http://geo.international.gc.ca/cip-pic/securitysystemreform-en.aspx and the statement of the Canadian Ambassador to the UN Security Council on 20 February 2007 at www.canadaninternational.gc.ca/prmny-mponu/canada.un-canada/statement.

17. See Center for Policy and Human Development, *Afghanistan Human Development Report 2007. Bridging Modernity and Tradition: Rule of Law and the Search for Justice* (Islamabad: Army Press, 2007), http://hdr.undp.org/en/reports/nationalreports/asiathepacific/afghanistan/nhdr2007.pdf.

18. For a complete list of these parties refer to the Central Intelligence Agency, *The World Factbook*, "South Asia: Afghanistan," https://www.cia.gov/library/publications/the-world-factbook/geos/af.html#Govt.

19. Ibid.

20. See Independent Panel on Canada's Future Role in Afghanistan, *Final Report* (Ottawa: Minister of Public Works and Government Services, 2008), http://dsp-psd.tpsgc.gc.ca/collection_2008/dfait-maeci/FR5-20-1-2008E.pdf., especially pp. 20-22. This document is hereafter referred to as the *Manley Report*.

21. These objectives have been challenged by the Canadian public with essentially the following arguments:
    - The money that goes to Afghanistan should go instead to poor and disadvantaged Canadians;
    - The Canadian involvement costs too much;
    - Canadian money is being spent on the Canadian military, not on the Afghan military;
    - Canadian resources should be invested in development, not in counter-insurgency actions;
    - Canada needs to revert to a traditional peacekeeping role (i.e., acting neutrally between opposing parties);
    - In Afghanistan, Canada acts as a lackey of the United States: Canada has been duped into a Global War on Terror (GWOT) that is based on false premises and is being ineffectively implemented;

- If Afghanistan is such an important issue, why are US/NATO allies contributing so few troops to the ISAF and imposing constraints ("caveats") that make it difficult or impossible for the ISAF commander to deploy them flexibly to deal with security threats as they arise in various parts of Afghanistan?
- If Canada were not involved, the Afghans would have to do the job themselves;
- It would be better to spend Canadian money on other places (i.e., Darfur); Afghanistan is a lost cause—there is no point in pursuing the Canadian involvement there.

22. This material is based on Duane Bratt, "Mr Harper Goes to War: Canada, Afghanistan and the Return of High Politics in Canadian Foreign Policy" (2007), www.cpsa-acsp.ca/papers-2007/Bratt.pdf, as well as on the *Manley Report*. According to Janice Gross Stein and Eugene Lang, the initial deployment to Afghanistan was also conditioned by reluctance on the part of the Canadian (Liberal) government in the years following 9/11 to participate in the modernization of NORAD, the US-Canada system for monitoring aerial threats to North America, into the US-led Ballistic Missile Defence program. With the United States wanting to focus more of its hard power on Iraq, Canada was happy to fill the void in Kandahar. For a detailed account, see Janice Gross Stein and Eugene Lang, *The Unexpected War: Canada in Kandahar* (Toronto: Viking Canada, 2007), 181. Some observers, such as Duane Bratt in "Mr Harper Goes to War," 7, have argued that the third deployment to Kabul in 2003 was, in part, a means for Canada to avoid a deployment to Iraq. Bratt also quotes the Canadian Ambassador to Washington explaining that the fourth deployment decision, in favour of Kandahar in 2005, was "linked to the failure to send troops to Iraq in 2003."

23. CBC News, "36 Percent Support Keeping Troops in Afghanistan through 2011 : Poll," *cbc.ca*, http://www.cbc.ca/canada/story/2008/07/07/afghanistan-poll.html.

24. The author is indebted to Jim Cox for his succinct rendering of this alphabet soup in "Afghanistan: The Canadian Military Mission," InfoSeries (Parliamentary Information and Research Service, Publication PRB 07-19E, 6 November 2007).

25. Prime Minister Harper announced the creation of the cabinet committee on Afghanistan and the Afghanistan Task Force within the Privy Council Office on 8 February 2008.

26. Foreign Affairs and International Trade Canada, "START – Stabilization and Reconstruction Task Force" (3 December 2008), http://www.international.gc.ca/START-GTSR/index.aspx.

27. See World Bank, "Afghanistan Reconstruction Trust Fund: The Benefit of Working Together" (World Bank Group, 2009), http://web.worldbank.org/WBSITE/EXTERNAL/COUNTRIES/SOUTHASIAEXT/0,,contentMDK:21698820~pagePK:146736~piPK:146830~theSitePK:223547,00.html.

28. *Manley Report*, 48.
29. Ibid.
30. Ibid., 47.
31. Cox, "Afghanistan: The Canadian Military Mission."
32. Ibid.
33. According to recent reports, the SAT-A unit is in the process of being disbanded and a new body, led by CIDA, is being constituted. This was one of the recommendations of the *Manley Report*.
34. Not to be forgotten in this picture are the non-state actors that design programs and/or support their delivery: first, the Canadian non-governmental organizations (NGOs) in both Canada and Afghanistan, as well the international non-governmental organizations and networks of which they are a part. For more information, see Canada's Coalition to End Global Poverty, "Canadian NGOs in Afghanistan (Briefing note, n.d.), http://www.devp.org/devpme/eng/pressroom/documents/pdf/NGOProfiles.pdf. Second, private military and security companies (PMSCs). While to our knowledge Canada has no such companies operating in or for the Afghan theatre, the United States does—and such companies can have an impact on both civilian and military activities carried out by Canadians. Ongoing research at the Geneva Centre for the Democratic Control of Armed Forces indicates that some ninety PMSCs are active in the Afghan theatre.
35. See "The Afghanistan Compact, Building on Success; The London Conference on Afghanistan," 31 January–1 February 2006, http://www.ands.gov.af/admin/ands/ands_docs/upload/UploadFolder/Afghanistan%20Compact.pdf; Government of the Islamic Republic of Afghanistan, "Afghanistan National Development Strategy Summary Report: An Interim Strategy for Security, Governance, Economic Growth and Poverty Reduction," http://www.reliefweb.int/rw/RWFiles2006.nsf/FilesByRWDocUNIDFileName/KHII-6LK3R2-unama-afg-30jan1.pdf/$File/unama-afg-30jan1.pdf.
36. See *Manley Report*, 25, and "Canada in Afghanistan. CBC News in Depth: Where the Mission Is and Where It Might Go Next," 22 January 2008.
37. This description is based on information from a NATO web page, "NATO in Afghanistan" (Factsheet, 5 July7 2005), http://www.nato.int/issues/afghanistan/040628-factsheet.htm.
38. *Manley Report*, 23.
39. For more information on the Norwegian model, see Norway – The Official Site in Afghanistan, "Norwegian Led PRT in Faryeb" (2007), http://www.norway.org.af/prt/faryab/.
40. Afghanistan is the single largest recipient of Canadian bilateral aid. Since 2002, Canada has contributed US$412.2 million (18.8 percent of the total) through CIDA to the World Bank-administered Afghanistan Reconstruction Trust Fund, making it the second-largest contributor after the United Kingdom. See World Bank, "Canada and the World Bank: Working Towards a Better Future for Afghanistan" (World Bank Group, 2009), http://go.worldbank.org/OZ869X45T0.

41. CBC News, "Afghanistan, by the Numbers," *cbc.ca*, 17 January 2008, http://www.cbc.ca/news/background/afghanistan/bythenumbers.html.

42. Scott Taylor, "Iraq and Afghanistan: Maybe We Should Admit Mistake" (Centre for Research on Globalization, 8 April 2008), http://www.globalresearch.ca/index.php?context=va&aid=8590.

43. CBC News, "Afghanistan, by the Numbers."

44. *Manley Report*, 26.

45. Editorial, *Globe and Mail*, 25 March 2008.

46. Government of Canada, *Report to Parliament: Canada's Engagement in Afghanistan – Setting a Course to 2011* (June 2008), http://www.afghanistan.gc.ca/canada-afghanistan/documents/q108/index.aspx?lang=en.

47. See, for example, "Afghan Civilians: Caught in the Crossfire," *International Herald Tribune*, 7 September 2008, http://www.iht.com/articles/2008/09/07/opinion/edafghan.php.

48. See Daniel Korski, "Afghanistan: Europe's Forgotten War" (European Council on Foreign Relations, January 2008), http://ecfr.3cdn.net/fcdc73b-8da7af85936_q8m6b5o4j.pdf; Paul Gallis and Vincent Morelli, "NATO in Afghanistan: A Test of the Transatlantic Alliance" (CRS Report for Congress, 18 July 2008), http://www.fas.org/sgp/crs/row/RL33627.pdf; International Crisis Group, "Reports by Region: Afghanistan," http://www.crisisgroup.org/home/index.cfm?id=1266&l=1.

49. Such shortcomings were at the core of a workshop on policing and justice issues organized by the Canadian Mission to the European Union in Brussels on 1 April 2008.

Chapter 15

Security Sector Reform in Afghanistan: The German Approach

Michael Brzoska

Introduction

This chapter assesses the largest security sector reform (SSR) support project the German government has ever been involved in: police reform in Afghanistan. After an introductory section outlining the German approach to SSR in general, the German effort to help establish a central police force in Afghanistan is sketched. The following section reviews successes and failures of the police program on a number of dimensions of SSR. Finally, the future prospects for police reform in Afghanistan are briefly discussed.

German SSR – An Overview

Germany has not published an official SSR policy statement or doctrine. The most authoritative statement is the "Interministerial Framework for the Support of Reforms in the Security Sector of Developing and Transition Countries," published in 2006 but available only in German.[1] This document has primarily internal functions—to serve as a guide for working units within the relevant ministries—but it is a good indication of the "German approach" to the extent that there is one.

The Interministerial Framework begins by referencing a diverse set of key international documents, most of which were elaborated with German contributions, such as the UN Security Council Resolution 1325 of October 2000, the European Security Strategy of 2004, the European Union Council's SSR concept of November 2005, and the EU Commission's SSR concept of May 2006, as well as documents on NATO partnerships such as the Partnership for Peace program, the Mediterranean Dialogue, and the Istanbul Cooperation Initiative. The Framework also mentions the OECD Development Assistance Committee's documents on SSR.

The main reference, however, is to the German federal government's "Action Plan: Civilian Crisis Prevention, Conflict Resolution and Post-Conflict Peace-Building" of 2004.[2] The Action Plan outlines an ambitious program including, somewhat unexpectedly given its title, activities by the Bundeswehr such as peace missions. The Action Plan has a strong emphasis on poverty reduction and governance, that is, traditional development cooperation concerns. However, the document also indicates that the security sector is of major interest:

> The overwhelming majority of current armed conflicts are domestic conflicts. They signal an inability of the state to adequately guarantee the physical safety of its citizens and certainty of the law. . . . Unless citizens are protected against violence and crime by a functioning state monopoly on the use of force, economic and social development is not possible. The socially disadvantaged groups within the population in particular are acutely dependent on a minimum level of physical and legal security. Reform of the security sector is therefore a key precondition for peace and sustainable development. This applies on the one hand to the reform of the state institutions responsible for guaranteeing the safety of the state and its citizens from coercion and violence (such as the military, the police and the intelligence services). But at least equally important, on the other hand, is a functioning system of civilian control of these institutions by parliament, the executive and the judiciary.[3]

Compared with such lofty statements, the number and scope of activities has remained rather modest. The first "Implementation Report" of the Action Plan, issued in May 2006,[4] lists a good number of projects—from legal reform in Latin American countries to the secondment of military advisers (up to thirty in 2006) to assist the armed forces of partner states in the development and reorganization of their ministries and command staffs, force structures, training courses, and logistical structures. No total financial expenditure is given, though it is said that the largest sub-program, on police reform assistance, was budgeted at €16.9 million in 2006, with most of the money spent in Afghanistan.

Based on German as well as international "lessons learned" in SSR support, the Interministerial Framework delineates three relevant dimensions of security:

- the absence of threats to territorial integrity and state sovereignty as well as to political and economic order;

- the existence of a "state monopoly of violence" as the "point of reference" of internal security; and
- the absence of threats to individuals within their immediate environment, that is, human security.

The objective of SSR according to the framework is to support reforms that cover all three elements of security. At the same time, these reforms need to correspond with democratic and legal norms, good governance, and human rights.[5]

Because SSR is such a comprehensive activity, it offers opportunities for a number of German ministries to contribute. However, for coherence and effectiveness, coordinated activity is "particularly important."[6] In order to improve coordination among the various ministries, an SSR Working Group was established in 2004 with representatives from the Foreign Office, the Ministry of Defence, the Ministry of Economic Cooperation and Development, the Ministry of the Interior, and the Ministry of Justice. It has, however, no executive function, except in the case of a small program on SSR in Indonesia, for which ministries (except Justice) pooled funds of €3 million over a three-year period.

With its emphasis on the two faces of SSR, namely, improving effectiveness of security institutions and ensuring their behaviour and control within a framework of norms, the German concept of SSR is very close to the international "mainstream," as enshrined, for instance, in OECD and EU documents. There are, however, marked differences. One is the strong emphasis in the German approach on the rule of law and thus legal reform. Although some elements of justice reform—primarily criminal justice and prison system reforms—are generally included in SSR documents, German documents tend to conceptualize justice reform more broadly on the basis of the importance of the rule of law for people. Another difference is the low importance given in German documents to the comprehensiveness of security sector reform across the security sector. The Framework document, for instance, contains a list of SSR "best practices," a compendium of projects sorted by security institutions but with little connection among them.

The specifics of the German SSR approach largely reflect German practice and resource restraints. Cooperation in SSR projects among ministries has been, and continues to be, very rudimentary. German development cooperation has traditionally been strong in justice reform, particularly in Latin America. Until recently, there was very little support for police and military reform outside of NATO. In both cases, German policy-makers had been "burned" by earlier scandals, such as the delivery of surplus weapons to Sudan within its military assistance program in the late 1970s, or police assistance to Ethiopia in the early 1970s and to Guatemala in the early 1980s.

Even though German representatives have been supportive of international efforts to improve the visibility and conceptual clarity of SSR, the investment of resources has remained very modest, with a few exceptions, such as Kosovo, Bosnia-Herzegovina, and above all, Afghanistan.

German Police Support in Afghanistan

The following discussion focuses on the police program. Germany supported some other activities that can be classified as SSR, such as seminars for judges and training for military units. These activities, however, were rather limited. Also, in German government presentations on its SSR support for Afghanistan, police reform dominates, if for no other reason than that it was by far the largest of all German SSR programs.

In the discussions among G8 donors to Afghanistan in early 2002, the international community agreed on the concept of "lead nations" to be in charge of reconstruction in different security-related areas. Germany, partly by default, partly by choice, and partly by history (German-Afghan police cooperation goes back to the 1950s), took charge of the construction of the Afghan National Police (ANP). Unfortunately, the concept of "lead nation" was never clearly defined with respect to either the share of contributions among donors or the relationship between the "lead nation" and the Afghan government. The German government saw its role as "lead nation" primarily in terms of "leading the way," but not in terms of being the only provider of human and financial resources.[7] This view, however, conflicted with that of other donors, who saw police matters as a German responsibility.

The German government also saw itself from the beginning as a "key partner" of the Afghan government (this term has replaced that of "lead nations" since the London conference in 2006), both in planning for a new Afghan police and in providing resources. However, as noted by Ambassador Helmut Frick, later responsible for the German police program, the mandate was unclear. As German police advisors were in Afghanistan on the invitation of the Afghan government, there was no international authority on which they could base their work.[8]

The notion of "lead nation" and its successor, "partnership," can be seen in different lights. The concept is in line with general pronouncements from the world of international donors concerning coordination, shared responsibilities, and division of labour among donors, as well as local ownership. However, this approach is also a good justification for limiting Germany's input of money and technical experts and for focusing on "core" activities of which the Afghan side was not capable.

The German government set its prime goal to establish a police force committed to the principles of democracy and the rule of law in which all ethnic groups and both sexes are equally represented. The German concept was that of a civilian police force serving communities and individuals and clearly separated from the military, with respect to both its functions and institutions. The German government sees the development of civilian police concepts in post-conflict situations as one of the great achievements of international peace missions since the 1990s.[9]

Strategically, German police support in Afghanistan was to concentrate on basic and further training for police officers, and equipment and infrastructure. Operationally, the first priority was the building and operating of a policy academy in Kabul and the training of police officers, first in Kabul and later in Kunduz, Faizabad, and Mazar-e-Sharif, incidentally all locations of German International Security Assistance Force (ISAF) contingents. Training at the police academy is thorough, lasting one to three years and covering all aspects of police work. In addition, shorter special training courses are offered by German instructors.

As a second priority, German officers helped to develop various central concepts for the police in Afghanistan—for instance, on training and on reform of the systems of rank and payments, recruitment and promotion—and collected these concepts in a 285-page catalogue known as the *Tashkeel*. These measures were officially adopted by President Karzai in mid-December 2005. Some objectives, such as those concerning the promotion system and pay increases, were implemented rather quickly, while others, such as those addressing the top-heaviness of the existing ranking structure, remain a problem.

As a final component, German officers were sent as advisors and mentors into the Afghan Ministry of the Interior and to various police units.[10] Mentoring is coordinated by the Interagency Police Coordinated Action Group, formed initially under German leadership with the involvement of the ISAF, the United Nations Assistance Mission in Afghanistan (UN-AMA), and other countries.

With respect to infrastructure support, in addition to the Police Academy, German priorities were the border police at Kabul International Airport, counter-narcotics and counter-terrorism authorities, and the country's Criminal Police Office. Germany's expenditures on these efforts were quite moderate compared with the costs of the German ISAF troops (close to €500 million per year) and development cooperation (about €120 million per year, including contributions to international organizations). Modest expenditure was particularly true of Germany's efforts to build up the Afghan police force to a planned strength of 62,000. Between 2002 and 2007, Germany spent a total of €12 million in bilateral aid per annum plus a contribution of €7 million to the Law and Order Trust Fund administered by the United Nations Development Program for the implementation of rank-and-pay reform.[11]

On average, about forty police officers from Federal and Land units were working in Afghanistan within the German police program, assisted by a project group at the Federal Ministry of the Interior. In addition, since the spring of 2007 some of the basic police training (for instance in Kunduz) has been provided by trainers from the Bundeswehr military police, the Feldjäger.

In June 2007, the German police mission officially handed over its responsibility to the European Union. The EU Police Mission (EUPOL) in Afghanistan is to be much larger than the German policy mission, with five times the number of external police advisors (195 at full strength) and three-and-a-half times the budget (€43.5 million for June 2007 to April 2008).[12]

Assessments of the Afghan Police Program

A good number of assessments are publicly available, and these documents provide important and detailed information.[13] The assessments agree on a number of key issues, the most important of which is that the Afghan police force continues to make an insufficient contribution to the establishment and maintenance of security for the Afghan people. In fact, on balance the police continue to be part of the problem for ordinary Afghans: "Since 2002, the Police have been a source of insecurity for communities across the country, rather than a solution to it."[14] Correspondingly, the image of the Afghan police is poor, despite some recent improvements.

The assessments give a number of reasons for this finding. At the top of the list is corruption, low pay for police personnel, low numbers of trained police, conflicting objectives of the police support program, and lack of functioning legal systems. In this section, the police program is measured against a number of criteria found in the SSR literature,[15] including reform success and failure, sufficiency of the effort, donor consistency, local ownership, and sustainability.

Reform Success and Failure

The German approach to police reform in Afghanistan—and justification for the focus of the program—emphasized quality training of civilian police. Quality was to trickle down from the top echelons and the best-trained personnel to the ordinary police officer. Has this worked?

Judging by the available reports, professionalism of the Afghan police remains low, except in some pockets. Partly this seems to be a question of numbers: because of high departure rates, the intended diffusion of skills and attitudes has suffered. The police also continue to be closely linked to traditional and newly emerged power structures. Despite major efforts (as discussed below), police from senior officers down to ordinary constables continue to extend their primary loyalty to persons rather than to abstract concepts such as the state or the law.

A core problem continues to be corruption. Police salaries have been raised and regularized with the implementation of the *Tashkeel*. The incremental raises beginning in 2005 helped to improve recruitment and retention rates but were too small to alleviate the endemic corruption. Considering the officers' level of education, and thus opportunities in other occupations, their salaries are still low at US$100 per month. However, police posts amount to licences to get rich through extortion,[16] at least in some parts of the country. Even though pressure from the international community has resulted in the removal of some prominent human rights offenders and corrupt officials from positions in the Ministry of the Interior (MOI),[17] corruption is still a major problem in the upper echelons. The principle of patronage, often linked to compensation payments, remains the most important vehicle for accessing the state and sharing its power.[18] Some contend that "the MOI is notoriously corrupt, factionalised and an increasingly important actor in Afghanistan's illegal drug economy."[19] Moreover, the police are commonly regarded by ordinary Afghans as acting arbitrarily, a perception that stems from the lack of adequate treatment of suspects in the justice sector. As a result, the public image of the police is poor.

Ethnic composition remains a problem despite major improvements in the recruitment of non-Tajiks. In the early days, the Afghan National Police was a dumping ground for AMF militiamen. Most of the high-ranking officers came from the Northern Alliance, particularly Tajiks. Tajiks remain overrepresented (about 50 percent of ANP members), Pashtuns fairly represented (43 percent), and Uzbeks (4 percent) and Hazaras (2 percent) underrepresented.[20] Among the highest-ranking officers, the ratios are similar to these.

The German police program wanted to help build an effective national police force in Afghanistan. Particular emphasis was put on accountability and gender: the police would operate within the law and under strong legal oversight, and the force would include many female police officers. In early 2007, however, there were still only 223 women in the ANP, which numbered close to 70,000.[21] In addition to the social, cultural, and religious barriers against women in many police functions, they also face problems inherent to the ANP such as the emphasis on physicality in recruitment and in performance criteria for advancement. The United Nations Development Program has observed that "a particular example of organisation bias is the uniform, which makes it difficult for police women to patrol in the streets. The cap, for instance, reveals some of their hair, contrary to prevailing Muslim standards in Afghanistan."[22] The German police program had to reluctantly accept that the recruitment base for women was small, and more importantly, that female police officers could take on only a select range of functions in Afghanistan.

The program tried to tackle a good number of the issues that contributed to the bleak picture painted here by focusing on professionalism, factionalism, and corruption. There were some concrete successes—for instance, in the selection of police generals in which the German police program intervened, and in the record of training many good police officers. Still, the overall assessment is damning.

Sufficiency of the Effort

In early 2006, the German government reported proudly that 3,600 police officers had graduated from the Kabul police academy, completing one-year or three-year courses, and 7,500 had received various forms of special training in short-term courses. Given this record, the German government still believed then that a total ANP establishment of 62,000 officers could be achieved by mid-2007, as indeed it was.[23]

However, the German police program has been heavily criticized for being too small and too slow. The German response has been that at the start a much larger Afghan input had been assumed. In fact, it had been expected that five or six years of external support for the buildup of the Afghan National Police would suffice.[24] However, the German program encountered major problems not only with the Afghan political decision-making process—particularly but not exclusively in the Afghan Ministry of the Interior—but also with the recruitment and retention of police officers. Recruitment of qualified candidates has been a major, and increasing, problem. The German police program had not expected such a low turnout of educated recruits for officer training. In many cases, reading skills had to be taught first. According to one estimate, fewer than 30 percent of recruits could read and write.[25] There are conflicting numbers on retention. The former minister of the interior, Ali Ahmed Jalali, claimed as a best estimate that of the 62,000 police trained as of early 2007, only about 50 percent were still with the ANP.[26]

One of the problems inherited by the police support program was the skewed hierarchy of the Afghan National Police. An objective of the pay-and-rank reform implemented in 2005–2006 was to rebalance this structure. Before the reforms in 2005, 2,750 of the 56,428 police were generals or colonels. The reform agenda aimed at 418 generals and colonels out of the planned 62,000 police complement. At the same time, the salaries of colonels and generals, ranging from US$95 to US$107 per month, were to be increased to US$400–$700.[27]

The German reaction to these problems was to stick with the original concept of thorough training. If there were not sufficient recruits for the more demanding programs, how could there be enough sufficiently qualified candidates for street policing? There was, in the view of the German Police Project Office, good reason to go slowly, as "absorptive capacity" was lacking.[28]

Conflicting Donor Objectives

Partly in response to the perception that Germany was failing to do the agreed-upon job, the United States started a massive training effort for both regular and auxiliary police in 2004. The quantities expanded, both in terms of advisors and money, to dwarf the German effort: US$200 million in FY 2004, $600 million in FY 2005, $1.6 billion in FY 2005, and $2.5 billion in FY 2007.[29] In April 2007, the United States had 447 external police advisors in Afghanistan, Germany had 39, and other nations had 58.[30]

Furthermore, the United States advanced a different conception of policing. Instead of quality, the emphasis was on numbers. This could be achieved only through short-term training—from six to nine weeks for the regular police, down to ten days for the Afghan National Auxiliary Police (ANAP) created in 2006. The United States pressured the Afghan government and the international donors to accept an increase in the planned strength of the ANP to 82,000. Also, the US concept focused on the police as a support force for the military charged, for instance, with holding territory occupied by the military. Correspondingly, the US Department of Defence, or rather the Combined Security Transition Command Afghanistan (CSTC-A), took over responsibility for the police training program from the US Department of State in the spring of 2005. This change was justified as follows: "The ANP's first mission was to conduct democratic and community policing at an international standard. Currently, the ANP is viewed as a key player in the overall counter-insurgency mission. The ANP's role today is different/expanded and may require different training, expertise and equipment."[31]

Ali Ahmed Jalali has said about the US police program: "It is clear that, from the beginning and under the influence of our international partners, the Afghan police was treated and was forced often to act as an extension of the military in the fight against the insurgency."[32] He also commented that "the Ministry of the Interior has been turned into a replica of the Ministry of Defence."[33]

How justified was the US criticism of the German program? The German program certainly was small considering its objectives. It is particularly striking that the program was not expanded when it became clear that security problems, including those that police had to deal with, were rising. The German justifications for the program, however, do have some merits. As will be argued below, there are structural problems to policing in Afghanistan that will, at best, take time to overcome. A forced approach to building up the police therefore has major drawbacks.

It seems that the United States, despite its massive program, is now encountering the same obstacles as did Germany—a small recruitment base, poor retention, and payment problems. In the meantime, the ANP is becoming more of an auxiliary force for the military, but without the training and self-protection the military has. Casualty rates among ANP and ANAP personnel are high, with 627 police killed since 2002, 200 of them between March and June 2007.[34] As a former police trainer said, "Not long ago, we were reforming the security sector while fighting a war on the side. Now we are fighting a war while reforming the security sector on the side."[35]

Initially, there was little communication between the German Police Project Office (GPPO) and the Combined Security Transition Command Afghanistan (CSTC-A). Following a meeting in Dubai, however, relations improved. In 2006 a formal coordination mechanism was established, the International Police Coordination Board. The differences in approaches, however, remain—even since the handover from the GPPO to EUPOL Afghanistan—despite the overwhelming quantity of the US effort.

Local Ownership

The German police program was initially built very strongly on the idea of local ownership. The idea was that Afghans would run the police program with German advice. Germany would not have much to do with the ordinary police constables—they would be recruited, trained, and led by Afghan police officers who had gone through the German police program.

This approach to local ownership proved overly optimistic. The loyalty of police personnel, both ordinary police and high-ranking officers, to traditional procedures, structures, and leaders was much higher than assumed in this approach. Afghanistan has not had a central police force before. Of course, there were enforcement specialists, but they were largely local. The rank reform helped to install more transparent and merit-based procedures in the ANP, but these improvements were, at least until recently, threatened and undermined by the Ministry of the Interior and by commanding police officers. The pay issue, which is linked to many other problems, including corruption and recruitment and retention rates, was also underestimated. The German approach has thus stepped away from a "light footprint" but has not turned into a "heavy footprint." This partial shift was particularly visible in the implementation of the Tashkeel and in the extension of the monitoring program. The German government, however, remains committed to its basic concept and does not support a different kind of mission under the auspices of the European Security and Defence Policy (ESDP).[36]

More generally, local ownership was highly problematic because of the distance of many of the objectives of the police program from the norms of Afghan society in terms of professionalism, tribal neutrality, corruption, gender equality, and so forth. These objectives probably are achievable even in Afghanistan and with Afghans in charge—but the time and resources needed have not been available.

Sustainability

Compartmentalization of the elements of the security sector in the "lead nation" concept, uneven levels of activity in the elements of the security sector, inadequate analysis of the problems in the security sector in Afghanistan—all these contributed to a lack of integration of the various SSR programs into a comprehensive framework and hampered efforts to achieve security sector reform.

The police program particularly suffered from the lack of progress in justice reform. In addition, the functional boundaries with the military became blurred with the growing insurgency. Police were given military tasks, resulting in very high casualty rates. The creation of the ANAP has further eroded the initial consensus on policing in Afghanistan. The current course of the police is not sustainable. It has become, in large parts, an auxiliary force of the military, for which it is not trained and equipped.

Another important point concerns financial issues. The buildup of security organizations and forces in Afghanistan has vacillated between requirements and resources. Early Afghan demands for large forces were turned down by the international community because it did not want to pay for them. With the growing insurgency, larger force goals were set, including for the police, but the question of how the personnel would be paid remains unsolved. At a salary rate of US$100 per month for the average police officer and an assumed average payroll of 75,000, salary payments run to more than US$90 million per year.[37] Including infrastructure and operating expenses, the costs for the ANP and ANAP were probably in the range of total domestic Afghan central government revenues of US$400 million in 2006.[38] Obviously, this is not sustainable: one of the sectors suffering from the lack of resources is the justice sector, where salaries for prosecutors are lower than those for police officers, and judges get on average US$100 per month.[39]

Currently, the payroll for the ANP is largely covered by the United Nations Development Program's (UNDP) Law and Order Trust Fund. From 2003 to June 2007, a total of US$315 million was spent, of which US$96 million since 2006 paid the salaries of 64,070 police. Recently, funds committed to the Law and Order Trust Fund, which have come primarily from the United States and the European Union, have fallen substantially short of the budget drawn up by the Afghan government and UNDP.[40]

The Future of Police Reform in Afghanistan and German SSR

The prospects for building up an effective, professional, law-abiding police force in Afghanistan remain distinctly mixed. Currently, the efforts of the Afghan government and the international community focus on having loyal police officers who are willing to play their part in subduing the insurgency. At the same time, the original program of creating a high-quality civilian police force continues on a low level, as part of EUPOL Afghanistan.

Current ideas as to the future of the Afghan police go in different directions. The US government has pushed for expanding the force to 84,000 police and may well aim for even higher numbers. Hodes and Sedra propose a large increase in the number of police, but based on the German approach. They compare Afghanistan to Iraq, a country with a similar population but with 152,000 police personnel to be increased to 190,000.[41] Wilder, on the other hand, asks whether, in the Afghan context, there is not a "case for a minimal role for the police. . . . Despite the best intentions and efforts of police reformers, there is a strong possibility they will continue to be a major source of insecurity rather than security."[42]

That begs the following question: Is it realistic to assume that, should the insurgency be defeated or subside through some political compromise, another attempt to create a modern, central police force would show better results than the previous one? On the one hand, the number of well-trained police officers is growing, as is the recognition that a reformed police force is necessary for the security of Afghan citizens. On the other hand, there is a continuing discrepancy between the objectives of police reform, at least in the German version, and the norms prevailing in many parts of Afghan society. Ironically, a political compromise with the Taliban might make it even more difficult to have a modern Afghan police force. Finally, the cost of a modern police force, alongside the various security sector elements and the many other requirements of the Afghan state, may prove to be too high for the Afghan government and even for the international community.

Afghanistan has been an unfortunate focus for the first large German SSR effort. The program was not based on sufficient knowledge of the situation in Afghanistan and was slow to react when the security situation worsened. It was too small to start with and did not grow when Afghans needed more police. Furthermore, it lost much of its impact when the United States decided to invest in police reform. By the end of 2007, not much of the German effort could be called successful, even though the basic approach—to create a civil police based on solid training—remained the one favoured by external observers who were most familiar with the history of the Afghan police program.[43]

Notes

1. German Federal Government, "Interministerielles Rahmenkonzept zur Unterstützung von Reformen des Sicherheitssektors," in *Entwicklungs-und Transformationsländern* (Berlin, October 2006), http://www.bmz.de/de/ zentrales_downloadarchiv/themen_und_schwerpunkte/frieden/rahmen-konzept_SSR_deu_Final_1.pdf.

2. German Federal Government, "Action Plan: Civilian Crisis Prevention, Conflict Resolution and Post-Conflict Peace-Building" (Berlin, 12 May 2004), http://www.forumzfd.de/fileadmin/PDF/Download-Dokumente/ action_Plan_BMZ_engl.pdf.

3. Ibid., 60-61.

4. German Federal Government, *Working Together to Strengthen Security and Stability through Crisis Prevention,* 1st Federal Government Report on the Implementation of the Action Plan "Civilian Crisis Prevention, Conflict Resolution and Post-Conflict Peace-Building" (Berlin, May 2006), http:// www.auswaertiges-amt.de/diplo/de/Aussenpolitik/Themen/Krisen-praevention/Downloads/Aktionsplan-Bericht1-en.pdf. This document is referred to hereafter as the "Implementation Report."

5. German Federal Government, "Interministerielles Rahmenkonzept," 6.

6. Ibid., 8.

7. German Federal Government, "Implementation Report," 60.

8. Helmut Frick, "Police Reform in Afghanistan," in *Zentrum für Frieden-seinsätze, International and Local Policing in Peace Operations* (Berlin Workshop, 14–16 December 2006), 85.

9. Frick, "Police Reform," 87.

10. German Federal Government, "Interministerielles Rahmenkonzept," S. 13.

11. See Bundesregierung, "Antwort auf die Große Anfrage der Abgeordneten Jürgen Trittin und andere," *Drucksache* 16/4243 (31 January 2007), 21.

12. Se the EUPOL Afghanistan website, http://www.consilium.europa.eu/ cms3_fo/showPage.asp?id=1268&lang=DE.

13. See International Crisis Group, "Reforming Afghanistan's Police," *Asia Report* 138 (Brussels, 30 August 2007); Andrew Wilder, "Cops or Robbers? The Struggle to Reform the Afghan National Police" (Afghanistan Research and Evaluation Unit, Kabul, July 2007); Cyrus Hodes and Mark Sedra, "The Search for Security in Post-Taliban Afghanistan," *Adelphi Papers* 47 (June 2007).

14. Hodes and Sedra, "Search for Security," 62.

15. See, for example, Michael Brzoska, "Introduction: Criteria for Evaluating Post-Conflict Reconstruction and Security Sector Reform in Peace Support Operations," *International Peacekeeping* 13, no. 1 (March 2006), 1-13.

16. Hodes and Sedra write, "The amount of money earned through corruption ranges from $200 per month for a patrolman to $30,000 for a police general." Hodes and Sedra, "Search for Security," 64.

17. United Nations, *Report of the Secretary-General on the Situation in Afghanistan and Its Implications for International Peace and Security* (A/82/345-S/2007/555, New York, 21 September 2007), 3.

18. Astri Suhrke, "Reconstruction as Modernisation: The 'Post-Conflict' Project in Afghanistan," *Third World Quarterly* 28, no. 7 (2007), 1302.

19. Wilder, "Cops or Robbers," xi.

20. United Nations Development Program (UNDP), *Afghanistan Human Development Report 2007* (Kabul, 2007), 82.

21. Ibid., 83.

22. Ibid.

23. Bundesregierung, "Antwort auf die kleine Anfrage der Abgeordneten Homburger et al," *Drucksache* 16/1046 (24 March 2006), 24.

24. Frick, "Police Reform," 86.

25. Wilder, "Cops or Robbers," 30.

26. Ali Ahmed Jalali, former minister of the interior, in Zentrum für Friedenseinsätze, *International and Local Policing in Peace Operations* (Berlin Workshop, 14–16 December 2006), 92.

27. Detailed data in Wilder, "Cops and Robbers," 39. The effects of the newly introduced merit-based selection process for the remaining high-ranking positions were thus cushioned. Officers could choose between accepting one year of severance pay or demotion to a lower rank. However, demotion often resulted in a higher salary than their previous rank.

28. Frick, "Police Reform," 86.

29. David Rohde, "Pentagon Spending $2.5 Billion to Revamp Afghan Police," *International Herald Tribune*, 18 October 2007, http://www.afghanconflict-monitor.org/2007/10/pentagon-spendi.html.

30. Bundesregierung, *Drucksache* 16/4243, 22.

31. Wilder, "Cops or Robbers," 44-45.

32. Jalali, Zentrum für Friedenseinsätze, 91.

33. Ibid., 92.

34. Wilder, "Cops or Robbers," 46.

35. Charles Barham, "Combined Security Transition Command, Kabul," in Zentrum für Friedenseinsätze, *International and Local Policing in Peace Operations* (Berlin Workshop, 14–16 December 2006).

36. Bundesregierung, "Antwort auf die Große Anfrage der Fraktion Bündnis 90/Die Grünen," *Drucksache* 16/6312 (6 September 2007), 24.

37. The number of officers may not correspond to those actually in the force, owing not only to absences but also to "ghost police officers" presented in the records by superiors. Higher-ranking officers receive higher payments; recruits get less than US$100. See Wilder, "Cops or Robbers," xx.

38. There are major efforts underway to increase the revenue base, but revenue collection has traditionally been at the core of the conflicts between the Central Afghan state and various local authorities. Tax revenues in 2005 covered 8 percent of all estimated income in the national budget, corresponding to

4.5 percent of the gross domestic product. The rest was provided by international donors. See Astri Suhrke, "Reconstruction as Modernisation," 1301. The overall cost of the security sector in 2005, prior to the latest expansion of numbers, was estimated at 17 percent of GDP by the World Bank. World Bank, *Afghanistan: Managing Public Finances for Development*, vol. 1 (Washington, 27 November 2005), 24.

39. Wilder, "Cops or Robbers," 60.
40. http://www.undp.org.af/WhoWeAre/UNDPinAfghanistan/Projects/sbgs/prj_law_order.htm.
41. Hodes and Sedra, "Search for Security," 64.
42. Wilder, "Cops or Robbers," 48.
43. International Crisis Group, "Reforming Afghanistan's Police"; Wilder, "Cops or Robbers"; Hodes and Sedra, "Search for Security."

The Contributors

Michael Brzoska studied economics and political science at the Universities of Hamburg and Fribourg (Switzerland), graduating with a diploma in economics. He obtained a PhD in political science in 1985 and a *Habilitation* on the subject of "Militarization of the Third World as a Problem of International Politics" in 1997. He has been scientific director of the IFSH and professor at the University of Hamburg since February 2006. From 1994 to January 2006 he was director of research at the Bonn International Center for Conversion. Prior to this he was, among other positions, research member and co-director of the Arms Trade and Arms Production Team at the Stockholm International Peace Research Institute, Solna, Sweden. His recent publications include *Promoting Security: But How and for Whom?* (2004), co-edited with Peter Croll, and *Security Sector Reform in Peace Support Operations* (2006), co-edited with David Law.

Colonel M.D. (Mike) Capstick retired from the Canadian Armed Forces in late 2006 after thirty-two years of service. In 1992–93 he commanded the 1st Regiment Royal Canadian Horse Artillery in Shilo and in the Nicosia Sector of the United Nations force in Cyprus. In 1997–98 he commanded the Canadian Task Force in the NATO Stabilization Force in Bosnia-Herzegovina. His final appointment was as commander of the first deployment of the CF Strategic Advisory Team – Afghanistan from August 2005 until August 2006. This unique unit, a mixed military-civilian team, provided strategic planning advice and capacity building to development-related agencies of the Government of the Islamic Republic of Afghanistan. He has also worked in Afghanistan as senior advisor to a cabinet minister and with an NGO. He is an officer of the Order of Military Merit and was awarded the Meritorious Service Medal for his service in Afghanistan. Currently, he is an associate at the Centre for Military and Strategic Studies, University of Calgary.

Mihai P. Carp is currently the deputy head of the Crisis Management Policy Section of the NATO Operations Division in Brussels. He joined NATO in late 1997 as a speechwriter for the Secretary General, and since 1999 has focused primarily on crisis management operations and political-military matters. Since 2003, he has been dealing predominantly with NATO's "new" missions, notably Afghanistan. He is the principal desk officer for Afghanistan. Prior to joining the NATO International Staff, he worked for the Department of State with assignments at the US Embassy Office Berlin (1991–94), Chisinau (1992), and Bucharest (1994–97). Over the years, he has authored numerous articles in Radio Free Europe/Radio Liberty's *Reports on Eastern Europe, NATO Review, Jane's Defence Weekly*, and selected foreign affairs journals. He completed his undergraduate degree at Georgetown University's School of Foreign Service in 1988, and received an MA from the London School of Economics in 1990.

Andrea Charron is a graduate of the Royal Military College of Canada, Department of War Studies. Prior to completing her doctorate at RMC, she obtained an MA in international relations from Webster University, Leiden, The Netherlands, a Masters of Public Administration from Dalhousie University, and a BSc (Honours) from Queen's University. She was a participant in Canada's Management Trainee Programme and worked as a policy analyst for various federal departments including Canada's Revenue and Customs Agencies and the Privy Council Office (Security and Intelligence Secretariat).

Hans-Georg Ehrhart is head of the Centre of European Peace and Security Studies (ZEUS) of the Institute for Peace Research and Security Policy at the University of Hamburg (IFSH). He received his MA and PhD from the University of Bonn. He has held visiting research appointments at the Research Institute of the Friedrich Ebert Foundation in Bonn; the *Fondation pour les Etudes de Défense Nationale*, Paris; the Centre for International Relations at Queen's University, Kingston, Canada; and the EU Institute for Security Studies, Paris. His research covers the broad topic of peace and security. Recent publications include "EUFOR Tchad/CAR: A Preliminary Assessment," *European Security Review* 42 (December 2008); *Civil-Military Co-Operation and Co-Ordination in the EU and in Selected Member States*, European Parliament, DG External Policies of the Union, October 2007; "The EU as a Civil-Military Crisis Manager: Coping with Internal Security Governance," *International Journal* (Spring 2006); and *Security Sector Reform and Post-Conflict Peacebuilding* (2005), co-edited with A. Schnabel.

Rainer Glassner is a freelance consultant and associate fellow at the Institute for Development and Peace (INEF). His particular focus is Afghanistan, with a specialization in governance, conflict, and development. Besides academic publications, he has produced policy papers for various institutions. He is regularly called upon to train or brief staff of the German police, military officers, and development workers prior to their deployment abroad. He is based in Germany but travels frequently to Afghanistan to conduct field research. He currently serves as an adviser for the Federal Ministry for Economic Co-Operation and Development, Afghanistan/Pakistan/Bangladesh branch.

David G. Haglund is a professor of political studies at Queen's University (Kingston, Ontario, Canada). His research focuses on transatlantic security and on Canadian and American international security policy. He co-edits the *International Journal*. Among his books are *Latin America and the Transformation of US Strategic Thought, 1936–1940* (1984), and *Over Here and Over There: Canada-US Defence Cooperation in an Era of Interoperability* (2001).

Roland Kaestner has served as a commanding officer and as a staff officer. He participated in the 30th General Staff course at the German Bundeswehr's Military Academy from 1987–89, and was a military fellow at the Institute for Peace Research and Security Policy at the University of Hamburg from 1989–91. He served as a battalion commander of the 252nd Paratroop Battalion from 1992–94 and worked in the headquarters of the German Army (Heer) from 1994 to 1995 as a consultant in charge of the Army/Special Forces air mobility concept. In 1995 and 1997, he was an instructor in military policy at the German Bundeswehr's Military Academy. In 1998, he worked in the German parliament as an academic consultant, and from 1999 to 2000, he supported the parliamentary faction of the German Green Party in security and defence issues. Since 2001, he has headed the strategic future analysis department at the Bundeswehr Transformation Centre; in 2005, he became a lecturer in strategy at the Military Academy.

Florian P. Kühn is a researcher at the Institute for International Relations at Helmut Schmidt University in Hamburg. He holds an MA in political science and German literature and linguistics, as well as an MA in peace and security studies. His PhD on "Security and Development in World Society" is to be completed in June 2009. His research includes the ideational foundations of security and development, with a special focus on their implications for policy in Afghanistan. His lectures at Helmut Schmidt and Hamburg University have included democratization policy, terrorism, international relations theories, and water politics in arid and semi-arid regions. He has taught preparatory courses for federal armed forces and NATO personnel. His publications include articles in the *Journal of Intervention and Statebuilding*, *Friedensgutachten*, *WeltTrends*, and peer-reviewed volumes. He is co-editor, with Berit Bliesemann de Guevara, of a special edition of *Security and Peace* (February 2009).

Janet Kursawe is research fellow at the GIGA Institute for Middle East Studies, Hamburg. She holds a degree in political science, cultural anthropology and psychology. She is a PhD candidate in political science at the University of Hamburg, researching drug policy and the impact of drugs on security matters in Afghanistan, Pakistan, and Iran. Additionally, she investigates the political development as well as the foreign and security policies of the aforementioned countries, which has led to various publications on domestic political developments in Iran and on drug trafficking in the Middle East. She has lectured at the University of Hamburg and at the Bundespolizeiakademie Lübeck where she helped to prepare police officials for deployment in Afghanistan.

David M. Law is a DCAF senior fellow and coordinator of the Security Sector Reform Working Group, doing research and writing on a broad range of issues pertaining to security sector reform. He is also editor of the DCAF *Backgrounders on Security Sector Reform and Governance.* Prior to joining DCAF in October 2003, he worked as a project manager and consultant. He directed the Russia-Canada Consortium for Economic Policy Research and Advice (CEPRA) and the Democratic Civil-Military Relations Program (DCMPR) for the Canadian government as well as a capacity-building research activity for scientists from the Commonwealth of Independent States on behalf of the European Commission. He was also employed by Business Environment Europe as a facilitator for scenario-planning exercises organized on behalf of various corporations and governments. From 1984–94, he was a member of NATO's international staff, where he worked as a policy analyst and principal advisor to three Secretaries General. He has lectured on European politics and strategic issues at Carleton University, Ottawa, the Canadian Royal Military College and Queen's University, and at l'Université du Québec à Montréal. From 1996–2003, he directed the course on European and international security for junior Swiss diplomats at the Geneva Center for Security Policy (GCSP).

Citha D. Maass is senior associate at the German Institute for International and Security Affairs (SWP) in Berlin. Having studied at Göttingen and Munich as well as Jawaharlal Nehru University, New Delhi, she received her MA and PhD from the University of Munich. After a four-year post-doctoral research sojourn at JNU, New Delhi, in the 1980s, she joined the SWP in 1990, working on South Asia. Since 1996 she has specialized in Afghan affairs. From late 1996 onwards she has repeatedly visited Afghanistan and was an international observer during the Emergency Loya Jirga in May-June 2002. From 2002 to 2005 she worked in Afghanistan on the electoral process. Since her return to SWP in late 2005, she has regularly published on Afghan and regional affairs and functioned as an advisor to the German parliament and government. Apart from security-related issues, she has again focused on the controversial forthcoming elections in Afghanistan in 2009 and 2010 and on regional approaches to the conflict.

Kim Richard Nossal is the Sir Edward Peacock professor of international relations in the Department of Political Studies, Queen's University. He is a former editor of *International Journal*, the quarterly journal of the Canadian International Council, a former president of the Canadian Political Science Association, and currently the chair of the Academic Selection Committee of the Security and Defence Forum program of the Department of National Defence. He is the author of a number of articles and books on Canadian foreign and defence policy, including *The Politics of Canadian Foreign Policy* and *Diplomatic Departures: The Conservative Era in Canadian Foreign Policy, 1984–1993*, co-edited with Nelson Michaud. His latest book, co-authored with Stéphane Roussel and Stéphane Paquin, is *Politique internationale et défense au Canada et au Québec*, published in 2007.

Lara Olson is co-director of the Peacebuilding, Development and Security Program at the Centre for Military and Strategic Studies, University of Calgary. She has extensive experience working with humanitarian, development, and peace-building efforts in conflict areas. Since the mid-1990s, she has worked as an aid practitioner and with innovative international projects to improve aid outcomes in areas of conflict, including directing the research phase of the Reflecting on Peace Practice project. She has worked with field-based NGOs in the Caucasus and Central Asia and on research into effective international approaches to address ethnic conflicts in general, and in the former Soviet Union in particular. She is a steering group member of the Peace Operations Working Group and affiliate of the web-based Peace Operations Monitor project. She has an MA in international politics from the London School of Economics, and a BA (Honours) in political science from the University of British Columbia.

Charles C. Pentland is professor of political studies and director of the Centre for International Relations at Queen's University, in Kingston, Ontario, Canada, where he teaches courses on international organization and global governance. He holds a BA and an MA from the University of British Columbia and a PhD in international relations from the London School of Economics. He has held visiting positions at Carleton University, the University of Manitoba, and the University of Cambridge. For the past several years his research and publications have focused on the external relations of the European Union, especially its eastward enlargement, its role in the Balkans, its relations with the former Soviet Union, and its Common Foreign and Security Policy. He has also written on Canadian foreign policy and transatlantic relations.

Christoph Reuter has a background in Islamic studies. He is a journalist reporting for, among others, the German weeklies *Der Stern* and *Die Zeit*. He has undertaken extensive research visits to Afghanistan and the broader Middle East. His field trips have taken him from the mountain valleys of Iraqi Kurdistan through barely accessible regions in Pakistan to the hot spots of Afghanistan. In 1997 his work was recognized with the Springer Journalist Award. He wrote the first book on suicide bombers, entitled *Mein Leben ist eine Waffe* (My life is a weapon), (2002), and the best-seller *Café Bagdad: Der ungeheure Alltag im Irak* (Café Baghdad: the incredible daily routine in Iraq), (2004).

Conrad Schetter is senior research fellow at the Centre for Development Research of the University of Bonn, where he is guiding a research group on governance and conflict. In addition to numerous articles, he is the author of *Ethnicity and Ethnic Conflicts in Afghanistan* (in German, 2003); and *Brief History of Afghanistan* (in German, 2004); he is co-editor, with A. Wieland-Karimi, of *Afghanistan in History and the Present* (in German, 2000); with Ch. Noelle-Karimi and R. Schlagintweit, of *Afghanistan – A Country without a State?* (2002); and with A. Wimmer et al., of *Facing Ethnic Conflicts* (2004). His thematic focus is on local structures of power and violence, international intervention, and collective identities.

Christian Wagner, PhD, is senior associate and head of the Asia research group at the German Institute for International and Security Affairs (SWP) in Berlin. He has studied political science at the Albert Ludwigs University of Freiburg and worked as a researcher at Rostok University and the Centre for Development Research of the University of Bonn. He has specialized in foreign and security policy in South Asia, focusing currently on India, Pakistan, Sri Lanka, Bangladesh, and Nepal as well as on regional cooperation and ethnic conflicts. His latest research papers include *Atommacht Pakistan: Nukleare Risiken, Regionale Konflikte und die Dominante Rolle des Militärs* (with Oliver Thränert); *SWP-Studie* S 03, January 2009; and "Pakistans Interessen in Afghanistan," in Peter Schmidt, ed., *Das internationale Engagement in Afghanistan: Strategien, Perspektiven, Konsequenzen, SWP-Studie* S 23 (August 2008).

Queen's Policy Studies
Recent Publications

The Queen's Policy Studies Series is dedicated to the exploration of major public policy issues that confront governments and society in Canada and other nations.

Our books are available from good bookstores everywhere, including the Queen's University bookstore (http://www.campusbookstore.com/). McGill-Queen's University Press is the exclusive world representative and distributor of books in the series. A full catalogue and ordering information may be found on their web site (http://mqup.mcgill.ca/).

School of Policy Studies

Measuring What Matters in Peace Operations and Crisis Management, Sarah Jane Meharg, 2009. Paper 978-1-55339-228-6 Cloth ISBN 978-1-55339-229-3

International Migration and the Governance of Religious Diversity, Paul Bramadat and Matthias Koenig (eds.), 2009. Paper 978-1-55339-266-8 Cloth ISBN 978-1-55339-267-5

Who Goes? Who Stays? What Matters? Accessing and Persisting in Post Secondary Education in Canada, Ross Finnie, Richard E. Mueller, Arthur Sweetman, and Alex Usher (eds.), 2008. Paper 978-1-55339-221-7 Cloth ISBN 978-1-55339-222-4

Economic Transitions with Chinese Characteristics: Thirty Years of Reform and Opening Up, Arthur Sweetman and Jun Zhang (eds.), 2009. Paper 978-1-55339-225-5 Cloth ISBN 978-1-55339-226-2

Economic Transitions with Chinese Characteristics: Social Change During Thirty Years of Reform, Arthur Sweetman and Jun Zhang (eds.), 2009. Paper 978-1-55339-234-7 Cloth ISBN 978-1-55339-235-4

Dear Gladys: Letters from Over There, Gladys Osmond (Gilbert Penney ed.), 2009. Paper ISBN 978-1-55339-223-1

Immigration and Integration in Canada in the Twenty-first Century, John Biles, Meyer Burstein, and James Frideres (eds.), 2008. Paper ISBN 978-1-55339-216-3 Cloth ISBN 978-1-55339-217-0

Robert Stanfield's Canada, Richard Clippingdale, 2008. ISBN 978-1-55339-218-7

Exploring Social Insurance: Can a Dose of Europe Cure Canadian Health Care Finance? Colleen Flood, Mark Stabile, and Carolyn Tuohy (eds.), 2008. Paper ISBN 978-1-55339-136-4 Cloth ISBN 978-1-55339-213-2

Canada in NORAD, 1957–2007: A History, Joseph T. Jockel, 2007. Paper ISBN 978-1-55339-134-0 Cloth ISBN 978-1-55339-135-7

Canadian Public-Sector Financial Management, Andrew Graham, 2007. Paper ISBN 978-1-55339-120-3 Cloth ISBN 978-1-55339-121-0

Emerging Approaches to Chronic Disease Management in Primary Health Care, John Dorland and Mary Ann McColl (eds.), 2007. Paper ISBN 978-1-55339-130-2 Cloth ISBN 978-1-55339-131-9

Fulfilling Potential, Creating Success: Perspectives on Human Capital Development, Garnett Picot, Ron Saunders and Arthur Sweetman (eds.), 2007. Paper ISBN 978-1-55339-127-2 Cloth ISBN 978-1-55339-128-9

Reinventing Canadian Defence Procurement: A View from the Inside, Alan S. Williams, 2006. Paper ISBN 0-9781693-0-1 (Published in association with Breakout Educational Network)

SARS in Context: Memory, History, Policy, Jacalyn Duffin and Arthur Sweetman (eds.), 2006. Paper ISBN 978-0-7735-3194-9 Cloth ISBN 978-0-7735-3193-2 (Published in association with McGill-Queen's University Press)

Dreamland: How Canada's Pretend Foreign Policy has Undermined Sovereignty, Roy Rempel, 2006. Paper ISBN 1-55339-118-7 Cloth ISBN 1-55339-119-5 (Published in association with Breakout Educational Network)

Canadian and Mexican Security in the New North America: Challenges and Prospects, Jordi Díez (ed.), 2006. Paper ISBN 978-1-55339-123-4 Cloth ISBN 978-1-55339-122-7

Global Networks and Local Linkages: The Paradox of Cluster Development in an Open Economy, David A. Wolfe and Matthew Lucas (eds.), 2005. Paper ISBN 1-55339-047-4 Cloth ISBN 1-55339-048-2

Choice of Force: Special Operations for Canada, David Last and Bernd Horn (eds.), 2005. Paper ISBN 1-55339-044-X Cloth ISBN 1-55339-045-8

Force of Choice: Perspectives on Special Operations, Bernd Horn, J. Paul de B. Taillon, and David Last (eds.), 2004. Paper ISBN 1-55339-042-3 Cloth 1-55339-043-1

New Missions, Old Problems, Douglas L. Bland, David Last, Franklin Pinch, and Alan Okros (eds.), 2004. Paper ISBN 1-55339-034-2 Cloth 1-55339-035-0

The North American Democratic Peace: Absence of War and Security Institution-Building in Canada-US Relations, 1867-1958, Stéphane Roussel, 2004. Paper ISBN 0-88911-937-6 Cloth 0-88911-932-2

Implementing Primary Care Reform: Barriers and Facilitators, Ruth Wilson, S.E.D. Shortt, and John Dorland (eds.), 2004. Paper ISBN 1-55339-040-7 Cloth 1-55339-041-5

Social and Cultural Change, David Last, Franklin Pinch, Douglas L. Bland, and Alan Okros (eds.), 2004. Paper ISBN 1-55339-032-6 Cloth 1-55339-033-4

Clusters in a Cold Climate: Innovation Dynamics in a Diverse Economy, David A. Wolfe and Matthew Lucas (eds.), 2004. Paper ISBN 1-55339-038-5 Cloth 1-55339-039-3

Canada Without Armed Forces? Douglas L. Bland (ed.), 2004. Paper ISBN 1-55339-036-9 Cloth 1-55339-037-7

Campaigns for International Security: Canada's Defence Policy at the Turn of the Century, Douglas L. Bland and Sean M. Maloney, 2004. Paper ISBN 0-88911-962-7 Cloth 0-88911-964-3

Understanding Innovation in Canadian Industry, Fred Gault (ed.), 2003. Paper ISBN 1-55339-030-X Cloth 1-55339-031-8

Delicate Dances: Public Policy and the Nonprofit Sector, Kathy L. Brock (ed.), 2003. Paper ISBN 0-88911-953-8 Cloth 0-88911-955-4

Beyond the National Divide: Regional Dimensions of Industrial Relations, Mark Thompson, Joseph B. Rose, and Anthony E. Smith (eds.), 2003. Paper ISBN 0-88911-963-5 Cloth 0-88911-965-1

The Nonprofit Sector in Interesting Times: Case Studies in a Changing Sector, Kathy L. Brock and Keith G. Banting (eds.), 2003. Paper ISBN 0-88911-941-4 Cloth 0-88911-943-0

Clusters Old and New: The Transition to a Knowledge Economy in Canada's Regions, David A. Wolfe (ed.), 2003. Paper ISBN 0-88911-959-7 Cloth 0-88911-961-9

The e-Connected World: Risks and Opportunities, Stephen Coleman (ed.), 2003. Paper ISBN 0-88911-945-7 Cloth 0-88911-947-3

Knowledge Clusters and Regional Innovation: Economic Development in Canada, J. Adam Holbrook and David A. Wolfe (eds.), 2002. Paper ISBN 0-88911-919-8 Cloth 0-88911-917-1

Lessons of Everyday Law/Le droit du quotidien, Roderick Alexander Macdonald, 2002. Paper ISBN 0-88911-915-5 Cloth 0-88911-913-9

Improving Connections Between Governments and Nonprofit and Voluntary Organizations: Public Policy and the Third Sector, Kathy L. Brock (ed.), 2002. Paper ISBN 0-88911-899-X Cloth 0-88911-907-4

Centre for the Study of Democracy

The Authentic Voice of Canada: R.B. Bennett's Speeches in the House of Lords, 1941-1947, Christopher McCreery and Arthur Milnes (eds.), 2009. Paper 978-1-55339-275-0 Cloth ISBN 978-1-55339-276-7

Age of the Offered Hand: The Cross-Border Partnership Between President George H.W. Bush and Prime-Minister Brian Mulroney, A Documentary History, James McGrath and Arthur Milnes (eds.), 2009. Paper ISBN 978-1-55339-232-3 Cloth ISBN 978-1-55339-233-0

In Roosevelt's Bright Shadow: Presidential Addresses About Canada from Taft to Obama in Honour of FDR's 1938 Speech at Queen's University, Christopher McCreery and Arthur Milnes (eds.), 2009. Paper ISBN 978-1-55339-230-9 Cloth ISBN 978-1-55339-231-6

Politics of Purpose, 40th Anniversary Edition, The Right Honourable John N. Turner 17th Prime Minister of Canada, Elizabeth McIninch and Arthur Milnes (eds.), 2009. Paper ISBN 978-1-55339-227-9 Cloth ISBN 978-1-55339-224-8

Bridging the Divide: Religious Dialogue and Universal Ethics, Papers for The InterAction Council, Thomas S. Axworthy (ed.), 2008. Paper ISBN 978-1-55339-219-4 Cloth ISBN 978-1-55339-220-0

Institute of Intergovernmental Relations

The Democratic Dilemma: Reforming the Canadian Senate, Jennifer Smith (ed.), 2009.
Paper 978-1-55339-190-6

Canada: The State of the Federation 2006/07, vol. 20, *Transitions – Fiscal and Political Federalism in an Era of Change,* John R. Allan, Thomas J. Courchene, and Christian Leuprecht (eds.), 2009. Paper ISBN 978-1-55339-189-0 Cloth ISBN 978-1-55339-191-3

Comparing Federal Systems, Third Edition, Ronald L. Watts, 2008.
Paper ISBN 978-1-55339-188-3

Canada: The State of the Federation 2005, vol. 19, *Quebec and Canada in the New Century – New Dynamics, New Opportunities,* Michael Murphy (ed.), 2007.
Paper ISBN 978-1-55339-018-3 Cloth ISBN 978-1-55339-017-6

Spheres of Governance: Comparative Studies of Cities in Multilevel Governance Systems, Harvey Lazar and Christian Leuprecht (eds.), 2007. Paper ISBN 978-1-55339-019-0
Cloth ISBN 978-1-55339-129-6

Canada: The State of the Federation 2004, vol. 18, *Municipal-Federal-Provincial Relations in Canada,* Robert Young and Christian Leuprecht (eds.), 2006.
Paper ISBN 1-55339-015-6 Cloth ISBN 1-55339-016-4

Canadian Fiscal Arrangements: What Works, What Might Work Better, Harvey Lazar (ed.), 2005. Paper ISBN 1-55339-012-1 Cloth ISBN 1-55339-013-X

Canada: The State of the Federation 2003, vol. 17, *Reconfiguring Aboriginal-State Relations,* Michael Murphy (ed.), 2005. Paper ISBN 1-55339-010-5 Cloth ISBN 1-55339-011-3

Canada: The State of the Federation 2002, vol. 16, *Reconsidering the Institutions of Canadian Federalism,* J. Peter Meekison, Hamish Telford, and Harvey Lazar (eds.), 2004.
Paper ISBN 1-55339-009-1 Cloth ISBN 1-55339-008-3

Federalism and Labour Market Policy: Comparing Different Governance and Employment Strategies, Alain Noël (ed.), 2004. Paper ISBN 1-55339-006-7 Cloth ISBN 1-55339-007-5

The Impact of Global and Regional Integration on Federal Systems: A Comparative Analysis, Harvey Lazar, Hamish Telford, and Ronald L. Watts (eds.), 2003.
Paper ISBN 1-55339-002-4 Cloth ISBN 1-55339-003-2

Canada: The State of the Federation 2001, vol. 15, *Canadian Political Culture(s) in Transition,* Hamish Telford and Harvey Lazar (eds.), 2002. Paper ISBN 0-88911-863-9
Cloth ISBN 0-88911-851-5

Federalism, Democracy and Disability Policy in Canada, Alan Puttee (ed.), 2002.
Paper ISBN 0-88911-855-8 Cloth ISBN 1-55339-001-6, ISBN 0-88911-845-0 (set)

Comparaison des régimes fédéraux, 2ᵉ éd., Ronald L. Watts, 2002.
Paper ISBN 1-55339-005-9

John Deutsch Institute for the Study of Economic Policy

The 2006 Federal Budget: Rethinking Fiscal Priorities, Charles M. Beach, Michael Smart, and Thomas A. Wilson (eds.), 2007. Paper ISBN 978-1-55339-125-8 Cloth ISBN 978-1-55339-126-6

Health Services Restructuring in Canada: New Evidence and New Directions, Charles M. Beach, Richard P. Chaykowksi, Sam Shortt, France St-Hilaire, and Arthur Sweetman (eds.), 2006. Paper ISBN 978-1-55339-076-3 Cloth ISBN 978-1-55339-075-6

A Challenge for Higher Education in Ontario, Charles M. Beach (ed.), 2005. Paper ISBN 1-55339-074-1 Cloth ISBN 1-55339-073-3

Current Directions in Financial Regulation, Frank Milne and Edwin H. Neave (eds.), Policy Forum Series no. 40, 2005. Paper ISBN 1-55339-072-5 Cloth ISBN 1-55339-071-7

Higher Education in Canada, Charles M. Beach, Robin W. Boadway, and R. Marvin McInnis (eds.), 2005. Paper ISBN 1-55339-070-9 Cloth ISBN 1-55339-069-5

Financial Services and Public Policy, Christopher Waddell (ed.), 2004. Paper ISBN 1-55339-068-7 Cloth ISBN 1-55339-067-9

The 2003 Federal Budget: Conflicting Tensions, Charles M. Beach and Thomas A. Wilson (eds.), Policy Forum Series no. 39, 2004. Paper ISBN 0-88911-958-9 Cloth ISBN 0-88911-956-2

Canadian Immigration Policy for the 21st Century, Charles M. Beach, Alan G. Green, and Jeffrey G. Reitz (eds.), 2003. Paper ISBN 0-88911-954-6 Cloth ISBN 0-88911-952-X

Framing Financial Structure in an Information Environment, Thomas J. Courchene and Edwin H. Neave (eds.), Policy Forum Series no. 38, 2003. Paper ISBN 0-88911-950-3 Cloth ISBN 0-88911-948-1

Towards Evidence-Based Policy for Canadian Education/Vers des politiques canadiennes d'éducation fondées sur la recherche, Patrice de Broucker and / et Arthur Sweetman (eds./ dirs.), 2002. Paper ISBN 0-88911-946-5 Cloth ISBN 0-88911-944-9

Money, Markets and Mobility: Celebrating the Ideas of Robert A. Mundell, Nobel Laureate in Economic Sciences, Thomas J. Courchene (ed.), 2002. Paper ISBN 0-88911-820-5 Cloth ISBN 0-88911-818-3

Our publications may be purchased at leading bookstores, including the Queen's University Bookstore (http://www.campusbookstore.com/) or can be ordered online from: McGill-Queen's University Press, at **http://mqup.mcgill.ca/ordering.php**

For more information about new and backlist titles from Queen's Policy Studies, visit http://www.queensu.ca/sps/books or visit the McGill-Queen's University Press web site at **http://mqup.mcgill.ca/**